1

# Thanks A Lot I've Had A Ball

### The Life and Music of
# Tommy Steele

**Derek Mathews**
**Discography by Morten Reff**

## A Biography

Thanks A Lot I've Had A Ball

**Cover Picture**

Tommy

For all the fans of this great artiste

# Contents

# Acknowledgements

I give my thanks to all those who have assisted me in the preparation of this book.

Barry J Barnes, Harold Fielding's Stage Manager on many of his big musicals.

Terje Dalene in Oslo, Norway for Scandinavian and Football information.

Morten Reff from Norway for the Discography.

Alan and Janet Smith from The Appreciation Society.

Souvenir Press Ltd, The Manchester Palace, The Manchester Opera House, The London Palladium, Northern Life Magazine and Southwark Local Studies Library.

Tommy Steele, for without him this book could not have been written.

And to all others I have been unable to contact but who have been mentioned in the book.

A very special thank you goes to Pat Richardson for passing on some of her memories.

# Foreword

In 1958, John Kennedy wrote Tommy's story.

Thanks A Lot I've Had A Ball takes us from the beginning, enjoyably and informatively to the present day, when Tommy Steele's talent is as formidable as ever. The author provides us with a wealth of information which will enchant not only Tommy's legion of admirers, but anyone who enjoys a good read

The 'epic' is a fine example of compilation and the narrative is so entertaining. But then it is about yours truly. It is a super piece of work.

Tommy Steele

# Prefix

## Where Tommy Steele lived – a short history of the parish of Bermondsey

Situated close to the river Thames the area where Tommy lived was once marshland, dotted with small islands, archaeologists discovered that the area's earliest inhabitants were from the prehistoric era. This was most probably why Tommy Steele called his first group 'The Cavemen'.

The name Bermondsey is thought to be of Saxon origin, deriving its name from Beormund's Eye. Bermondsey Street was built up as a causeway across the marshy land. In the first instance it was an access way to a religious foundation on the site of Bermondsey Square.

Four monks from France with the help of a wealthy Londoner, Alwyn Child, established the Priory of St. Saviour in the eleventh century, a miraculously discovered cross, the 'rood of grace' made the priory a place of pilgrimage.

The parish of Bermondsey was in the Hundred of Brixton, in the County of Surrey. The manor was mentioned in the Doomsday Book as being held by the King, Earl Harold having held it previous to the conquest. In 1094 William Rufus gave the manor to a monastery founded in this place in 1082. In 1399, the priory became Bermondsey Abbey, it received many gifts from royal and noble donors; it was surrendered to King Henry the Eighth, who granted it in 1541 to Sir Robert Southwell, who in the same year sold it to Sir Thomas Pope.

Sir Thomas Pope, the founder of Trinity College, Oxford pulled down the priory church and constructed an impressive

13

mansion from the ruins of the buildings. This afterwards became the residence of Thomas Ratcliffe, The Earl of Sussex, who in 1583 died there. Masonry from the abbey was also used in the construction of the houses that lined Bermondsey Street. (Evidence of this has recently come to light as the result of work on construction sites.)

The parish consisted of 514 acres with very few houses; by 1708 there were 1500 houses, a mere village. In 1717, the parish and the manor were sold to Peter Hambly, their family still held it in 1868.

In 1739 there were 1900 houses and by 1792 this figure had rose to 3100. In the census of 1801 a population of 17,169 inhabitants was recorded living in 3203 houses. The census of 1861 showed that there were 8455 houses and a population of 58,212 inhabitants. Although inhabitants of the area were subject to plague, fires and flooding that affected all Londoner's, it flourished as an area of successful artisans and manufacturers. In the 17th and 18th centuries, life revolved round the parishes of St. Mary Magdalen and St. Olave churches.

South of the river and outside the city walls the area attracted trades that were obnoxious and unpleasant. It became known as an area associated with leather, especially the tanning process. Allied activities such as wool stapling, hat manufacture and glue production ensured that none of the products of the leather trade were wasted, by the end of the 18th century; the noise and the smells of the area were driving out all but the most resilient. The owners of the companies were living in pleasant houses in the new suburbs. The area became overcrowded as workers flocked in from elsewhere to seek jobs at the former Peek, Frean & Co. factory where Tommy's mum worked it was probably the best-known food processor in the area.

Houses that were built in 1819, were still housing families in 1936. By 1900 Bermondsey's population was all working class. In between 1940 and 1945 German bombing raids killed many local people. Much of the housing was substandard and early in the 20th century the council carried out extensive slum clearance and other social reforms.

Today Bermondsey is one of London's trendiest areas, with Bermondsey Street at its heart, the area blends history with modernity and has a strong sense of community. The area now boasts some of the top London restaurants.

At the southern end of Bermondsey Street on the site of the Bermondsey Abbey is Bermondsey Square – home since 1949 of the Friday morning New Caledonian Antiques Market.

To the south of the area lies the Old Kent Road with many large food stores. Property is very much in demand at the moment and many new estate agents have sprung up to service this demand, the area is now home to many celebrities from stage and screen.

From Tommy's eighth floor apartment on the bank of the Thames he can see Bermondsey the place where he used to play as a child. When he moved into it he quoted.

"It has taken me almost fifty years to move less than a mile from where I was born."

# Introduction

Tommy Steele (born 1936) is a British entertainer and is regarded as Britain's first rock 'n' roll star. His cheeky Cockney image, combined with the boy next-door looks, won him success as a singer and later a variety entertainer. He was the first London based artist who started their career in the famous 2 –I's Coffee bar. His co-manager, Larry Parnes, once said, "Tommy was the greatest entertainer I had on my books. His rise to fame as a teenage star was probably attributed to his charisma rather than simple sex appeal".

In the early 1960s Tommy moved into acting and soon became an established family entertainer. He became a master of stage musicals.

Luck, publicity, personality and talent are the four things that have all played a major part in transforming Tommy from a back street boy into an international celebrity. Tommy is the first to admit that he has had a lot of luck, and the bulging scrapbooks of his fans testifies the enormous amount of publicity he has received in national newspapers and magazines throughout the world. But luck or publicity can ever make a star of someone lacking personality or talent.

"Rags to Riches", "Overnight Success", "One Leap to Stardom" – are all phrases, which are used in show business, but all of them are true when it comes to talking about Tommy, whose meteoric rise to fame left everyone gasping. His personality registered the moment he bounced on to the stage, the moment the film or television camera picked him up, the moment the microphone caught the first note. He is a personality performer with the rarest of gifts – the ability to project his personality across the footlights. It is not merely a pleasure to see him it is an experience that makes one shares his joy of living.

This book is the story of a person who, according to Trevor Peacock "was the wildest thing imaginable in the days of television shows such as "6-5 Special". Tommy has made records, become an actor, has produced shows, has made films – in other words, he is an all round entertainer. During the last six decades Tommy Steele has become synonymous with the Palladium, starring in productions such as Dick Whittington, Hans Andersen, Singing in the Rain, The London Palladium Show and Scrooge.

In 1958 John Kennedy, in his book 'Tommy Steele.' (Souvenir Press) he wrote about a teenage idol and gave an inside picture of show business.

But who was John Kennedy, and what were his dealings with Tommy?

John Kennedy was as well known in Fleet Street as he was in Tin Pan Alley. He was born in Rangoon, where his Scots father was a merchant; he was brought up in New Zealand. He first wanted to be a sea captain, and on a variety of ships as a deckhand, visited every port worth knowing from Boston to Bombay. The lure of the sea eventually faded away. In Canada he turned to photography and crossed the Atlantic – to Fleet Street. There he worked on various papers and magazines; then he made a change into the publicity field. He was recognised as one of the shrewdest men in the business, even before his phenomenal success with Tommy Steele. He lived alone in a West End flat, where he collected antique pistols, grew indoor plants, and played records well into the night. He was always well dressed and used to browse around the street markets of London in search of paintings. He was always talking about the holiday he never had. He said he had no ambitions to go into show business – until the night he met Tommy Steele.

John Kennedy wrote in his book that Tommy was like any other normal twenty-one year old. "I have to be brief as that because to try and give a picture of Tommy is asking the impossible. He is just like any youngster who has just reached manhood. But put him under a microscope and the difference sticks out a mile. Look at him objectively and you realise that he had to be different to get where he is – yet he had to be the same as the kids who followed him or he would have had no appeal to them. He is of average height about five foot seven or eight. His physique is strong and wiry, as you would expect from someone who has knocked around the world and spent hours in a gym keeping fit. His eyes are pale blue these he fixes on you when talking, and they never wander away until he has finished. Whether he is good looking or not is a matter of personal opinion. One thing Ann will never have to worry about is his food tastes – he could spend a fortune on eating if he wished, but his favourite dish is sausage egg and chips. He likes this above all else, although he enjoys an entrecote steak well done or stuffed hearts. But what he does like when he's in London is to go down to Jamaica Road, Bermondsey and have a lunch of eel pie, pie and mash or jellied eels. Poor Ann, who neither likes pies or eels, has to sit outside and wait whilst Tommy drops in for a quick snack. He sleeps late as a rule and when he gets up will only have a cup of tea or coffee, then after an hour or two will eat a large breakfast. He loves listening to records like Frank Sinatra, Ella Fitzgerald and Hank Williams. He loves driving and playing golf, which he started to play whilst on tour in Llandudno, and horse riding.

Tommy hates women who drink too much. He used to say, 'to see a man drunk is bad enough, but to see a woman drunk is unforgivable. He also hates dressing up; he is at his happiest when he can wander round in old slacks and a soft sports shirt. He has an aversion to moths and wasps. At night if there is a moth fluttering in the room he will not go in until it has been chased away. Wasps he dislikes on sight and for some reason they don't like him – for some reason they seem to be attracted to him and when he tries to flick them away he invariably gets stung. If Tommy makes up his mind not to do something, nothing in the world, be it by force or persuasion, will make him do it. Tommy is a wealthy young man, leaving out those who are wealthy because of inheritance, and must be one of the richest in Britain. Two stories about him best shows what affect this dramatic 'rags to riches' success has had on his character. One concerns the house he lives in, the one he bought for his mum and dad. A fashionable designer laid out the contemporary interior. Money was lavished on the job. Think of those glossy magazines with pictures of coloured ceilings and odd-looking furniture and pottery. That will give you a slight idea of what lies beyond the front door.

But now walk with me past the cream telephone in the hall into a small room at the back of the house. It is like opening the door to the past. Indeed it is a door to the past. A fire burns in the room and bric-a-brac is scattered all over the dresser. The carpet looks as if it came from the corner shop. If you have an eye for taste and if you like contemporary surroundings then this room is an appalling mixture of the two. But this is the place where Tommy spends most of his time. This is the room where Tommy composes his music or discusses five figure contracts with Larry or me. This is the room where the old terraced house in Frean Street lives on. It is almost a replica of that dining room, nothing changed.

The other is this. One day we were having a meal with Ann and Tommy and with a friend outside of show business. As we got up Tommy noticed an almost whole cigarette that Ann had stubbed out when the meal had arrived. He picked it up and put it into his pocket. 'Waste not, want not,' he said. The friend looked at him and said. You have enough money to buy a cigarette factory yet you pick up a stubbed out fag. I know he said, but there's a lot of people in the world tonight who'd give anything for that stubbed out fag. I could have done with it myself at one time. I don't want to forget what's going on out there".

Number 12 Mason Street 2006

# The Beginning

Like everyone else, Thomas Hicks doesn't remember his beginnings. All that he knows is that he's as old as his nose but not as old as his teeth. About his very early childhood, he can only relate to what his Mother told him.

He was the second child to be born to Elizabeth Ellen and Thomas Walter Hicks. His Mother's maiden name was Bennett. His elder brother, Colin, whom he never knew, died before he was born with double pneumonia and whooping cough. Colin was only ten months old.

Before Tommy was registered at Southwark the family moved to a two bedroom flat in 12 Mason Street, a row of little blackened terraced houses just off the Old Kent Road. The registration details can be found in Volume 1d, page 19, 1937.

For all the early years of his life Tommy was a sickly child. His Mother told him he was never out of hospital for more than three months at a time. It may be because he was sick all the time that he grew so close to his Mother.

In 1957, he wrote in "My Story":

"Yes I do love my Mother and I am not ashamed of putting it in to writing or speaking about her. I wrote that then because of all the comments that were appearing in the newspapers."

Tommy always stayed faithful to his Mother."

Tommy went on to write.

"They are the queer ones for not loving theirs. In families like mine where seven kids came along one after the other, a

Mother has to be as loving as an angel and as tough as a professional boxer. My mum was just nineteen years old when she had me. My dad was then a professional backer – in other words, he worked the racecourses, - there was no pretending that it was a steady job. It was always as changeable as the weather.

My Mother went through plenty of hardships and plenty of sorrows in those days. But my mum always kept us clean and tidy and 'brought us up decent'. She is the one person who always made me nervous when I knew she was in the audience. Because I never knew what she was thinking of me, it didn't matter whether I was buying a new guitar or taking out a new girl, I still asked my mum of what she thought.

My mum and dad had had plenty of pretty hard times, when you think about it. She was a tin basher in a metal box the factory in south London when my dad met her.

He was driving a horse and cart at that time. My mum never got tired of telling me how smart a chap he was. Said Tommy 'No matter what happened dad was always good for a laugh.' He was always telling the story of how they first met. 'He took her down to a boozer in the old Kent Road. He thought he was on to a good one for she was knocking back the whiskies one after another.' Well he thought to himself 'I hope she doesn't carry on like this all night!' But when he was taking her home she was as sober as a judge and he got it out of her that she had been pouring all the drinks he had bought her into an aspidistra plant.

One thing about being in hospital all those years, my Mother helped me with my reading, see used to spend hours teaching me how to read."

When Tommy was two years and nine months old, war was declared.

In the November his Mother had his first sister, Betty. She was a lovely child; during the blackout his mum who was carrying her was knocked down. Betty was killed, with a fractured skull. His mum had concussion. When she got better the doctors decided that she should be evacuated along with the rest of the Mothers and young children. But she wouldn't have any of it. For a while she went down to Cornwall, taking Tommy with her. His Dad was still staying in London at the time and she missed him terribly, so they soon came back home. They had just got back into the city and the air raid siren sounded. Mrs Hicks tells the story. "We rushed to the shelter and when it was all over we found out we could not return to our house in Mason Street, because it had been blitzed. In the same raid I lost all of my family, when the house in which I was born in got a direct hit. We never used to sleep in the air-raid shelters at night because the noise was so horrendous. People would be playing mouth organs, singing, laughing and telling jokes, and it was like a big get-together every night. The Germans would drop parachutes with flares on them so that their bombers could see where to drop their bombs."

Tommy takes up the story.

"We used to go to bed naked. (There were no pyjamas in those days.) When the sirens went there was no time to stop and get dressed. You had to get down to the shelters as quickly as you could. Most nights, I'd be seen running through the streets naked, carrying all of my clothes under my arm. My mum never knew her Mother. She died in childbirth. An aunt had brought her up, and that aunt was killed in the same air raid along with another aunt, an uncle, and three of her cousins. Almost every day there was an air raid and many other houses and factories in the area were raised to the ground. We moved into another street in the area but that was bombed as well. We were put up at the Tuscan Hotel in Shaftsbury Avenue wearing the only clothes we were standing up in. Because my mum was expecting again she went back to Cornwall, whilst I stayed in the city with my dad. Then we moved into Frean Street. Frean Street was listed as condemned when we moved into it but it stood up to the bombs that Hitler sent over. There was no bath or indoor lavatory but it was home."

Tommy was ill in bed with measles, when his Mother came back from Cornwall to have Colin. When he arrived they all went to stay in Cornwall with Mrs Uren who had a farm near the coast. He shall never forget the long walks that they took along the cliffs with the gull's screaming overhead and the roar of the sea below.

A few years later Mrs Hicks had another boy. He was named Rodney He seemed a healthy baby until he was eighteen months old and then his mum's world crumbled. He went into Lewisham hospital, and was diagnosed with bowel cancer.

Seven weeks later he was dead.

Shortly after Rodney died the family moved into Nickleby House (a block of flats.) They lived on the second floor of the building.

Tommy said, "The first school I attended was just across the street from where I lived it was called St. Joseph's, and I could go home for my dinner. One day as all the kids were returning to school the Germans came over in a retaliation raid. Their fighters came in lower than ever with their machine guns blazing. Most of the kids just stood in the playground while the bullets rang out around them. As quickly as possible the teachers came out and ushered all of us inside."

One of the things Tommy remembers about his boyhood was the time when he was taken to see a circus at the Elephant and Castle. The next day he ran away from home to join the circus. He was out of the house all day and his mum was frantic. He was found by a policeman and taken home, as it was getting dark. When he told his mum that he wanted the leading lady to be his Mother she was really upset. Another time he remembers was when he was down in the new forest with his brother Colin. The Sunday school camp, he had said, was all 'do this and do that!' So he told Colin that they were getting out of the place. After walking across some fields and a wood they found a main road.

"Which way shall we go?" he asked Colin.

Colin pointed one way and he decided to go the other. When they did a head count at the camp they found out that they were missing and rang their mum. But she wasn't kept in suspense for too long because the first place they went into when it started getting dark was a police station and was brought home to another good tanning. Quite soon after this he went to the big school. It was called the Bacon's, in Grange Road. It was founded in 1718 with money left by Josiah Bacon. His mum took him there on the first day, as he was terrified. He had heard all about the place. If you looked up from your desk, he was told, you got the cane.

When he was eight years old he had to be rushed into hospital again. This time a blood vessel had blocked and burst in his stomach.

One of the finest men he ever met during his school days was a Mr Binger. He used to talk like a sergeant major, and he ran the school with a rod of iron. This school was the toughest in London. Another of the teachers he used to worship was a man called Mr. Creswell.

After school the boys used to have gang fights in the bombed out houses. The boys who lived in Nickleby house had to join the Hicksey Mob, the boys in the next street were called the Knights. Because Tommy lived in Nickleby House, he had to join their gang. The Hicksey Mob would always try to get the better of the Knights; if the Knights broke six windows the Hicksey's broke seven. It was always bad luck if one gang member was caught out on his own by the members of the other gang, as they would scuff him up. That's what started all the trouble with rival gang's parents, new clothes were hard to come by during the war years, so a rule was put in force that if a boy was wearing anything new, he would not get scuffed up. After that day they always changed into their old clothes when they came home from school. One day Tommy learned a lesson he would never forget: that is never try to fight in a pair of Wellingtons on a bombsite! There was this boy in his class who he used to fight every week. He was a member of the Knights' gang. One day Tommy saw the boy coming down the street in his old clothes. Tommy had on his feet a new pair of shoes, so he rushed inside the house and put on the first thing he saw in the hallway, and that was a pair of Wellingtons. He pulled them on as quickly as he could and met the lad outside the door. Tommy dragged the lad over to the bombsite and set about him. First Tommy hit him and then he hit Tommy, and Tommy overbalanced on the bricks. In wellybobs you can't get up properly as anybody who has worn welybobs knows. The lad set about Tommy whist he was on the ground. He made a hell of a mess of him! Then his dad saw them and he knew the trouble that he was in. He went over and dragged Tommy home. That was awful. To be pulled out of a fight by your dad was the worst thing that could happen to a chap. The word soon got around amongst the gangs, and for weeks Tommy was called a Ninny.

Just before the war ended the family moved back into Frean Street. By this time his dad had got a job as a bookies clerk and tic-tac man. He was always away from home and the money was not too good. To keep his children properly fed and clothed, Tommy's mum had to go out to work as well. She used to start work at five in the morning, scrubbing other people's floors, and then she would come back home to get the children's breakfasts ready and get them off to school. When they were all in school, off she would go, looking after old people. Then, she would go to work at the Peek Frean Biscuit factory. When she came home she would say to the children, "I'm going to have half an hour so see you all stay nice and quiet". Well they would sit quiet and watch the clock and after the time was up they would then start making loads of noise again. As Tommy was the eldest, he had to look after the house and the rest of the family as well. That meant he had to be prepared to fight anyone at the drop of a hat. Many a time when he came home from school, one of his brothers or sisters would come running into the house telling him that he had to go and sort somebody out.

Bermondsey was known as the toughest spot in London.

Since the incident with his dad he never picked a fight again on the bombsites. He said, 'I tell a lie! I did have one big fight and that was with a boy in my class', it had all started in the classroom. The lad started telling Tommy the facts of life during one of the lessons; well Tommy didn't believe what he had said. Tommy told him he was disgusting and filthy and that he would smash his face in at the playtime – they had a terrific fight and they were sent to face the headmaster. All that night Tommy lay awake thinking of what the lad had said; in the morning he still didn't believe it. You see at that time he believed that parents saved up all their money for a special kind of pill, which they got from the doctors, and that was that. The next day at school he was on detention. In those days, Tommy's main interests was listening to the radio and writing short stories – and that was how he got a special job at the school. It all began one day when one of the teachers had to go out into the playground for something. Tommy was betting that it was for a quick fag, the teacher had told Tommy to keep the children amused, so he told them one of the stories he had written the night before. When the teacher came back, instead of stopping him he just sat down and listened until he had finished. It wasn't very long before all the teachers in the school knew that Tommy could tell stories and they started asking him to tell them as well. It was Mr Cresswell who got him to write them in his composition books. On Fridays the school always had a free period and all the children in his class used to fight about whose turn it was to read the stories Tommy had written that week. One morning Tommy thought that Mr Cresswell must have had a bad night, for when he came in to the classroom his desk lid was up and he took hold of it and slammed it down. Tommy thought it was funny and started laughing. Mr Cresswell did not think it was funny and called Tommy to the front of the class. Without even looking at him he took out the cane from its stand. He caned Tommy on both hands and sent him back to his desk. Trying not to cry at the pain Tommy put a slight grin on his face. After about thirty seconds Mr Cresswell called out loud, "Hicks there is nothing in my class that I can see that is funny. Now come out here." When Tommy got by his side he held out his hands and Mr Creswell gave him another two tastes of the cane for good measure. Tommy was bursting to cry but held back, looking Mr Cresswell straight in the eyes, as he walked back to his desk. He was bursting to cry by this time. "Hicks" Mr Cresswell roared at the top of his voice; "get back here this instant," and gave him two more tastes of the cane for good measure. Just at that moment the next teacher came in to take over the lesson. Just as Mr Cresswell left the room, Tommy burst into tears. Tommy wanted to leave school there and then, but he still had a few years to go.

For a holiday Tommy's family went to the farm in Cornwall. On the farm was an old horse named Faithful, which he and his brother used to ride. They rode on him everyday. In the mornings his mum would send him out to find Colin and he would often find him upon the old horse's back. Tommy would call him off and get on himself. By the time they got back to the house, breakfast would be cold and they would get their backs sides tanned.

Tommy developed 'Porphyries' an enzyme deficiency, which affected his nervous system that meant he had to have months of treatment. When he got better his dad took him in a taxi for the first time to see a show at the London Palladium. He vowed there and then that one day he would captivate an audience on that stage. Little did he know then that fifty-eight years later he would be making his 1,727th performance upon that stage.

At the age of twelve Tommy started to write plays and they would be put on in the school assemblies. He only did them because his friend wanted to get off maths. "He used to die beautifully," said Tommy. "In one of the plays there were fourteen deaths in the first act, and red paint all over the stage." The headmaster told Tommy, not to kill off so many people in his next play. To further his career in writing Tommy thought of travelling the world and even this might not have happened if it hadn't been for one of his School Teachers. Mr Binger caught him in class one day with a few of his mates drawing a log cabin and some canoes.

"What are you doing"? Mr Binger asked him.

Tommy told him that they were all planning the place where they would live out in Australia. They were all going to stow away on a ship and see the world. They often stood on the side of the Thames and watched the boats going through Tower Bridge and wondered where they were going.

"Well one day we are all going to find out", said Tommy.

Mr Binger said. "Look, boys from Bermondsey don't get to go travelling the world". Well that got Tommy going.

He said, "They don't, do they not? Well you wait and see".

When Tommy was 15 just before he left school he was told that the Minister of Employment was coming along.

"We were all ushered into the headmaster's office in turn. Instead of finding someone to give us inspiration, we discovered a grumpy old soul, whose one object was to put us off what we wanted to do and stick us in a factory, said Tommy. Nine out of ten accepted this. I did not accept it. On that day I probably had the first argument with an adult in my life. I did not see why the representatives of the Minister should be given the job of talking people out of it. I wanted to go into the navy. So no matter what the grumpy old soul had to say it went in one ear and out of the other."

His mum thought that, because he was only four feet eleven in his stocking feet he would make a good 'bell boy' at the Savoy Hotel. Well, like the good lad he was, he went along for an interview. Mr Toye was so impressed with him that he said; he would fix up a date when Tommy could start. But his dad had other ideas. Since the age of eleven he had been taking him to the racetracks with him.

"When you are old enough to leave school." He would say. "You could come and be a tic tac man like me".

Well Tommy knew what the money was like – it was not much good and besides, all the time he was thinking of what he had said to Mr Binger, about wanting to see the world. One night he went to a party with his mum and dad and there at the party was a deck hand named Ritchie. He was very tall and had a great suntan. He started talking to Tommy about having a healthy life, and then Tommy told him about how he had always been a sickly child.

"Get some fresh air in your lungs," he said.

Ritchie told Tommy that he would get him fixed up with an interview with a Mr Haddon of the Canard Line in Leadenhall Street. Tommy went to see Mr Haddon the next day without telling his mum. He also was very impressed when Tommy told him his story about wanting to travel the world. Mr Hadden told Tommy he would think about it. A few days' later two letters came for Tommy. One of the letters asked him to join the staff at the Savoy and the other, to go to the Gravesend Sea Training College.

So there he was at the crossroads. What should he do?

Join the hotel life or go to sea?

He made up his mind there and then. Tommy chose to go to sea! "I was 15, two weeks after I had left school and I went into the Merchant Navy", he said.

For two months Tommy was back at school again learning how to lay tables and balance plates. He told to his mates in the college that he could have been doing this at the Savoy and getting tips for doing it. Then came another two weeks learning to tie knots and another two weeks of navigation. He didn't like the atmosphere at that place. He told his Mother all about it but he got no satisfaction from her. She told him that he'd chosen it and that he'd have to stick with it! Tommy hated the food and decided he would have been better off if he were in prison. He did learn while he was there, that it had been a military prison during the war years. He passed out of the college with flying colours. He had a couple of weeks at home and then he got a telegram telling him to report to Southampton Docks to board the ship called Scythia.

It was a day he would never forget.

When he read the telegram out to his family his Mother cried, and his father put his hands on his shoulders and said to him. "Whilst you're away Tommy, always stick up for yourself and don't let anyone take a liberty with you!" It was the advice he had always given to him, and it was this advice he was always glad to remember.

Tommy said of the Merchant Navy, "One thing you learn in this service is to fend for yourself even more than in Bermondsey, and you learn to control your temper."

Tommy's first ship

# Days at Sea

The Scythia was a 19,000-ton liner on the Southampton to Quebec run. Tommy had to report to the ship at Southampton on the 21st April 1952. The telegram he received stated that he had to be aboard the ship at eight o'clock in the morning. There was a train that got him into Southampton, from Waterloo, by quarter to eight, so instead of risking that, he set off at two o'clock in the morning. When he got to Southampton at five o'clock, he had three hours to kill. He found an all-night café, got some toast and a cup of tea and went back to the station and settled down on a bench. Soon he was fast asleep. When he woke up and looked at his watch, it was almost half past eight. Panic stations! He raced out of the station and caught a bus to the docks. What would they say? Would the ship have left port without him?
Were his seafaring days over before they had even begun?
Why was the bus driving at such a snails pace?
Did the driver not understand that he was in a hurry to get to the docks?
After getting to the dock gates, he then had to find the ship. He finally found it and raced up the gangplank, and reported for duty. All that worrying and nobody even noticed he was late.
After signing in Tommy was told that his cabin was RC45; he thought he said R45, so he then went on a journey around the ship looking for this cabin number. After a while he found it.

31

It was right next door to the tourist pursers' office. He thought to himself that he must be the bloke who looks after the bellboys.

The door of cabin R45 was open so he went inside. The cabin was absolutely fabulous, it comprised of three beds, a telephone, a bell push, a mahogany wardrobe, a writing desk and it even had its own bathroom. He picked the best bed in the cabin – the one next to the porthole and dumped his gear in the wardrobe and lay down on the bed for a while waiting to see if anybody else turned up to share the cabin with him.

When nobody came he got up and went into the tourists lounge and signed on with the rest of the crew. There he met some of the lads from the training school. One of them was crying. 'I don't think I can stand this, I can't live down there.'

Tommy told him, "Don't worry you'll soon get used to the all the teak and polish."

"Hi' Tom," they all said "are you on this ship?"

He told them that he was.

"What cabin are you in, they asked"? '

"R45" he answered.

They looked at each other not saying anything. The lad who was crying said, "I'm in R45 too."

Tommy said, "Why don't you come up later and have a coffee?"

We will," they answered in unison.

They never said anything whilst they were having tea so Tommy went back to the cabin and had a lie down. He thought about ringing The Rising Sun a pub on the corner of his street back home and asking them to let his mum and dad know that he had settled in ok! But he changed his mind and thought he'd better have a kip instead. He was just nodding off when one of the stewards came in to the cabin with some towels. He apologised for waking him and said,

"Sorry sir, I didn't know that you had boarded, I didn't think that this cabin was being occupied until tomorrow morning."

"Carry on," Tommy replied.

Well the steward knew what the score was and reported back to all the other crewmembers that he was in the cabin that he'd said he was in. Tommy was just having a stretch when they all piled in and started laughing. They picked him up, piled all his gear on his chest and carried him down the corridor, down the stairs, along a dark and dingy corridor and into a place that resembled a chicken run with the wire taken out. Then they threw him onto a bunk. 'This is the cabin you should be in!" they told him. It was awful. It had twelve bunks and lockers with not enough room to swing a cat around. It smelt of stale sweat and unwashed socks. Tommy was nearly sick. That night when they turned off the lights he cried himself to sleep. He began to think perhaps he should have gone to the Savoy after all. At least he could have gone home every night and slept in his own bed. The next morning he was assigned to work in the pantry. As soon as the passengers were boarded the ship set sail. Within the hour Tommy was as sick as a dog. This lasted for seven days until the ship docked in Quebec. He had a couple of days on dry land, then after the ship set sail he was sick for the next seven days until the ship returned to England's shores. He got used to being a sailor. On future trips he was never again seasick. When he got back to his post he was sent to the purser's office for a long stand.

He knocked on his door. "Come in" called the purser.

Tommy like a good sailor went into his cabin and stood to attention.

"What do you want?" asked the purser.

"I have been sent to you for a long stand sir," Tommy replied.

"O.K." said the purser; "Wait there; don't move an inch till I get back!" Then he left the room. Well Tommy stood to attention for about an hour, not daring to move. When the purser came back empty handed Tommy asked him. "Sir, where is the long stand?"

The purser replied, laughing, "I think you have stood there long enough don't you. Now off you go back to your post". When Tommy got back it was dinnertime in the crew's mess and they all sat there laughing at him.

Life on board a ship was never boring. The older members of the crew were always playing tricks on the youngsters.

Tommy had to get up early every morning but he soon grew to love it. The wages he was paid were two pounds and five shilling per week, out of which he put away thirty shillings for his mum. When the ship reached Quebec all the crew had a couple of days leave, not that Tommy had anywhere to go as all the letters he had written to his mum were posted on the ship. Anyway he didn't have much money left out of his wages. After serving on the ship for a few months he was given some leave back in England – one of the reasons being that he had got dermatitis. Tommy had not been home long when he got severe pains in his back. His mum sent for the doctor, and he was rushed straight into hospital. When his mum and dad turned up a little later they were told that he had got spinal meningitis. Then the fever started. The doctors told Tommy's mum that there was little hope of a recovery. They believed he would not last the night. The next morning he was diagnosed as being critical and totally paralysed below the waist. On the doctor's advice his mum and dad left him to continue his fight for life. All his mum could do was cry and pray. The next morning, the doctors checked him over again. The fever had receded and his legs were beginning to feel sensations.

He was on his way to making a full recovery.

His Mother called it a miracle.

Then Tommy told his mum of his recollections. He told her that as he was lying there he heard the sound of a child laughing. He looked around and a brightly coloured ball landed on his bed. He reached for it and threw it back over the curtains. Then it happened again and again but each time the ball went a little further away from him and each time he threw it back it again came back over the curtains. The last time it came over it landed on the floor and he had to get out of bed and throw it back. When they drew back the curtains and his was the only bed in the room he began to wonder what was going on. Then his Mother began to tell Tommy a tale about his brother Rodney and that his favourite toy had been a brightly coloured ball. "He used to wake you up in the mornings, throwing the ball at you, she had said. Tommy said to his Mother, "Do you think my brother came back because he knew I was not was well?

"Yes," she had whispered into his ear!

A few days later he was moved into a ward with all the other people. One day just after lunch, a busker came into the ward to entertain them all with his guitar. He saw Tommy watching him after he had finished playing. He went over and started talking to Tommy.

"Does it take long to learn to play one of those?" Tommy asked him.

"To play it properly it does' the busker replied.

"Could I have a try?" Tommy asked. The busker spent the rest of the day teaching young Tommy the chords and notes.

Tommy was in the hospital for four months having physiotherapy. One of the physiotherapists brought him in an old guitar, but to Tommy it could have been a new one. It was the best present anybody could give him.

When he was eventually allowed to go home his legs were so thin that his Mother had to massage them every morning and evening, he had to do exercise three times a day. After a few weeks of this, the doctors said he was fit enough to return to his ship.

Tommy bounced back to sea, taking the guitar with him. First he had to get up the gangplank. His mates laughed at him with a kit bag on one shoulder and a guitar as big as himself on the other. He said that it had been "a struggle." Once out to sea and back to his duties he felt better. During his breaks he practised his chords, much to the annoyance of his mates, who threatened to throw it, and him, over the side if he didn't learn to play it properly.

His next ship belonged to the Furness Withy Line. It was called The Queen of Bermuda. It sailed out of New York. The Queen of Bermuda (22,575 girt, 580 ft. long) was delivered in 1933. An armed merchant cruiser, later a troop transport, during WW2, she resumed sailings for Furness Bermuda Line in 1949. She was sold for scrap in 1966. Tommy was taken on as a bellboy. His wages were twenty-five pounds a month. It meant that he was away from home for almost two years, but he wrote home and sent money every week. After twelve months, he was offered the job as an officer's steward. The wages for that job were sixteen pounds a week all found. The Queen of Bermuda took thirty-six hours to sail from New York to Bermuda with a day off at the end of each run. In New York he would go on the town and listen to jazz being played in the clubs. One of his favourite places in New York was the Market Diner in Basin Street.

"There were some terrific guys in there," said Tommy – "Dave Brubeck, J. J. Johnson, Cootie Williams and the famous guitarist of the day, Freddy Green.

As for Bermuda Tommy says – "Well its paradise. – It's always summer there and everybody seems to be laughing. Most of the Bermuda men used to join the ship at some time or another, sometimes as deck hands, and others times, as laundry men. You were a 'nobody' in Bermuda amongst the Bermudan people unless you had been to New York. They used to go for the flashy suits and the fast life that was so far different to the life in Bermuda. In Bermuda there are lots of great hotels whose terraces ran right down to the waters edge, there were also plenty of high-class exclusive nightclubs where the rich people used to go to. But for the poor people there were always the warm beaches where they would sing calypsos with the fishermen for hours on end. After thirty-six hours at sea, it was heaven to leave the ship and be my own boss".

By this time Tommy was playing his guitar almost every day and he was getting so good at it that he was invited to do a turn in the ship's concerts. One day in Richmond he heard a different kind of music. It was called rock 'n' roll. The leader sing was Buddy Holly. It was so good that Tommy decided to put it into his act. It went down with the captive audience a treat.

He had four months leave due to him, so he set off back to England and his family. He arrived in England around two-thirty in the morning and as he was walking along the Old Kent Road towards his home a police car pulled up beside him.

"What's in the bag, son?" they asked.

"My kit'" said Tommy.

"Get in the car, son," they said, and they took him to the police station. Tommy told them that he was a sailor and was returning home on leave. He was asked to empty all his bags on a table, and they searched through everything he had before they turned him on to the street – miles away from where he wanted to be. "You'd better give me a note. I don't want pulling over again and having to go through all this rigmarole again before I get home", he said.

After a week at home Tommy decided to go to New Zealand to learn how the Maoris played their guitars. To raise money while he was there he got a job playing and singing with a band in a club. He said, "It was a fantastic experience".

When he got back home he signed on as a tourist waiter on a ship called the Mauritania. The pay for that job was seven pounds five shillings per week. For most of the time the ship sailed into New York, so he visited the places he'd been to before. This time he listened more intently to the music they were playing, and put the songs he'd heard into the ship's concerts. He even had a dresser; his name was Kurt Littner, an Austrian. He worked with Tommy in the tourist lounge and they even shared the same cabin. Tommy had a name which he thought at that time was a good one – 'Chick Hicks.' Kurt would pretend that Tommy was a famous star and he would brush his clothes before he went out on the stage.

Tommy said Kurt "used to lay out my clothes, be my manager, be my band and my audience, applauding every time I used to practise a new number, or a play a joke on him. Kurt was always telling Tommy that I was wasting his time working on boats and that he ought to go on the stage. "Let me tell you, one day you will be a big star and he would laugh. "Whenever

Tommy was down in the dumps he would know, for he would start telling Tommy stories of the days when he was in the Foreign Legion." In the months that followed, Kurt and Tommy would make up sketches and Tommy put them in his act.

For five months the ship went out to the West Indies taking in Nassau, Jamaica, Panama, Havana and Haiti. On that trip the ship crashed into a collier and made a great hole in her side, so the ship had to stay in Havana for a couple of weeks until it was repaired. Havana girls are some of the most beautiful girls in the world. Three things he thinks which make Havana a dream island is the sun, the girls and its music. In Havana Tommy learned the Spanish method of playing his guitar, rated by many as the hardest method. On this trip Tommy got a job as a swimming instructor, he reckoned it was the best job on the ship. All he had to do was sit in the sunshine and get as black as coal and even play his guitar.

The next job Tommy got he said, "Was as a gym instructor."

The ship spent two days in New York to take on provisions before they set sail for England – so Tommy went round his old haunts. On the way back to England Tommy was put on fire duty. It was a horrible night said Tommy. "The rain came down in buckets". He was so fed up that he went into a corner to have a cigarette, but he was discovered and he was dragged in front of the captain and suspended from duty. He was paid off from the Mauritania on the 7th August 1956.

As he walked down the gangplank at Southampton he saw his brother walking up. 'Where are you going?' he asked, to which his brother replied.

'I am going to sea like you did and this is my first ship.'

Tommy wished him well and set off towards home.

In 2006 he was asked, what did he learn in the four and a half years he was at sea?

"Everything I know", he says "Self-preservation, the need to trust your fellow man, loyalty, tolerance, cultural differences. I even learned how to play the guitar from a black plate cleaner in Bermuda. Seeing Buddy Holly on stage in Norfolk, Virginia, was a road to Damascus moment, I thought to myself I could be doing what he is doing, I could already play the guitar and I loved performing."

When Tommy got home he found out that his mum had been taken ill. Now it was his turn to look after her. He washed the dishes, made the beds, got the children off to school and he even made their teas and got theirs and his dads sandwiches ready. When he came home his dad used to say, "Right lad, now off you go and enjoy yourself. I'm here now to take over".

During his earlier leaves from the ships, Tommy used to meet up with a few of the boys from the coffee bars where they would listen to music and of course pick to up girls. They were a mixed lot, said Tommy. "A couple of them worked at the ice rink, a couple were barrow boys. One was a van driver. One was an electrician and then there were those who just said they were 'in business'. But all of them, Lefty, Spike, Rocky, Buckingham, Brompton, Fabian and the rest had two things in common  - they all liked music and a laugh. They would all pile into the back of a tradesman's van and hop around to the 'Bread Basket' off the Tottenham Court Road or to the 'Cats Whisker's' where they played rock 'n' roll".

On Tommy's last trip home he went out on his own and called into a place called the Yellow door. It was packed. He squeezed in, ending up in a corner with Mike Pratt. Mike Pratt was a piano player, whose ambition was to become a songwriter. Tommy took out his guitar and had a sing along with a few of his mates. They were Johnny Yorke who played the tub bass, Wally Whyton who played guitar, and Lionel Bart. By the morning they had formed themselves into a group, with Mike playing the piano. Within the week they had their first booking. They were all convinced they had hit the big time when they were offered a booking for two pounds each. "We called ourselves 'The Cavemen.' Said Tommy."Then we started going round the coffee bars. We heard of a new coffee bar that was due to open so we went along to see if we could sing there when it opened. They said it was O.K. to do so.  At first the coffee bar was a financial disaster, and then it was taken over by Paul Lincoln and Ray Hunter. Within three weeks the place was packed to the doors".

Tommy had to return to sea and the group broke up.

Whilst he was away, Johnny Yorke, Lionel Bart and Wally Whyton and Mike Pratt reformed as 'The Vipers'.

There are lots of stories going around of how Tommy started in show business. Let Tommy tell you the real story:

"I suppose, in an odd way, it was my Mother who inadvertently set me up on the road to show business! Money was short and to earn a few bob, I began going round the coffee bars in the West End, almost literally singing for my supper. Skiffle was taking its hold and espresso froth was all the rage. I would start off an evening at a place near Euston Station. There I'd play for a couple of hours and get a spaghetti dinner for giving others pain. Then I'd go on from one place to another, playing and singing, ending up about four in the morning at a terrible place in Charing Cross Road where tramps and frustrated writers sat around in half darkness. It was about this time that an old shipmate of mine asked me to a party in a bombed out house in Waterloo Road. It was a weird place that it hardly had any roof, and its windows were boarded up, but I remember there was a beautiful yellow front door with a brass knocker and a letterbox. There were people living in that house who were an assortment of poets, writers and musicians. Amongst them was a small fellow with a beard who came from the East End. His name was Lionel Bart. We became very good friends. The following night I went into the 'Bread Basket' and Wally turned up. I sat in with the band playing some of my bits and him singing some of his bits at the end of the night. Wally said to Johnny Booker, "Monday at the Two-Is?"

Johnny replied, "No, it's been cancelled. We are not doing it!"

Tommy said "But there was something in the way he said it that made me think it was not true. So I went home. On Sunday the night I was sitting with my mum and dad, and I said, "I think there's something strange going on", and my dad asks "what?" and I told him the story. Dad looked at me and I said, "I think that fella Wally Whyton has taken my place.

"Well what can you do about it?" His dad replied.

"There's nothing I can do about it!" Tommy replied, "But what annoys me is that they have told me an untruth, and that's what I don't like."

"Well", said my dad, "There's only one-way to find out, my lad. Go over there and check it out".

So I went there. When I arrived at the Two I's there were these songs I'd played coming up from the basement. I went down there and there were all these photographers taking pictures of the 'Vipers'. Well I looked at them and said, "Is this a mirage, or are you really down here playing?" Well, once I was on the stage I wasn't going to get off until I'd sung a couple of numbers I'd heard in the states five days before. So I picked up a guitar that was lying around, and sang them and a couple of numbers of Hank Williams that I used to sing in my act on the ships, I walked off the stage and left.

A man with deep-set eyes and a long white mackintosh followed me into the street. He came up to me and said as I walked towards the 'Heaven and Hell' coffee bar.

"Who are you?" And I told him.

"I am Seaman Tommy Hicks"

"How would you like to go into show business" he asked.

And I said, "No, I wouldn't." When he asked why not, I replied, "'Cause I'm a seaman. I only do it for fun." He said, "If I can make you a star would you go into it?"

I said, "Look, whatever your gonna do, you got ten days to do it in." I gave him my address. When I got home I told my mum and dad what had happened.

I had just got up, when John Kennedy came round to my house.

"Sorry I'm not ready," I said, looking at him in his suit and me in my vest and pants. "I went to another coffee bar after I left you and got home rather late, don't just stand there, come in and meet my mum and dad."

# Skiffle and Rock

As far as popular music was concerned, Great Britain in the mid-fifties was a colony of the United States. All vital impulses came from across the Atlantic; British singers and musicians were – often literally – pale imitations of their American models.

The impact of rock 'n' roll was, at one level, just like that of other musical styles.

By the end of 1955 'Rock Around The Clock' had brought new music to everyone's notice, and in the first months of 1956, the impact of Elvis Presley, Carl Perkins and other Americans demonstrated that this was something more than just a passing fad. Then local talent began to emerge in the shadow of the U.S. singers, rock 'n' roll groups started to be formed, taking Bill Haley and his Comets as their model.

The first real rock group in England were Rory Blackwell's 'Rock 'n' Rollers' who started working in September 1956, soon to be followed by 'Tony Crombie and his Rockets'.

In late 1956 a 'Rock 'n Roll Jamboree' was held at Wimbledon Palais, this featured other new bands including 'The House Rockers', Leon Bell's 'Bell Cats' and Oscar's 'Hot Icebergs'.

The wildest group at that time were known as 'The Rocking Sinners', who started in the film 'Rock You Sinners', Britain's answer to the U. S. rock films. These groups never attained mass popularity, but they provided a background of intense activity from which solo stars could emerge.

In November 1956, Tommy Steele was first billed as Britain's answer to Elvis Presley, and soon a stable of rock 'n' rollers began to emerge under the management skills of Larry

Parnes; Terry Dene, Marty Wilde, Dickie Pride, Vince Eager, Johnny Gentle – all gyrated to the new tunes they were learning, and when they were billed together they squabbled over who was to sing the most popular of Presley hits.

The most successful of the British rockers and also one of the Parnes group was Tommy Steele who quickly made his way towards showbiz respectability while the rest had no more than a whiff of the real revolution going on about them, although they did fit snugly into the package tours they undertook. The Saturday night dances they played at soon became an unwavering tradition. But the British music scene was too small and too centralised for any development.

It is true that the new medium – Television – provided rock into the U.K. with programmes such as '6.5 Special' on the BBC and later 'Oh Boy' on Independent TV, brought the new music to more people than otherwise would have been possible.

During the 1950s popular music was controlled by the four major record companies – EMI, Decca, Philips and Pye – and was broadcast to the nation through the channels of the BBC and Radio Luxembourg, the latter becoming the outlet for the big record companies. The only available outlets where rock bands could be seen were old-fashioned 'variety' theatres dotted around the countries and major cities, but Moss Empires that worked in tandem with the agents controlled these. Singers were normally presented as part of a package deal ensemble which included a juggler, a conjurer, a dance act and a comedian – hence the term 'Variety'.

It was hardly fertile ground for the emergence of rock and roll. There was at that time another level to Britain's answer to rock that held possibilities for the future music and that was 'Skiffle'.

'Skiffle' may have been based on American music, Kevin Colyer as a blues-based form of black folk music introduced it in this country.

In 1954 Lonnie Donegan, guitarist and banjo player with 'Chris Barber's Jazz Band' recorded 'Rock Island Line'. When it was released as a single in 1955 it became a hit.

Lonnie became famous and a Skiffle craze began in Britain.

In the wake of his popularity only three groups reached more than a small audience; 'Chas Devitt Group', Johnny Duncan and 'The Vipers'.

By the end of 1957 the craze was losing momentum and by 1958 the boom had ended. Lonnie Donegan might have been king as his publicity agents called him of Skiffle – he had two hits in 1957 –'Don't You Rock Me Daddy O' written by the Vipers lead singer Whally Whyton and 'Cumberland Gap' he was not the Skiffle creator. It came from the coffee bars all over London's West End, places where Tommy Hicks used to go – 'The Bread Basket', 'The Gyre and Gimble', 'The Nucleus' and the 2-Is. Although the Skiffle boom had collapsed, Donegan continued playing it at the major showbiz venues. In May 1957 he recorded 'Putting On The Style'. He revived his career in 1959 with the single 'The Battle Of New Orleans's' and in the following year his biggest success, 'My Old Man's A Dustman' which sold a million copies. In the late fifties he topped the bill at three major variety venues successively – The Hippodrome, The Prince Of Wales and the mighty London Palladium and for the next twenty years played in Working men's clubs and miners welfare centres which to him were his bread and butter. After some initial resistance, rock and roll was accepted in the USA as a perfectly normal manifestation. The British culture, however, regarded it as some form of alien art form. The new music did not make a full impact on Britain until mid 1956 with the arrival of Tommy Steele who had the credentials of both singing talent and youthful image. He was promoted as a new discovery from the coffee bars of London, but, in fact his much-publicised amateur status was a myth.

In 1975 Tommy reminisced "I'd been to America when I was at sea. The story about docking one day and being discovered in Soho the next is true, but I'd docked as a semi-professional. For two years I'd worked with Jack Fallon as lead vocalist in places like American Servicemen's Camps that was in 1954 and 1955. In 1955 also I played second guitar behind Josh White for quite a bit when he'd tour clubs and things. I was lucky I was the only teenager around that could play a guitar and who had his own ideas I'd picked up abroad. It was just fortunate, they were looking for someone who could play this new American music and that I was this sort of answer just walking around the streets."

During the summer of 1956 he was already receiving offers of management from a number of agents. He became involved with two business men – Geoff Wright and Roy Turvey who had recruited John Kennedy to arrange advanced publicity for their protégé. John Kennedy managed to persuade Tommy's parents to let him manage him and the story is old news. Tommy was to say, "I never felt like a pioneer although I was the only one singing country music. On my first tour, a good third of my act was country music. The origins of rock 'n' roll are in country music, when the beat is accented the second and fourth beat of the bar from the drums that is rock 'n' roll. The BBC said they'd created this new show 6.5 Special for me. I was doing rock 'n' roll for three years – I started in 1956 and finished in 1959. There had never been a British teenager singer before me, so there was no president for what I was doing. When others came along, they could be surprised or disappointed by what was happening because they had seen me. Larry Parnes used to ring me up with names, "What do you think of 'Marty Wilde' or 'Billy Fury'? "Yeer, that sounds nice." And, to be honest, they were far more committed than I was. I never went looking for screams and gyrating and quivering my lower lip. In Sweden they had a poll to find out exactly who was the best rock 'n' roller – and believe it or not, I beat Elvis. That was purely on my personality, I think – my records weren't as good as his!

Jack Good said, "Tommy was a complete natural, a star from the moment he stepped on the stage. Before I met him, he had absolutely no technique, Tommy would say, Well, Well, Well, does anybody want to hear 'Giddy Up A Ding Dong?' and the whole audience would scream. He was fantastic. He wore a pastel blue bellboy outfit, he was full of energy, his eyes twinkled and his mouth was full of wonderful teeth. He must have been marvellous because his band was not the worlds best rock 'n' roll band, as we didn't have anybody who could play rock 'n' roll, but Tommy was so good and I didn't mind that he didn't have threatening aspect which I liked in a rock 'n' roll artist. Tommy wasn't on the 6.5 Special very much because the BBC wouldn't pick up his options and two months after it started we couldn't afford him 'cause the price was double the budget for the whole show. I was only on £18 a week myself. Rock 'n' roll was a stepping-stone for Tommy, he wanted to be an all round entertainer. In 1957 he starred in 'Goldilocks And The Three Bears' at the Royal Court in Liverpool and climbed the ladder to international fame.

Tommy said, "That was the first show I ever did where I could act and dance and it was the turning point of my career. That's why I have a great love for Liverpool. I used to sail from Liverpool and most of my shipmates were Scousers. My career has had some wonderful moments in Liverpool. My friends at the Liverpool Press Club taught me so much about handling the press, I've always been grateful to the city and its people."

# The John Kennedy Version

I was in the 2.Is coffee bar on the 19th September 1956 in the heart of the London's red light district taking some pictures of the group on the stage when Tommy walked in and started a commotion.

He got on the stage, had a bit of a bust up with the lads and started singing a few songs. He was dressed in a bright blue jersey and a pair of jeans that had seen better days. His thick blond hair was unruly and kept tumbling across his eyes, but in those days that was the fashion. His voice bounced off the walls and hit you like a tidal wave as the children dressed in every kind of crazy getup let the music carry them away.

At the end of his songs there was complete silence.

But then the applause started, and it went on and on.

Tommy was not handsome but he had a smile that drew you to him. He sang another song 'Heartbreak Hotel' and in seconds he had dominated the room. I leaned forward listening to every beat of the music. I turned round. The girls were staring at him and biting their nails down to the qwicks. I could feel the effect myself. I found myself tapping my feet and beating time with my hands on the table. Then I knew if I could get hold of that lad I could take him to the top. As quickly as he had come into the room he was gone. I looked around and caught a glimpse of him heading for the door.

Once the group started playing again I was no longer interested in them. They were good, but for my money were not going to put a crisis in Tin Pan Alley. But the lad I had been listening to would.

I was out of my seat quickly and followed him into the street. He was heading towards another coffee bar and I asked him his name.

'Tommy Hicks" he replied. "What's on your mind?"

I told him I could make him a star!

I told him that I thought he had got plenty of talent and ought to stop what he was doing and go into show business with me as his publicity agent.

He said," I wish you were right, but I'm a seaman in the merchant navy and I only do this for fun. On board I often do turns in the ships concerts. Blokes are always coming up to me and saying the same sort of thing. Look at these he says pulling out from his jeans pocket a stack of cards. All these have asked me to contact them; well I've done that. I've been to auditions. I've even been on the 'tele' in the States, but they don't want me. They say my act is too much like Norman Wisdom's".

"Norman Wisdom"? What are you talking about?"

"Well" Tommy says. "That's my act, I do a few songs, tell a few gags, fall over, get up, play my guitar and a bit on the piano."

I told Tommy, "You are a singer, not a comedian". I asked for his address and told him I would call round in the morning but before then I had lots of telephone calls to make, and wondered, what on earth I was going to say to him. The next morning I took a cab to Tommy's house and knocked on the door.

Tommy himself opened the door. He looked as if he'd just got up. His hair was all over the place. He was dressed in his jeans and a vest. He invited me inside. It was a typical terraced house with a long hall with two doors off it; he invited me into the parlour or best room. We had a short chat. Then he said, "Come and meet my folks!"

We went into the back room. "This is my dad. My mum is in the kitchen making some tea".

Mrs Hicks popped her head round the door, "You must be the man Tommy has been telling us about" she says.

"John Kennedy" I replied.

"Pleased to meet you, Mr Kennedy, I won't be a minute," she called back as she entered the kitchen. "Just making a pot of tea". Tommy's dad was reading the paper. He put it down as Mrs Hicks brought the tray from the kitchen, and began clearing a space for her to put it down on the table.

"Do you have sugar and milk in you tea Mr Kennedy?" She asked.

"Put in your own sugar," she said and passing me a cup.

As she sat down she came straight to the point. "Now what's this you have been saying to Tommy? What are you trying to do to him?"

"Without any hesitation I came to the point. I confessed that I knew a great deal about publicity but very little about managing an entertainer."

She told me all about Tommy, how she had wanted him to go to the Savoy and about him going to sea behind their backs, and how he had been ill and nearly died.

I talked about myself and what I had done, concluding with the fact that Tommy had a better chance with me making him famous, than any other person in the entertainment business. I told them of my plans to get him talked about in the newspapers and that people would be coming to me to book him. Take a look at this house, the street, and the people. Tommy is a natural. The children need someone like Tommy to fall in love with. He is the boy next door. He comes from the same kind of street they live in, he went to the same kind of school, he has had the same illnesses and he talks the same way. I say to you that I shall get him to the top. Whilst we were talking Tommy just plucked at his guitar.

The tea had gone cold by this time and Mrs Hicks rose from the table and said, "I don't understand why you want him? We don't even think he can sing or play his guitar properly yet do we dad."

Mr Hicks looked embarrassed.

Mrs Hicks broke in, 'Well' she said, "If you think he will be a big star then we will just have to take your word for it, but don't make fools of us. We are only humble people and don't want people talking about us, or having people look into the way we live. Whatever you do we are in your hands."

We signed no contract. We just agreed that I would be Tommy's manager and left it at that. I told Tommy to be at the Two Is at eight o'clock that night, what for – I had no idea, but I knew I had to do something fast.

I left his house and made my way to my office in the city to make some telephone calls. The first one that I made was to George Martin, a friend, who worked for a famous record company. I asked him to come down to the 2-Is that night with a view to getting Tommy a recording test. The next phone call was to the 2-Is manager, asking him to get the Vipers to back Tommy so that the fellow could hear Tommy singing with a group. At eight o'clock the '2-Is' was packed to bursting point. When George Martin heard Tommy singing  he walked out. I was after him like a shot.

"Well what do you think of him?" I asked.

He replied, "No chance, - you'll never get anywhere with him, he can't sing."

Yet inside the coffee bar the crowd were going wild. I never told Tommy anything about what had been said.

I told Tommy, "Be back tomorrow at the same time".

The next day I rang Hugh Mendl of the Decca Record Company to have a meal with me at a venue quite close to the coffee bar. Over the meal I told him about the lad I had found. I must have sounded enthusiastic because he said he would come along and hear him sing.

I had arranged with Tommy to keep singing until I gave him the nod, but once inside the coffee bar I could not even see him.

After the fifth song Hugh pushed his way out of the coffee bar. Out on the street I asked him what he thought.

After a moment he said, "He's good, very good. I like him. Bring him down to the studios tomorrow for a sound test".

After fighting my way back inside the coffee bar I found that Tommy was still singing I waved him off the stage.

"I thought you were never going to get me off. I was beginning to run out of songs to sing." Said Tommy

"Well done mate" I said. "You were great. I have arranged a sound test tomorrow with Decca Records".

"Make a record?" he asked. "You had better write it down on a piece of paper. My mum will never believe it"

I told him that Hugh Mendl wanted him to find two songs one – for the A side and another for the B.

I contacted a few friends from the papers and told them to be at the Decca studios first thing in the morning.

I met Tommy at the studios.

The conditions under which "Rock With The Caveman" and Rock around the Town" were recorded were absolutely crazy. Tommy's mum and dad were there, his baby sister Sandra, his young brother Roy and his dog that growled at everyone who came near it. Hugh Mendl almost had a fit.

The very first time they recorded the "Caveman" it sounded great to me – but not to Mendl's ear.

He made him go through it again and again.

On the thirteenth time the smile on Mendl's face told me all was going well, then half way through the number, young Roy let go of the dogs lead and it rushed across towards Tommy, barking like mad, another take ruined.

Mendl was livid.

He rushed out of the control room.

"Just one more interruption and every body will leave the studio," he roared at the top of his voice.

Take eighteen was note perfect, but just as Tommy sang the last lyrics, Roy and Sandra began clapping and the dog started barking. The disc was ruined again. At the next run through Mendl was happy at last and the record was in the can.

Hugh Mendl asked, "Who had published the music?"

Tommy answered. "No one, I wrote it with two of my pals from the coffee bar".

"Well you had better get a publisher, and then you'll be able to get royalties from any sheet music sales". Said Mr Mendl.

"What about a name for the lad? Hicks doesn't sound good for a recording star", asked Mendl

"We already have worked that one out!" Said I. Tommy's paternal grandfather's name (of Scandinavian descent) was Thomas Stil-hicks. Thus if we drop the Hicks, and a change it to an English version we get the name Tommy Steel.

"Tommy Steel, that sounds absolutely great," said Mendl.

"Tommy Steel it is!" I said

That afternoon Tommy and I went to see Jimmy Phillips, a music publisher for the firm Peter Maurice. He paid us £150 advance for fifty per cent of the royalties.

The "Caveman" side of the record went up to number thirteen in the hit parade and made for us several thousand pounds. When the record came out his name had been spelt Tommy Steele.

The next thing I had to do was make sure that Tommy never went back to sea. To do that I had to get him some bookings, after the publicity I got for him he was on the way up.

Tommy' first professional booking was at a small club 'The Condor' in Waldour Street for one night only – his pay for that night was three pounds.

After that I tried club after club but they all turned him down.

His first proper booking was at the Stork Room.

The day after the Stork Room finished he was invited to appear on BBC's "Off The Record".

On the way home from the recording studios I invited Tommy for a drink at the local pub and he told me "I don't drink".

"Why" I asked.

"Well" said he, "Once when the ship was in stopped in New York. I went with some shipmates to a bar and they started on large rums. Everyone said to be a good sailor you had to like a drink, so I just kept up with them. After the sixth rum I fell on the floor and they carried me back to the ship and put me in my bunk. It was two days later before I felt any better. I was dragged before the captain and lost all my shore leave, I had spent more than I could afford, and swore I'd never touch another drop as long as I live."

The following is an extract from an article that appeared in the 'Record Mirror,' written by the editor, Isidore Green.

"Into my office on the Saturday afternoon following his appearance on 'Off The Record' were ushered two sprightly and smiling young men, one I immediately recognised as John Kennedy who was a photographer for the magazine in its early days, and the other was Tommy Steele.

John Kennedy had been to see me some four or five weeks before to tell me he was packing up his photography career and going into show business as a manager for a young man named Tommy Hicks, I guarantee that when I call on you next time he'll be big news.

This was the 'next time' and certainly John's guarantee had been fulfilled.

"I've brought Tommy along, so that anything you want to know about him you'll get first hand."

Tommy, a slightly built youngster with quite a baby face, his blond hair flowing down his forehead, relaxed into one of the green armchairs, He said very quietly:-

"I sure don't know what's hit me. Less than two months ago I was a bell-boy on one of Cunard Line's ships, at everyone's beck and call and now I'm told I'm going to top the bills at variety theatres up and down the country."

I asked Tommy, "Are you deliberately imitating Elvis Prestley?"
Tommy was emphatic in his reply.

"Absolutely not! When I was in New York a few months ago – on shore leave – I saw him on television and I went crazy about him, but I developed my own ideas about singing long before I saw him. All my life I've had dreams about singing fast numbers in my own way and everything I do comes naturally with no thought of anyone else. I sing from the heart. I put feeling and power into my numbers. I want to make everyone happy when I give out that I want everybody to feel the same way."

Some artist's – I should say, most of them – have to bash away for years and years before cracking into the big time, most of them knock themselves out all there lives without even smelling it. How is all this reacting on him? Do you feel any different today than, say, three months ago? Said Mr. Green.

Tommy replied, "I promise you it won't go to my head. I'm happy, of course I am. It mean's I can sing like I want to. It means that my mum and dad will be able to live more comfortable. It means joy for them and joy for me. Max Bygraves was my idol, he came from Bermondsey, too, you know. I want everybody there to be as proud of me as they are of him."

Mr Green replied "It's up to Tommy, if I'm any judge of character, I think you will be a big hit without getting a big head.

Tommy at 'The Stork Room'

# The Hugh Mendl Version

I decided within a matter of minutes to put the lad on to a disc.

We older people have tended to get far too conventional in our approach to singing. For example, no matter how competent the drawing room baritone or the ordinary vocalist may be, we in the industry have to be ready to foster any vocal style, which has appeal. Watching those children in the coffee bar, I knew he had appeal. I felt then that this lad was a fine artist. He had the vitality and the freshness, which our record company so needed in those days.

Decca had the reputation in the disc world of not wasting time, and I felt that the needle didn't drag in the groove on this occasion.

I asked John Kennedy to bring the lad down to the studio the following day. John and the lad arrived early with his family and his dog and Lionel Bart plus a host of press people. They were shown round the studio whilst I attended to finish some business. After a few minutes I went into the recording section and I asked John if he had he brought his backing group. He replied, "No only Lionel. So I fixed them up with two guitar players and a drummer I picked up off the street.

After a few practices I said, "Right let's do it" and went into the control room.

The songs he had chosen were 'Rock With The Caveman' and 'Rock around the Town' which the lad told me he had written only the night before the recording.

After nineteen takes, many of which had been ruined by his family clapping or the dog barking, the record was in the can. It was 24th September 1956.

The next day, although much of the press had covered the recording, only the Musical Express recorded the event. However it was vital to get things moving. A lot of people think that after making a record, stardom follows automatically. Well that is not the case. Hundreds of singers are put on disc on a daily basis but they don't sell. If that happens after several trials, they don't renew the contract and the rest get scrapped.

Kennedy was taking no chances. He planned his campaign on three fronts; one to get his lad on a disc, two to get him noticed by the press, and three to get people talking about his public performances. But first he had to get the lad a good name. Tommy Hicks would not sell records. Nor would the name he went under in the ships concerts – Chick Hicks. Kennedy had already decided with Tommy that, to sell records, his name would be his grandfather's name, Tommy Stil, changed to Steel.

When the record was produced somebody had put an E on the end of the spelling and the name stuck.

When Kennedy tried some of the larger West End Clubs they didn't want to know. There were others, in various departments of show business, who didn't want to know either, but Kennedy kept trying to boost Tommy's confidence. He booked him into a small club, The Condor on Wardour Street, for one night. Tommy was paid three pounds. Not a lot, but it gave him the confidence he needed. At that time 'genuine' bookings didn't come easy as club after club turned him down. Then there came an element of luck. Around that time reports of frenetic behaviour at Elvis Presley shows were coming across the Atlantic. They were soon to be followed by the large-scale press coverage of audiences rioting during the showing of the Bill Haley Film, 'Rock Around The Clock'. Had the Steele, Kennedy venture started three months earlier it would have been rough going. It could have flopped right then and there. Yet as luck would have it, they came along just at the right time.

Tommy's first big press break came with the 'Sunday People' newspaper with a circulation of four and a half million readers. Kennedy sold them the idea that Tommy had been invited to entertain at a swanky rock 'n' roll party and a photo feature came out the following morning with the heading 'Rock 'n' Roll Hits the Smart Set.'

It gave Tommy valuable publicity.

It was on 30th September when John Kennedy did some hard talking to Bill Offner, a well-known London club land proprietor of the Stork Room in Regent Street. Offner knew the business well and wasn't easily impressed, but he took a liking to Tommy and decided to try him out.

He gave him an audition in the afternoon and he liked him so much sent him on the stage that night without even a run through.

Tommy Steele went down well with the sophisticated diners – as well as he did with the coffee bar clientele. The only way to get Tommy off the stage was to turn off the lights. He was signed up that night for a two weeks run – the reported fee being twenty pounds per week.

It was possible that John Kennedy could have booked Tommy for many weeks on the West End club scene, but he was after bigger and better things for his artiste. But before he could go after them there was one question to be asked, "How was the record selling"? I reported to him that it had had several playing's on 'Radio Luxemburg and that many people were beginning to buy it. That as far as John Kennedy was concerned was good enough; he could now tackle the big impresarios.

It was whilst Tommy was at the Stork Room that Kennedy took on a partner.

He knew that Tommy had the voice, he had the publicity know how, and Larry Parnes had a shrewd business head and money to invest.

Larry wanted to know what kind of contract he had with Tommy.

John informed him it was a handshake agreement only. After the show that night Tommy was consulted and he agreed that a proper contract should be drawn up.

The following day John and Larry visited Mr and Mrs Hicks in Frean Street. They would have thirty per cent of his earnings; a good booking agent ten per cent and Tommy had the rest.

It was agreed and the contract was signed.

To get more money for Tommy John Kennedy started asking one hundred pounds per week for him and quite a few of the impresarios said that he was off his head; he could have lowered the price and just accepted a trial week at some obscure music hall. He could have, but he didn't.

He took the opposite course. He put Tommy up for two hundred, plus top billing.

He got no offers.

The press interest was on the increase.

On 15th of October 1956 Tommy made his first appearance on 'Off The Record' for the BBC. Record returns for 20th October for 'Rock With The Caveman' took the record to number seventeen in the charts on the 26th it got to 13.

On 23rd October Tommy made his first film, 'Kill Me Tomorrow'.

The film Kill Me Tomorrow starred Pat O'Brien, Lois Maxwell, George Collouris and Wensley Pithy. It was a black and white movie, which lasted for eighty minutes. Tommy had two scenes in the film as a nightclub singer singing 'Rebel Rock his only appearance. The film was made in Britain by Delta.

By the 2nd of November the record ' Rock With The Caveman' moved up to number thirteen.

Suddenly Tommy Steele was the name that everybody wanted. The top line impresario Harold Fielding sent Ian Bevan, head of his agency, to take a look at him and then he took a calculated risk booking Tommy for a six week run with a handsome salary, at the number one venues as Top of the bill. I don't know what was going through the minds of Fielding, Bevan, Kennedy and Parnes, but Tommy was greatly perturbed to be catapulted to a point where the major responsibility of the show rested with him, billed above artistes who had been in the business for years. It left him weak at the knees. As it happened, none of them need have worried.

Tommy Steele's first date was at the Sunderland Empire.

He opened on 5th November 1956; fireworks flew that night for the lad as fans packed the theatre night after night. The teenagers were all outside the stage door screeching for their newfound hero. Nottingham, Sheffield and Brighton took Tommy to their hearts and voted with their feet.

On Monday 3rd December the show came to Finsbury Park Empire. It was a sell out and those who could not get tickets stood in the foyer hoping to hear anything of his performance. I went to the theatre and the young Steele gave a fresh, active, and crowd pulling performance. His boyish disarming manner sold him to his audience with his bobbing about, flicking his guitar as if it was a bren gun, He fired away 'Rock with The

Caveman' and 'Giddy Up A Ding Dong' with so much gusto that the girls went wild. But not every body liked what he was hearing Dick Hall reporter wrote in a newspaper,"Mr Steele, What a phenomenon Rock-n' Roll singer and guitarist Tommy Steele is!

A phenomenon because on Monday, in his London Variety debut at Finsbury Park it seemed little short of a miracle that this 19-year-old youth could receive such a rapturous ovation for the little musical talent that he displayed. The audience gave Steele one of the biggest first-house receptions I have ever heard. But Steele appearing in skin-tight white flannels, green jersey and white cravat, offered them little in the way of entertainment, his voice lisping and at times sounding like Johnnie Ray, and was frequently out of tune, his intonation was also bad. Perhaps it would be kinder not to mention his guitar playing. His accompanying group, the Steelemen, provided an adequate backing for Steele's vocal contortions. The best act in my opinion was the multi-instrumentalist Johnny Laycock.

"The rest of the story is common knowledge," said Mendl. "He made a mint for the Decca record label with his run of fast selling discs."

Tommy had proved himself to be more than just a freak of the rock 'n' roll craze. Since he first sprang into the limelight, seats in theatres that once were empty are now being filled when he is on the stage.

In the 1956 N.M.E. poll Tommy was rated as the eighth outstanding male singer and the twelfth outstanding British Musical personality.

On Christmas Eve of the same year his contribution to the BBC's 'Off The Record' production he sang 'Singin' The Blues.' Eighteen days later this record reached number one in the British Charts. However Tommy might have missed out having another number one in the charts as Lionel Bart recalls.

"I wrote this song for Tommy. It was called 'Give Us A Kiss for Christmas.' It would have suited Tommy perfectly, but he overslept on the day of the recording. The choir were there at the studios. The orchestra were ready and waiting but he never showed up. "What shall we do?" said the manager; so I said to him, "I'll sing it myself. Decca put the record out the following week and it made the charts getting to number four, even with my voice".

Lionel recalls the making of 'Rock with the Caveman'.

"When we got to the studios I had just the top line of the music. Hugh Mendl brought in three other guys – Ronnie Scott, Dave Lee and Benny Green. They were all excellent jazz musicians and they arranged it there and then. Ronnie Scott knew nothing about rock 'n' roll, but his solo on that record rivalled Rudy Pompillis's playing for Bill Hayley. The record sold hundreds and hundreds of copies but all I got for the session was £6. I thought Tommy was very talented but we weren't aware of what was going on as far as rock 'n' roll was concerned at that time. In 1960 Tommy found his own style and recorded a song called 'What A Mouth.' Tommy said, "I did that song for one person only – my father. He said to me, "You think you can perform and know what you're doing but until you can sing like the Two Bills from Bermondsey, you've had it. The Two Bills sang 'What A Mouth' and I listened to it and thought, I'm gonna do that. And he did."
Hugh Mendl died in 2008.

# Ode to the greatest Personality In Show Business

By Adrienne Parker… East Sheen.     By courtesy of Pat Richardson

Fair hair flopping to and fro
A figure of rhythm from head to toe
Feet astride and nibble fingers Plucks his guitar, a tune that lingers
Bright red shirt and tight blue jeans
Receiving an ovation of shrieks and screams

A stamp of his foot, a nod of the head
His fans all shout aloud with glee
He sings with his heart and soul you see
It's as if he were singing just for me

The stage lights dim except for one
Which shines on the face of one so young
The music throbs to the song he sings
And at the end the applause he brings

Echoes through the concert hall
As he takes his final curtain call
Now that it's over it doesn't seem real
But that last act was my own Tommy Steele.

# Entertainment Agents, Managers

Trawling the local circuit for paid work will inevitably introduce entertainers to the local 'Entertainment Agent or Promoter'. Both provide an essential service to artists/bands by removing the hassle of finding gigs. Their main function is to find the acts on their books as many gigs as possible; some may even help to put together a sensible gigging strategy. A good agent will be in touch with other agents and promoters who may exchange information on who they currently have touring or swap/share gigs. This gives their artists the opportunity to open a show close a show or appear with a more established act or deputies for a late cancellation in a venue otherwise unavailable.

An Agent can either negotiate on the entertainers behalf with the venue or promoter for a fee and charge them a commission for arranging the booking or the agent will 'buy' the band for a fee, and then 'sell' the band on to a venue for a higher fee. The difference between the purchase and selling price is the agent's profit. He/She may switch between the two methods depending on the type of show that the venue requires. The standard commission fee is between 10% and 15% of your GROSS earnings on each booking they provide and for each subsequent rebooking in the venue. Sadly many agencies are charging 20% but avoid paying more than 15% if at all possible and don't bother with those that charge more unless they getting you loads of work for lots of money!!

Since registration with the DTI ceased to be a requirement anyone can set up his or her own agency. There is very little regulatory control, many agencies are here today and gone tomorrow or have been know to collect artist fees but not pass them on, so do be careful, check them out prior to using, chat to other performers using their services, contact local venues for recommendations. There were some rumors that the DTI regulations where going to be re-instated we don't have any further information at this time. Seek advice from local artists/bands, use long-standing agents with good reputations and read the trade newspapers for news of agents who have defaulted or stopped trading.

Up-front fees are prohibited!! Agencies that charge up-front fees to entertainers, models and extras before finding them work have finally been outlawed in legislation published by the Department for Trade and Industry.

The Entertainment Agent - deals mainly with all styles of 'Covers Acts, Bands and Entertainers' ranging from Classical to Cabaret and Comedy with a myriad of artists on their books all pushing for more work! Their range of venue varies depending on the reputation of the agency and the chosen area of specialisation. Most local agents are independent and book acts/bands for pubs, clubs, local and some corporate events whereas others concentrate on providing entertainment for Cruise Ships, Theatres, Hotels and International Venues.

The only way to tell which area the agency specialises in is to visit their sites or find their advertisements in local and trade papers, directories etc. If you are searching for one agent to represent you look at their past endeavours and talk to musicians who have used their services before signing an exclusive contract. Unless an agent can guarantee regular work it is not productive to use one agency, most have many artists on their books and are required by their bookers to provide a variety of entertainers. This limits the amount of paid bookings you are likely to receive, so find several reliable agents who like your act and are perceptive enough to place you in venues that are going to appreciate your style of music.

The Entertainment Agency - is made up of several agents, each of whom may cater to a different type of venue. Some specialise in new artists and original bands but the majority are similar to the independent agent and deal with a variety of entertainers including dancers, singers, musicians, comedians etc.

The Music Promoter - books covers, tributes and original acts/bands for regular Showcases, Festivals or Venues, sometimes runs a circuit within an area to promote specific styles of music. The Promoter is not an agent but organises events where they book acts to appear. Many promoters work on behalf of a venue and do not charge a commission to the act/band. More established promoters will often give local original artists a support gig for one of their more popular or major acts/bands with 'Audition or New Band' nights to encourage and promote live music.

Payments to the artists vary with many promoters handing out tickets to the band members who are counted after the gig and a small percentage of the takings paid to the artist/s. More established and headline acts/bands may be offered a flat fee. The promoter either takes a percentage of the door fee or is paid by the venue. It's true that many artists have lost money through dodgy promoters however, those that are not on a weekly wage invariably pay out all expenses, advertising, p.a. hire, sound engineer and other staff fees from the door money!! In other words, don't expect to get paid if there isn't much of an audience unless you have signed a contract or made prior agreement with the promoter on a standard fee.

It's a totally different ball game for signed or popular artists, who can command a fee, specify P.A. & Lighting requirements plus provide their own sound engineer.

In the first instance John Kennedy took Tommy on without signing any agreement with him.

When Larry Parnes came on the scene he signed an agreement with Tommy's mum and dad because Tommy was under age when the two of them Kennedy and Parnes arranged that the both of them should be his managers.

Harold Fielding never signed an agreement with Tommy and that's what Tommy liked about him, he was always true to his word that he would look after him and he did.

When John Kennedy decided to part with Tommy another agreement would have to be signed between Tommy and Larry Parnes.

When Larry Parnes decided to part, Harold Fielding took on Tommy full time.

When Harold Fielding could no longer manage Tommy, Tommy changed over to International Artists again another agreement would have had to be signed

In April 2010 Laurie Mansfield left International Artistes and formed a new company Laurie Mansfield Associates taking Tommy amongst his long list of established artistes.

Each time Tommy Steele signed the agreement it was done under his birth name of Thomas Hicks.

A TOMMY STEELE PERFORMERS/AGENTS CONTRACT WITH HAROLD FIELDING MADE 16TH JULY 1961. CONTRACT NUMBER 1296

Harold Fielding Limited Fielding House, 13 Bruton Street, Berkeley Square, London, W1 Telephone Mayfair 3151.

An agreement made on the 16th day of July 1961 between HAROLD FIELDING LIMITED, Fielding House, 13 Bruton Street, W.1 hereinafter called the Management of the one part, and TOMMY STEELE ENTERPRISES LTD, to provide the services of Tommy Steele hereinafter called the artiste of the other part, witnesseth that the client hereby engages the artiste and the artiste accepts an engagement to appear in accordance with the terms and conditions contained hereafter is being understood and agreed that for the purpose of this engagement the conditions of Schedule 1 and also Schedule 2 (if any) overleaf shall be read and present the artist at the Venue on the dates stated in the schedule hereto; To make the appearance in each of the two concerts at the Opera House Blackpool on Sunday 16th July 1961 at 6.20 and 8.15 p.m. To make the appearance in each of the two concerts at the Opera House Blackpool on Sunday 17th August 1961 at 6.20 and 8.15 p.m. For an Inclusive salary of (left out for privacy) for each of the two Sundays detailed payable by cheque from the Harold Fielding Limited office on the Friday following the termination of the engagement. To make the appearance in each of the two concerts at the Winter Gardens, Bournemouth, on Sunday 29th August 1961 at 6.20 and 8.15 p.m. For an Inclusive salary of £? (Left out for privacy) payable by cheque from the Harold Fielding Limited office on the Friday following the termination of the engagement.

Pp. Tommy Steele Enterprises Ltd

Signature ......Thomas Hicks...

The signature is signed over a stamp note, not with his stage name of Tommy Steele but with his birth name Thomas Hicks.

The new partnership together

# Top Of The Bill

Tommy recalls, "After the first two weeks at the Stork Room as top of the bill Al Burton came into the dressing room with a booking form in his hand. John went outside to talk with him. After a minute he came back. '

They want to book you for another two weeks. Your pay will be twenty five pounds per week," he said.

"When we got away from the dressing room we walked into the city and looked for a newspaper stand.

One of the large newspapers had promised to do a big write up on me being Britain's own Elvis Presley. We picked up the early edition and looked through it. It was not there!

Where is it"? I asked John. My mum has told everybody to buy the paper; they are all going to laugh at her now!

Then John had an idea - why not get my mum and dad to come to the club themselves.

It made the papers the very next day.

By now I decided that I was not going to go back to sea!"

One night whist Tommy was performing at the club a friend of John's came in - his name was Larry Parnes.

"I liked him at once," said Tommy, "and we spoke together for a long time, at the end of which John suggested that they should have a proper contract signed instead of just shaking on it like they had done in the first instance. I agreed, and both John and Larry became my managers."

When his parents signed the contract, they walked down to the local pub and had the document witnessed by the pub manager who knew his dad quite well. Larry suggested champagne, but Tommy said, "Don't be daft my dad will have a bitter and my mum will have a stout, and you can make mine an orange juice".

Then John and Larry got to work.

Mr. Harold Fielding took on Tommy without a contract being signed. Harold made him top of the bill at the Sunderland Empire opening on the 5th November 1956. His pay was reported at one hundred and fifty pounds per week.

When they all arrived at the dressing room in Sunderland, they let Tommy go in first, and he got the biggest surprise of his life!

There in the centre of the dressing room was his old mate from the ship – Kurt "Brushes" Littner. He rushed to him and at once burst into tears.

He was so pleased to see him. He thought Kurt had come to see the show, but when John told him, "You talked about him so much in the first weeks of starting out I just had to have him as your dresser".

He could have killed John for not informing him.

Just before he went out onto the stage, Mike and Bernie Winters came into his dressing room to wish him luck. Reg Thompson followed those two.

These were the true veterans of the business and although they were true professionals and they were wishing him luck.

Him, Tommy Steele a mere lad of nineteen with the responsibility of the show on his shoulders luck, he thought. He needed more than luck as he stood at the side of the stage. He could not move.

He felt a push in his back and a voice calling out "Too late to be nervous now Tommy."You're on".

He kept on moving and shaking as he sung the songs.

After six curtain calls they finally closed the curtain. He was exhausted, not from singing, but from the noise of applauds and cheers. When the curtain finally closed, Tommy just stood there staring at it, as the crowds in front yelled for more.

John came back to the dressing room after watching the show from the front of house and said to Tommy,

"I had dreamed of success for you but I never dreamed it would be like this".

Some of the girls who had seen the show forced their way past the stage door and were calling his name.

As the stagehands were trying to get them outside, Tommy stopped them and invited the girls into his dressing room. When they saw him they just stood in awe as he signed their autograph books. One even looked into John's eyes and cried out, "Oh he's wonderful!" When they had all left, Tommy sat in a chair and had a cigarette.

At every theatre they went to after that, the crowds grew larger and larger.

Outside the stage doors it got so bad that the theatre managers had to call the police to stop the crowd from breaking the doors down.

On Monday, December 10th 1956 he opened up at Birmingham's 'Hippodrome Theatre' for six nights doing two shows per night. On the bill with him were the Hippodrome Orchestra, Marie De Vere Dancers, Reg Thompson, Len Young, Thunderclap Jones, Josephine Anne, Harry Worth and the Steelemen.

After a few days break he was informed by his managers that he was to appear at the Café de Paris, home of the international stars.

Tommy heard what was being bandied about - that he would not go down well with the swanky set. He knew they would be wrong, as he had already gone down well with the customers of the Stork Room.

Tommy knew at the back of his mind that a flop at the Café de Paris would send him back to sea and he didn't want that. He had begun to like what he was doing.

Harold Fielding began to get the jitters.

He spoke to John and Larry to call it off, but the contract had been signed.

The opening night was 21st January 1957.

The dressing room walls were decorated with telegrams and flowers from his friends in the business. Tommy had seen the people outside waiting to come in and there was not a teenager amongst them, and he was nervous for the first time in his life. Tommy got even more nervous when they told him that every national newspaper had sent a representative.

Then came the report, "Mr Steele your on!" and he made his way to the top of the stairs on which he had to dance down. At the Café de Paris the light went on him as they made the announcement! "Welcome to the nineteen-year-old sensation of show business, Mr Tommy Steele". His brain went into gear. The first number went well, and just as he started his second song the mike died. Tommy could feel that something was wrong and stopped the band from playing. The audience started whispering and tittering, so he got the staff to turn on all the house lights. There, seated at the very front seats, were his mum and dad.

Tommy nearly died.

He could do nothing, so he shouted at the top of his voice, "Can you hear me at the back?"

A small voice came back, "No we can't."

"There must be a fault with the mike." He said,

"While we get it fixed I'll tell you a story!"

Everyone sat quiet not knowing what to expect. He told them the story of a pack of cards. Everyone leaned forward, not wanting to miss a word. When he had finished the story he looked at his mum, and she was crying.

The mike by this time had been fixed and the audience were on his side.

He yelled at the top of his voice, "Come on let's rock". Some of the youngsters that John had brought in got upon the floor.

The headlines the following day were as follows, "The kid from Bermondsey knock's them in the Old Kent Road.'It was Tribal and they loved it", "A success story to end all success stories".

During his run at the club he recorded the record 'Elevator Rock'. Tommy wrote the flip side, 'Rebel Rock', on the way to the studios.

He found out after the first week that the proprietors wanted him to stay on for another fortnight, but his managers had other plans. Tommy had been offered, and his managers accepted, a six weeks' tour of the provinces. This tour changed his life completely!

One night at the Chiswick Empire, Lionel Bart, one of his song-writing partners, brought in a girl. John had always insisted that girls were never allowed into his dressing room after the first experience, but this one, wow! She was introduced to him as a dancer from the Windmill Theatre.

When John looked at Tommy in a lull in the conversation, he could see it was love at first sight.

Lionel called her by her stage name Annette Donati.

Her real name was Ann Donoghue.

Tommy said "She was wearing a marvellous seafarer's hat, which was a kind of blue and green stripe, and a cloth raincoat with a high collar. It was fitted and reached about three inches below her knees. I asked her if she was staying to watch the show. After the show that night, instead of going out to eat with John, I went out with her and Lionel Bart instead, to a coffee bar. When Lionel Bart left us on our own I found out that she came from Leeds and was born on 27th May 1936, and that she came from a show business family.

Ann was one of eight children, and she had first appeared at the Windmill Theatre in London in February 1952."

John Kennedy was livid because Tommy started taking her everywhere with him.

A week later, Tommy took Ann along to a television interview. That was when John and Tommy had their first row.

The next big thing that happened to Tommy was the making of the film of his life 'The Tommy Steele Story' at the Beaconsfield Studios.

This was great fun, but it entailed a lot of hard work, as it was so different from the stage act he had done up to then. It was a GB film in black and white. It was based on the story of his life as a rock 'n' roll singer. The film starred Hilda Fennimore and Lisa Danielly. In the USA the title was changed to 'Rock Around The World' this included some extra scenes featuring the American DJ Hunter Hancock.

"My life", he said. "It seems that only a few weeks ago that was at sea. Most people think that a film studio must be a fabulous place to work, but it is boring."

He was glad that Ann came to see him everyday or he would have gone mad.

A number of people were asking who she was and John kept telling them that she was his secretary.

After the filming finished he went on another tour, which took in the Manchester Palace and the Empire at Sheffield. On the bill also were Camilleri, the world's greatest accordionist, Reg Thompson, The Dehl Trio, Paul and Peta Page the puppeteers, Mike and Bernie Winters and Harriott and Evans coloured entertainers.

In the March his managers fixed him up to appear in the 'Six-Five Special' series for the BBC television. Six five Special was intended to run for only six weeks. The first show was presented by Pete Murray and co-producer Josephine Douglas and was played in and out by Kenny Baker and his jazzmen. Michael Holliday contributed a couple of ballads and Bobbie and Ruby and the King Brothers provided the rock 'n' roll. The show developed a strong association with Skiffle (Lonnie Donegan, Chas McDevitt and Willie McCormick all made regular appearances) and Tommy Steele was an early guest as was Vince Eager.

Tommy recalls his time on the Six-Five Special show-

"Jack Good had glasses and wore a silk suit. He had an Oxbridge accent and I didn't believe he would have had anything to do with rock 'n' roll. He looked like a headmaster and had a brimful of ideas. Every one thought he was a crackpot but he knew how to get through to the children. I was a bit sceptical when he asked me to appear on the first show, and I was successful enough to be in the following five. The viewers thought it was my show, which of course it wasn't. The show became the forerunner of 'Top Of The Pops."

Trevor Peacock, who wrote the scripts, told Tommy; "Jack Good took me down to the Finsbury Empire to see this strange young man who had burst on the scene and it was you and I knew at once we should have you on because America had produced Elvis and one or two others so it was about time we produced one of our own." He also said that Tommy was at that time the wildest thing imaginable.

It was the beginning of a new era.

Tommy's second record never even made it in the charts at all. But the exaggerated entrance in 'Singin' the Blues' is one of rock 'n' roll's classic elements, it went on to sell more than 2.5 million copies in various versions.

When it was recorded Tommy said, "It was not planned, I was standing in the booth when somebody pointed a finger at me and it just came out, and the record producers left it in."

Newspapers can be kind, but they can also be very bitter. It was reported at one time that Tommy was trying to dodge being called up for the armed services. Well that was not true. He had had the medical, but because he had so many illnesses as a youngster plus flat feet, they turned him down.

"I have never tried to dodge anything in my whole life," he told John Kennedy. "If that's what they thought of him then he vowed he would go back to sea."

He had another row with John over the affair with Ann.

He told him, "There are no friends in this business and even you have turned against me because of my friendship. I know what I shall do. I will call Larry and tell him to let the press know, and they can go to town with the story".

It made John very ill and Tommy had him shipped into hospital.

When John got better, Tommy apologised and made it his business to put his medical condition into the papers. This brought boos at a charity concert at the Coliseum and at the Albert Hall people even started walking out before he had finished his first song.

On 3rd February 1957 he appeared at De Montfort Hall, Leicester along with Steelemen and The Ken Mackintosh Orchestra and other Artists. By this time he had been on stages up and down the country for months, he had made two films and was getting tired of the whole business.

John and Larry knew it and so did his agent Harold Fielding, who told his managers that he had lost his sparkle.

Harold Fielding said, "What Tommy needs is a holiday."

And that's where he went, along with his mum and brother Colin.

The next day the headlines in the newspapers stated that 'Tommy had Been Killed'.

Tour Programme 1957

# Rushed of my feet

In June of 1957, Tommy wrote an article for the Hit Parade magazine - I'm being rushed of my feet - but I like it!

"So much seems to have happened to me since I last wrote for you that I don't know where to start. I have been to a lot of towns around Britain since then, and also managed to take a few days off for a holiday in the Mediterranean with my mum and my kid brother. Then there were five weeks filming on my life story. That was a great new experience for me. It seemed like a different world. I made a record, "Knee deep in the Blues," and appeared on the B.B.C. in the 'Six five special.'

But let's begin with the present. At the time of writing I'm just starting on the first leg of my tour with the American rock 'n' roll group, Freddie Bell and his Bellboys.

Don't believe the press reports you may have read about Freddie and I not getting on with each other. Right from the start we've been the greatest of pals, and it's been the same all along. Of course there were the usual problems to be ironed out, the main one being that unbeknown to each other, Freddie and I had both planned to feature the song 'Hound Dog' in our acts. Freddie had intended to sing it here long before he arrived in Britain. As for me, well, as you know, it's been a regular number in my variety act for some time. I think that Freddie had a hand in writing it, so he was naturally disappointed that he wasn't able to perform it on his first British tour. But we soon sorted everything out between us.

He agreed to let me sing it. In return he agreed he should sing 'Long Tall Sally' another number we both had planned to feature. After that we got along like a house on fire.

I went straight into this show after a ten-day holiday in Majorca.

It was the first break I'd had since I started touring in variety last year, so I was glad of the chance to relax. But it didn't turn out as exciting as I thought it would. My Mum and Colin (my seventeen year old brother) seemed to enjoy themselves all right, but I got bored after the first few days. I don't know whether it was the time of the year or what, but we found very few young people there. There were no girl friends that Colin and I could spend the day on the beach with - what is there for two blokes to do? As for the food, well, I just didn't get on with that at all. I don't know whether you have tried any of that Mediterranean stuff or not but give me a plate of fish and chips any day."

Tommy returned from the holiday with his mum and Colin fit and well. He had had all the rest he had needed and was now ready to do anything his managers asked, which included a big variety tour with a big American rock 'n' roller Freddie Bell and the Bellboys. They were both heading the bills, but Tommy's managers insisted that Tommy closed the show.

During the tour he had to return to London to record "Butterfingers."

During the tour with Freddie every seat was filled for the whole of the tour. When they reached London, Tommy's name was in lights twice as big as Freddie's. They opened at The Dominion Theatre on 20th of May 1957 six months to the day from when Tommy was asked to sing at that 'Debs Ball' John had arranged.

By this time Tommy could not walk down a street without being recognised and mobbed for autographs. Every night of the week at the Dominion, Herbert Smith of Anglo-Amalgamated Films, who wanted Tommy to do a film for them, pestered John. A few weeks later Tommy recorded, 'Water Water' and 'A Handful of Songs.'

Top Record Stars book 1957 wrote "Tommy is at twenty-one years of age, the most controversial figure in British show business ... "they" said he couldn't last - "they" said he was just a teenage pan-flash..."they" were wrong! And "they" - the Old Moore of Charring Cross Road, the sages of the theatre - also showed a certain amount of sourness at this kid's continued fame. This guitar-playing rock 'n' roll idol knows the freezing - point of some of the stars shoulders. He hasn't climbed rocker-style to fame without arousing a certain amount of envy. Yet in spite of the animosity of certain names Steele wins, wherever he goes. He is a Cockney kid, a natural, unaffected youngster from the back streets who has something to sell and is conscious that there may come a day when it will be a buyers' and not a sellers' market. What effect has he had on the population? Everyone is aware that he exists. Few can have missed his frequent occupation of the nations' newspapers front pages. The high-powered publicity drive drove teenagers to storm hotels to be near him – they tore his clothes, ruffled his hair: became modern slaves of a blue-jeaned idol. When Tommy started making his new film, "The Duke Wore Jeans", at Elstree the telephone operators screamed! Not at Tommy – their screams of anguish came as the switchboards jammed for three hours with call from teenagers agog to see their golden boy on the set. But he would have been an unusual sight for the youngsters - he was 'sans' guitar! Said Tommy: "Guitar? Look, I'm starting on a new career in musical comedy ... forget the 'banjo' for a while and give me a chance as an actor" And act he does. In fact, he is two actors, because his part sets him in a duel role. Each is a contrasting type: the first as a young aristocrat, eager to become a great breeder of show-cattle, the second as a young Cockney kid looking for employment. June Laverick played the part of "a tempestuous princess in an oil-bound Central European kingdom".

At Christmas Harold Fielding wrote in the souvenir brochure of Cinderella; - "This Christmas, for the first time in my sixteen years as a theatrical impresario, I am presenting a pantomime. By a lucky combination of circumstances, I have been able to secure wonderful team of actors and producing talent. I have secured a superb score by Rodgers and Hammerstein, and with the co-operation of Mr Prince Littler and Sam Harbour, a theatre, which is by far, the best suited in London for a really spectacular presentation. It has cost £100,000 to bring this show to the stage. The ballroom scene alone (a masterpiece of theatrical design) has cost £12,500. The cast is the most expensive that has ever been assembled for a West End production, and includes three of the top variety stars of our day, Jimmy Edwards, Kenneth Williams and Ted Duranti, as well as three equally famous personalities of the day, Tommy Steele, Yana and Bruce Trent." "Tommy Steele's the 'golden boy' of British show business celebrated his twenty-second birthday the night before he opened at the London Coliseum, his very first starring role in a major West End production. It is amusing to recall that four years ago (when he was based in New York as a British merchant seaman) he appeared on an American television programme for nothing. It was an amateur talent show, and Tommy's contribution was an impression of Norman Wisdom. He was a complete failure, because none of the American viewers had ever heard of Wisdom. Since then he has become not merely a national celebrity, but an international star of major proportions. "Happiness," he says is the keynote of his success. The unique quality, which makes him a star, is that he can 'project' his happiness through the camera and over the footlights. Star quality must be backed up with talent, and Tommy is fortunate to be blessed with a photographic brain a natural sense of rhythm and a nimble body, which enables him to fulfil the most exacting demands of film and stage directions. But talent can only carry a performer part of the way. It is the elusive and very rare 'something extra' which carries him to the absolute heights. One does not need to be a teen-ager to know that Tommy has that 'something extra' which spells stardom with a capital S."

For the rest of the summer Tommy played at the Winter Gardens in Blackpool, whilst John stayed up in London looking after the fan mail. At that time Tommy was receiving several thousand fan letters per week. Tommy was staying at The Majestic Hotel in St Annes and travelling to the theatre every day. One night he decided to have a go on the organ in the bar, much to the disgust of the manager, and he was asked to leave his hotel immediately. The newspapers got hold of the story. The story was bad enough but what made it a calamity was the follow up story, which put Anne's name in print, linking her with Tommy for the first time.

John Kennedy went to Blackpool immediately.

By this time Tommy had a new member of his management team, - John Edwards, an ex-newspaperman.

Outside their hotel were reporters from every single national newspaper. Tommy had another row - this time about Anne with John and Larry, as the sounds of Blackpool went on outside. Tommy and Anne had secretly become engaged without letting anybody know. The story appeared as the headlines in most of the newspapers that Anne and he had split up - but they hadn't.

Tommy Steele's ex-girl friend, showgirl Anne Donati, 21, spoke angrily about the other women in the life of the twenty-year old rock 'n' roll idol, wrote one newspaper.

Whilst another wrote, "Anne who parted from Tommy on Wednesday said: "It's not the usual case of another woman coming between us. In my case there are thousands of them - his fans. I'm afraid the odds are too great."

Anne was Tommy's first steady girl friend. She left him in Blackpool, where he is in a show, and travelled to London.

She said, "You would be surprised how many fans think of Tommy as a little boy. Women who are Mothers seem to think of him in that way. I know ... I was his secretary for eight months and I had to reply to them. You don't expect sweet little boys to have steady girl friends ... so I have left for the sake of his career. It was put to me that it would be best for him in view of his fans. Finally I agreed, but it took a lot of courage."

Anne also said "Mr. Larry Parnes, one of Tommy's Managers, told her it would be better if they parted "because people were talking about us - it had been rumoured we were engaged."

She went on: "I do not hold it against anyone. I like to think that this has been done just for Tommy's sake."

Would she see Tommy again?

"If he was in town and asked me to see him I wouldn't refuse." she said.

The reporter told her that Tommy was heart broken.

She said, "I am very sorry. But I wish him every success in his career."

Another article appeared in the newspaper 'The Pictorial' (closed in 1990) Tommy Steele: Wed? Not Me!

Tommy Steele last night denied that he and the ex-Windmill girl Annette Donati were married in secret on Thursday. This Rumour - the latest in a series of rumours about Tommy's romance with Annette - has been sweeping through the world of rock 'n' roll. But Tommy said, "We are definitely NOT married."

These are the facts behind the 'secret marriage' rumour:

"Last week Tommy introduced twenty-one year old Annette to friends as "my fiancée." Next day, disguised in a cloth cap and dark glasses, Tommy saw Anne off at Darlington (Durham) station for a TV appearance in Scotland. They kissed in the compartment before the train left. Then Tommy went back to the hotel where he had been staying during his stage appearance at nearby Stockton.

Anne had been staying at the same hotel.

Before she left she told a Pictorial reporter: "I love Tommy and hope one day we'll be able to marry."

Said Tommy's manager, John Kennedy: "It would be silly now to deny that Anne is his girl friend (first reported in the Sunday Pictorial of May 12)."But I have told them they must not think of marriage – certainly not yet." "It would ruin our plans for Tommy. I have presented him as a boy who is within the reach of every factory girl." Last night Tommy left Stockton for Blackpool where he appeared in tonight's ATV "Meet The Stars" show.

When Tommy left Blackpool he went off to the studios to make the film "The Duke Wore Jeans," Tommy talked the company into providing him with a caravan instead of staying in a hotel. When the film was finished he owned the caravan he had lived in for seven weeks. 'The Duke Wore Jeans' was a British film that lasted for eighty-nine minutes. It was in black and white. Tommy starred with June Laverick, Michael Medwin, Alan Wheatly and Eric Pohlmann.

By this time, every fan in the world knew his house in Frean Street. Even his mum was pestered for autographs every time she left the house to go shopping. The fans had even started carving pieces out of the windows and doors.

Tommy said, "John was always pestering me, to move my mum out of the house, but I would not have it". A few weeks later John found out that the house had been condemned.

Tommy spoke to his mum. "What is going to happen with the street"? "It's being pulled down," she said. "Something to do with slum clearance the letter says. We are to be re-housed in a new council flat."

Tommy said, "John had a word in my ear."

"You can't let your mum and dad live in a council flat with all the money you are earning. What will people think about you"?

He was right.

Tommy said, "If I bought her a new house, someone who was homeless could have the flat instead".

John agreed and took time out to look for a suitable property. Eventually he found Tommy's mum a nice property she liked, on Ravensbourne Park Road, Catford.

On 1st September 1957, Tommy gave a house warming party at the new house in Catford. At the house warming were his managers John Kennedy, Larry Parnes, Desmond Lane, Mike and Bernie Winters, Vic Lewis, Hugh Mendl, Max Bygraves and Terry Dene.

Godfrey Winn talked to Mrs Hicks about the house Tommy bought for her, in an article 'The Hearts of the Stars.' He wrote: "I don't know how far Catford is from Bermondsey as the crow flies. But it is a whole world - and just one year of fantastic fame (plus intensive hard slogging) divides the former six-roomed house of Mr and Mrs Hicks and the house that their eldest son recently bought them with love and gratitude. The area looks like any other neat; quiet residential area of four-bedroom semi detached houses, each with its patch of garden in front and behind. The only thing that makes the Hicks home different is the milling group of teenagers that hang around the front gate with autograph books in their hands. From time to time the static crowd of sightseers swell with excitement as a car draws up. Who is it? A fellow star like Max Bygraves, whom Tommy looks up to in admiration, and who was there for their house warming party, or a friend of the family? I wondered how his parents reacted to this eternal barrage of fans. I wondered, too, how they were all settling down in their new family nest, with its startlingly modern décor and its brilliantly papered walls, so different from the home in Bermondsey they had left behind. I felt at home the moment that I was greeted in the hall by Mrs Hicks with a real Bermondsey welcome. Tommy's Mother was wearing a working black dress with an apron over it. 'Mind you keep your apron on for the photographs.' I suggested. I needn't have worried. For her instant reply showed her true character. 'I wouldn't dream of taking it off. I don't feel comfortable if I'm not wearing an apron'.

Mrs Hicks is a handsome woman, as dark as Tommy is fair, with fine eyes and an air of natural dignity that is most becoming. 'Son' she called up the stairs 'are you dressed yet! And don't forget to brush your hair'... 'Not that it makes any difference whether he does or does not. It's such fine hair; he can't do anything with it. I know its late (it was quarter to two in the afternoon) but it's so important that he gets enough sleep. He's still growing. I tell him. And after a show, he can't go straight to bed. He has to unwind himself first, he keeps explaining to me, and I see how it is.

'And I suppose he can't eat before a show'? 'Your right, he's so keyed up, and he can't digest anything then. I always say to him; Son, I don't mind what hour I cook a meal for you or your friends. I would much rather you brought them home. The only time I worry is when I don't know where he is. And I don't like him staying in those posh hotels when he's on tour. I went down to see him at one of them one time. I took one look, and I said you move out of here quick and go to a nice private boarding house, where you will get proper looked after. Of course, it can never be the same as being in your own home, can it."

I was standing in the dining room at the back of the house, looking out on to the garden where Mrs Hicks washing was freshly pegged across the line. Each wall of the room was a different colour with a wide panel over the fire place painted black with silver stars of different sizes dotted all over it.

Mrs Hicks saw me looking at it. 'Tommy wanted it all contemporary and what I say is he has a right to choose after all he has done. Mind you, I haven't settled down here myself yet. I do so miss the neighbours and the old dears I used to look after when I went out as a home help."

We moved into the little room next to the kitchen, which had cream walls. "It's just as the last people who had it, I specially asked that it should remain as it was" said Mrs Hicks. This room went with her apron, and the hands that were never idle for one minute of the day.

"There's one thing about this house that Tommy has bought us," she exclaimed with a smile. "A bathroom! I still can't get used to having hot water at all hours of the day, just by the turning of a tap. None of us can. Sometimes when Tommy was small he used to watch me carrying a pail and he'd say, "Mum one day I'm going to buy you a house with a proper bathroom." It was a kind of happy secret between us, but the wonderful thing is it's all come true."

"What made you choose Catford?" I asked. "Everybody asks the same question. Tommy used to say when he was young "where'd you like the house to be?" And I'd answer, "Well not too far from Bermondsey."

"About as far as Catford?" he'd ask.

"Yes I'd say, never dreaming it would really happen."

Just as I was leaving two children rushed up the path with autograph books, and I said to her, "Couldn't you ask them to leave Tommy alone, and give him some private life?"

She replied, "It doesn't seem fair; it really doesn't, neither for him or the rest of us. I wanted my boy to make a name for himself, but I didn't think for one moment it would be like this. Before I left she said.' I'm going to tell you something now that I've never told any body else who has come to my house. My Mother died when I was born. I spent my own childhood, first with one aunt and then another. That's what made me so determined, when I had children of my own, to give them all the love I never had. That's why Tommy and I are so close and always will be."

On September 29th Tommy appeared on the Jack Jackson's 'Off The Record Show on ITV, his next appearance came on the 18th October.

For the film 'Shiralee' Tommy recorded two songs 'Shiralee' and 'Granddad Rock'.

Tom boarding the aircraft

# His Tours Abroad

Tommy flew over to Scandinavia on a goodwill tour to publicise the release over there of the film, 'The Tommy Steele Story.

John Kennedy stated – "I knew Tommy was known in places like Copenhagen, Oslo and Stockholm - but I never expected in a hundred years the kind of reception that awaited us. We arrived in Copenhagen at about eight o'clock and invited by the police to go to a giant playing field for children. The scene on arrival was more fabulous than anything we had experienced in Britain; in the darkness there were some 15,000 children and teenagers. Tommy went upon the platform where a group of five boys had been playing. He looked out to a sea of faces and a wave of foreign voices filled the air. One of the words we did understand was these thousands of voices all shouting in unison - Tommy, Tommy. He took a guitar from one of the boys on the stage and walked to the edge of the platform and held up his hand. He made signs for quiet, and the fans did just what he wanted. They may not have understood a word, which he sang but the clapping was drowned by screams and shouts for him. With a police escort we were driven away to our hotel."

In Sweden these scenes were repeated again and again. It frequently needed police escorts to travel from town to town.

The Palladium where the film 'Ung Mand Med Guitar' (Young Man With a Guitar) the Danish name for the film 'The Tommy Steele Story' had a stage only about a yard wide in front of the screen which the film was to be shown - the Steelemen used this. Tommy had to stand on the cinema organ.

Tommy, who had bought a phase book gave a short speech in there own language - after that the children were ready to make him their lord mayor.

He had flown out of London expecting a rest but that was not to be.

The film ran for nine record-breaking weeks.

Historical Flashback to 1957

In Norway, the history of rock 'n' roll starts with Tommy Steele, about a year after the riots in connection with the film 'The Blackboard Jungle' in 1956.

England's answer to Elvis, Tommy Steele held two concerts in the Colosseum Cinema in Oslo.

The newsreels of the day showed Tommy descending an aircrafts stairs waving to the fans who had come to greet him at Oslo airport. This time he was coming to open his film 'The Tommy Steele Story'. In Denmark it was named "Ung Mand Med Gitar."

The film was an enormous success and was seen all over the world

In 1957 it was rated as one of the top films of the year.

Aflonbladet, a Swedish newspaper arranged a poll to decide who was the best - Elvis or Tommy? The poll result was Tommy got 6380 votes to Elvis 6330.

'Filmjournalen' number 15/16 1957, The English Rock 'n' Roll king Tommy Steele got proof of his enormous popularity when he visited Oslo. The Colloseum building was about to fall apart the minute Tommy and his musicians entered the stage. The audience roared and screamed and made so much noise that nobody heard anything. At the end of the show people began to jump on to the stage and his managers were afraid, but before they got to Tommy Leif-Eric Bech of the Fotorama Film Company warned the audience if they did not go back to their seats the show would be cancelled, they did and the show went on.

'Se og Hor' a Danish magazine, ran a competition the winner having a day out with Tommy. On the 13th September 1957 edition the winner is shown in the magazine.

Tommy Steele Og Hanna from Aalborg (Tommy meets Hanna from Aalborg) He sang for her alone in the Tivoli, Copenhagen.

Took her out for a meal, (breakfast for two), went to a restaurant for dinner. Went to a local coffee bar - Willis Soda Fountain, where he showed her how he made his living playing the guitar.

As Tommy was once a sailor Hanna showed him a place called Nyhavn and they went aboard a boat. They managed to escape the cameras and Hanna was told the story of his life. They went dancing in the evening at a restaurant in Copenhagen and the last photographs show them heading towards an SAS aircraft on the tarmac of Copenhagen airport.

The same magazine fourteen years later 22nd July 1971. They meet again at the Tivoli. Hanna is now married (as was Tommy) and she has two children of her own and Tommy has one, his daughter Emma.

Her children were amazed that their Mother knew the star of the free concert he gave for the children outside the Tivoli where he sang the song 'The Ugly Duckling'. They had listened to his records from being very small and now they were meeting the singer.

Terje Dalene (a Norwegian fan) got a cigarette of Tommy's on this day, which is kept in a case on the wall of his small specially adapted cinema called 'Steelorama' in Oslo. Terje is a very big fan of Tommy. He was hooked on him and rock 'n' roll way back in 1958 and has followed him ever since.

He says, "The first time I saw Tommy was in a local cinema called 'Valhalla Kino' at Kjelsaas, a suburb to Oslo. I remember I saw 'The Duke Wore Jeans.' I was hooked at once and could not get this likeable fellow out of my mind. Then I saw the film 'The Tommy Steele Story'. He represented something quite the opposite to the Elvis style. We talk about the happy fifties and that's just what it was. There were two camps, you were either for Tommy or against Elvis or the other way around - at school we were always quarrelling or fighting to decide who the best was for me. Tommy always came out on top. My first record of Tommy's was a seventy-eight of 'Elevator Rock'. This record has a special story behind it. I used to be a ski jumper at school. One day whilst I was in the arena, this record came over the loud speakers. My trainer knew that I liked Tommy and promised me that if I jump well he would give me the record as he had one at home. Well that day I jumped badly, but my trainer gave me the record anyway because he felt sorry for me. I still have that record to this day amongst my collection of memorabilia."

Because of his interest In Tommy, Terje from Lorenskog, near Oslo, was the only foreigner, invited to participate in Tommy's Fan Club Party celebrating his forty years on the stage. This was in November 1996. From that party Terje took home two things - a signed print of a painting by Tommy and a piece of cake. That cake he was supposed to eat at the party, but instead he put it in his pocket and brought it back to Oslo. It is kept in his freezer at home. He takes it out on many occasions just to show his friends.

'Bildjournalen' number 18 May 3 -10, 1958 (a Swedish Magazine) wrote;

Don't Forget About Me.

By now the English youth have got the first rock superstar to appear on the Scandinavian stage, Tommy Steele, back in their country, but it will be a long time before we forget the time when he toured Sweden.

And we are sure he will not forget Sweden either, for since he has got home he has been sent thousands of Swedish fan mail. One of the letters was from the girl's school next to where Tommy was staying.

Dear Tommy, We are many writing this letter, we all admire you we hope you will come and visit us again. As you understand, Tommy, we can only listen to your records or watch you on films; in the end we have difficulty to believe you were a real person. But now we have seen you in the flesh, you look so good. Tell us Tommy, is it not lovely to be a Rock-King and look around the world? Are all your fans hanging around to close? YOUR FANS THAT'S US, Lasse, Barbro, Gittan and all us here, have your photo hanging round the wall of our rooms.

What do our Mothers say?

They only shake their heads and look mysterious; they can't remember their own youth. We love you so much. Will you please come and see us again. Love from your Swedish fans.

When Tommy sang in Jonkoping, the whole police corps, and the mayor, sat in the first row, just in front of the stage. At first they looked surprised at the screaming audience, but after a while they clapped and screamed themselves. Nobody could actually hear the songs Tommy was singing. The magazine showed a picture of a girl's school, which was next to Tommy's hotel in Linkoping. There is a girl in the window with a ring around her face. The magazine promises her that if she writes in they will give her one of Tommy's records.

In Sweden Tommy was always smuggled out through the back door of the hotel in which he was staying. In Linkoping, however, the fans discovered this and the girls from the school ran after his car. When they found it parked behind the hotel they covered it in lipstick messages. Each of the girls kissed the car, and wrote their name underneath their lip marks. Inside the sports hall in Linkoping, Tommy talks to his manager,

"John, make me a drawing of that stainless steel water mug. I want a thing like that in my new house. It will remind me of this place".

The magazine wrote, "The Swedes will not forget him and we will not forget the Health Authority in Eskilstuna who brought a machine into the theatre. The machine measured 117 phon when the noise in the theatre was at its highest. Only an airplane at high-speed ready for take off, makes more noise than the inside a concert hall during a Tommy Steele concert. We will not forget when Tommy did a ju-jitsu demonstration with John Kennedy before a concert in Orebro. We will never forget the small extra concert Tommy gave at Roxtuna, playing together with Tony's Skiffle Group. Those fifty boys living in a hospice felt they were in heaven. We will not forget when 2000 people tried to get into Tommy's hotel room and only three were allowed in. They listened to Tommy's records half the night, and the guard who said, "You must promise not to touch Tommy or you will be thrown out!"

We will not forget those two thousand people left outside the concert hall in Jonkoping, because there were no tickets left. We will not forget the representative from a Swedish match factory who gave Tommy a huge box of matches, and he said at a concert, 'turn the lights off and everybody light a match, it will bring us all luck.' We will never forget the face of a little boy at the Savoy hotel who used his new camera to take a picture of Tommy, the boy got so nervous he could not find the trigger, in the end Tommy took some pictures of the little boy instead. So now there is a boy in Jonkoping looking at some pictures of himself, knowing that Tommy Steele has taken those pictures. He will never forget you neither.

Neither will the two little girls who stood in a cafe in the middle of nowhere when a man started to sing and dance in the middle of the day. First Tommy puts a coin in the jukebox, and he sang the song coming out of the loudspeaker and he sounded just the same as the record. The girl who was serving in the cafe, dropped a cup of sugar on the floor as she whispered," It is him."

"It's who?" asked the little girls

"The man on the record - Tommy Steele! Ask him will he give me his autograph?

The jukebox went silent and Tommy sat down at a table and ordered two warm hot dogs. The two little girls went up to him and smiled.

Tommy smiled back and asked them how old they were.

"I'm eight and my sister is six. My name is Elisabeth and that is Margareta" pointing to her sister.

Tommy smiled, rolled his eyes and laughed.

"I have a sister at home who is nine. Her name is Sandra".

Margareta and Elizabeth were thrilled because he had spoken to them.

Little did they know that he had just left thousands of girls in Jonoping who would have given a month's salary, to be there right now.

"Can she sing too?" asked Elizabeth.

"Sure," said Tommy. "How about you? Can you sing?"

"Yes"- said Elizabeth "I sing in the school. Will you come and sing at our school?"

"If your teacher will let me, I would not mind," Tommy replied.

Whilst Tommy was in Sweden he asked to be shown an experimental centre for young criminals. He was so impressed with the place he gave them an impromptu concert.

Then it was on to Brussels where on the last day of the tour, he appeared in a 'Charity Show' in aid of the Belgian Press Fund.

The Tommy Steele Story film played for nine weeks at the Palladium Cinema in Copenhagen and it showed that John Kennedy was right; Tommy was safe and popular with all generations and nationalities.

Whilst Elvis smouldered, Tommy just smiled.

He was never a sex symbol; he was always the boy next door. It wasn't intentional - it was just him. Presley was playing Presley, he wasn't playing at being Presley, and he was just playing himself.

Tommy says, "To get into show business the easiest way is to be you."

"I remember my first pantomime. It enabled me to act and dance. I regarded that as a turning point in my career. I got the feeling in the rock 'n' roll business I couldn't come up with the goods, the travelling was getting me down and I was not overjoyed with the one night stands. It wouldn't have been so bad if the place we went to had been planned, it was like bingo, as if the places had been pulled out of a hat. The worst thing was playing one night in Norfolk, the next in Ayr and back to Bournemouth for the next."

After a brief appearance in Belgium he went on another tour of England taking Ann with him. Whilst he was tour he returned to London to record "A Handful Of Songs" which won the Ivor Novello Award. His mum accepted it for him. John and Tommy made a quick visit to his home only to find out that his love for Ann had found its way into the newspapers.

A reporter photographed them and this made front-page headlines. Again John went mad. He thought that the photographs would harm his career, but it didn't. Many of his fans started asking the fan club for pictures of them together.

Tommy knew that he had a busy schedule ahead of him, so his managers decided it was time for another holiday. This time it was off to Nice. He took Ann with him.

When he got back home he found out that he had been voted Britain's Top Musical Performer gaining second place to Elvis Presley.

Just before he left to go to Nice, the BBC called him to do a show to celebrate his 1st year in show business; it was to be produced by Ernest Maxim.

It was called - 'The Golden Year' His co-star was Ruby Murray. Larry Parnes and John Kennedy wrote to Tommy: - We congratulate you on your first year in show business – which can only be described as fabulas. Besides handling a great artist, it has been wonderful working with you on your road to fame.

On 21 October, Tommy started work on his next film.

On 26 October and the 2 November Tommy was on the TV with 6-5 Special series.

On 4 November Tommy was presented to Her Majesty the Queen at the Royal Film Performance in London of Les Girls.

On 18 of November Tommy was invited to appear before the Queen again at the Royal Variety Performance, to close the show. It caused a lot of jealousy among some people who had been passed over, but it was a wise choice when you remembered his popularity. Not only had he been asked to perform but he had been given the spot of closing the performance. Proceeding Tommy on the bill were some of the greatest stars in the world, all there talents had been presented then it was Tommy's turn.

The curtains parted and he ran onto the stage, he only got a mild reception from the ageing audience. His first number was 'Long Tall Sally', Tommy called out to the audience, "Everybody clap your hands", but nobody took any notice of him. Harold Fielding, Larry Parnes, John Kennedy and Tommy's mum started to clap but the audience turned in their seats and stared at them as if they were doing something rude.

John Kennedy suddenly noticed the people in the seats in front of him not looking at the stage but at the Royal Box. There was the Queen's Mother resting her hands on the edge of the box smiling and clapping her hands in time to Tommy's strumming on his guitar, quite soon all the Royal Family was clapping. The tension broken all the audience joined in. He sang his final number 'Singin' The Blues', in front of the curtains just before he finished the song they parted to reveal the whole cast holding miniature guitars and joining the chorus. Tommy left the stage to a thunderous applause.

He says, "To me, the most wonderful thing about the Queen is that when you meet her you are a bag of nerves, and find that she is a bit unsure, and you fall over yourself trying to put her at ease. In this way, she makes you forget all about your stage fright."

Appearing on the programme was Gracie Fields making her eighth performance on a Royal Variety Show, Tommy admired her so much that he insisted having his photograph with her. In her Biography written by David Bret he writes "The next morning Gracie and Boris met the journalist John Lambert for breakfast at the Dorchester - Gracie let rip - I know that I'm an old woman now - old in years, anyway. I don't pretend to understand what young Mr Steele has got - I can't even understand the words he is singing. His is the only sort of act that'll fill variety hall these days. They're all alike these kids. They wear jeans, they imitate Elvis Presley, and they last five minutes. In 1962 when she visited England she was the quote that she had 'revised her opinion' about Tommy Steele, telling Tony Barrow from Decca, 'Now there is a true artist. He can handle an audience and he knows how to move on stage - unlike some of today's young singers. God help them without a microphone!"

Tommy returned to the city of Liverpool, to do the pantomime 'Goldilocks' at the Empire Theatre. The report that follows said that Tommy was a sensation in this medium. "His confidence and his easy style, plus a very terrific personality enable him to move in the tradition of pantomime with the ease of a veteran. He works extremely hard and he is becoming an all round entertainer".

Tommy says, "1958 started with me still playing in 'Goldilocks' and I was blamed by some headmistresses for very poor examination results in the area. All the girls in the country were in love with me. I was asked by one newspaper about marriage and I told them. It's impossible, it would ruin all me plans, I've got 20,000 girlfriends at the moment and I am not prepared to disappoint 19,999 of them. I was asked how many girls I liked and I told them. I like a lot of girls, but they do really not zonk me. My agents have signed me for a radio series and later film deals so I'm too busy to think about girls till they are finished."

A week after the pantomime finished, Tommy was at home with John when the telephone rang. Tommy picked up the receiver and the operator asked him to hold the line as she had a call from South Africa. A man then came on the phone and said. "This is Mr Ken Park. Is Mr Steele there?"

Tommy replied, "No! I am his agent."

The man carried on speaking "I want to book Mr Steele for a two week tour of South Africa at the end of February - could you inform me be the cost of such a booking would be?

Tommy replied, "Oh £6000 plus expenses."

The man replied. "I'll think about it and ring back tomorrow".

The next day the phone rang again.

This time John took the call.

"Mr Park here, the £6000 fee plus expenses will be fine."

John replied, "I said the cost would be £8000 plus expenses for the band, the managers, the hotel bookings and a first class ship. You must have misheard me yesterday - it was a bad line."

Mr Park replied, "Hold on a moment and the line went dead."

He came back on a few moments later, "Yes £8000 plus all expenses, I'll post the confirmation tomorrow." Then the line went dead again.

When the contract came, John signed it for him to appear in South Africa without telling Harold Fielding.

Harold Fielding was livid because he had signed a contract for Tommy to sing in America and it had to be cancelled.

A man who asked for his autograph approached Tommy a few weeks later.

Tommy said, "I was so pleased, that I gave him a few".

Then the man gave Tommy a piece of paper tied up with a ribbon.

Tommy asked, "What it was?"

And the man replied, "It's a writ."

Tommy rang John.

Harold Fielding had taken his managers to court.

It was all over the papers, 'Tommy Steele's Managers Sued!"

Tommy says, "All I can remember about the case was a remark made by Justice Hardman who in the legal argument asked, how long this Tommy Steele can last? Five Months?

John had to be stopped from getting to his feet and telling the judge that he thought "I would be still packing theatres for years to come."

The case brought the wrong kind of publicity.

John hated falling out with Harold Fielding, but from their point of view they had made a point. Half way through the case, the writ was withdrawn, but because of the case the tour of South Africa was in doubt, as the theatre managers were holding back the bookings for fear that he, or his managers would cancel the tour.

On 24 December 1957 Tommy appeared on the ITV Christmas Eve Show, singing 'Princess' to his little sister Sandra.

Forty-eight hours before they were to board the ship to South Africa, his managers were in consultation with Harold Fielding. They all agreed that the tour was risky and really should be cancelled, but Tommy stuck to his guns.

"The children ought to get to see what they have paid to see, and I'm not going to disappoint them. They won't blame Ken what's his name? They'll blame me Tommy Steele."

So the trip went ahead as planned.

Tommmy meets up with Cliff

# He almost gets killed

Tommy said, "We boarded the Winchester Castle for the voyage down to Cape Town. This was long before touring South Africa was a political issue, but I told my managers that for every white concert I do I'll also do one black one".

According to the ship's radio, Cape Town had been playing Tommy's records and informing the people that he was on his way.

"On board the ship, I got up to my old tricks and performed in the ships concert," said Tommy

The first people who were to ask for his autograph when they reached Cape Town were the customs officials who boarded the ship just outside the port. The pilot who was to take them into the port itself followed them. The pilot informed John Kennedy that the fans were waiting for Tommy at the port and along the main streets of the town. There was no knowing just how many fans were there. They had been arriving into the town on every available contraption for the past two days. He said that the mass was an uncontrollable mob.

When the ship reached the port and Tommy looked over the side of the ship he could not believe how many people there were on the quayside. John had set up a room on board the ship where Tommy could be interviewed. Tommy was there for over two hours.

Tommy says, "Thousands of pictures must have been taken of me in that time but I never got the chance to see any of them".

Meantime the fans on the quay waited. Then there was trouble; John informed Tommy that the money for the tour had not been paid and that he and the ship were returning to England. Tommy told him straight, "Those children down there have waited hours, days, even, to see me. We can't let them down. Were going ashore no matter what! We can't hide up here. They want to see me, and see me they shall."

When he looked over the side of the ship again he reckoned that if he started signing autographs at one end of the quay he would be there at the end of the fortnight, so they stayed there.

They stepped down the gangplank to rapturous roars, and there waiting for Tommy was a red and yellow convertible with its hood down.

"This is supposed to take us into town?" "No chance." said John.

They got into the car anyway. As soon as the car got through the dock gates, the youngsters burst through the police cordon. The car pulled away from them but further up the road they were mobbed. Tommy heard the driver say to Larry, "Tell them to get down on the floor" and then all hell broke loose. "How we got out of it I shall never know!" said Tommy later.

Tommy did twelve shows in South Africa and each was more successful than the last. "The white ones were boycotted because I was doing black ones and they also had the impression that I was bringing over decadence. When I did a show in Cape Town the first twelve rows were full of professional men who sat there throughout the whole of the show with their arms folded in protest. To tell the truth I didn't have a great time over there." But they couldn't have been happier than when the last song was sung and they were on the boat heading towards home. As soon as the ship left the port Tommy went to his bunk and slept for eighteen hours.

When Tommy got home, although he was dead-beat, he recorded the song 'Nairobi,' which got to number three in the hit parade. Record info from London Records, New York, March 24, 1958: This is the kind of release to please all 'pop tastes. Tommy Steele, one of England's hottest recording artists could increase, his stock here in the states with his latest release, a rock novelty entitled 'Nairobi'. This side jumped from nowhere to 12 this past week in England. Tommy joins forces with tricky female sounds and puts it over with a relaxed ease. 'Neon Sign' on the reverse, is a slick rocker which bubbles along with a beat that get the crowd swaying.

Then he had to fly over to Scandinavia to do some shows.

On 27 of April he was in the town of Odense, Denmark, the birthplace of Hans Christian Andersen.

Tommy was so impressed by the cleanliness of Scandinavia and the fitness of its people he wanted to extend the tour. He liked the complete lack of snobbishness and the informality of life there.

He was to remark, "This is the place I'd like to retire to one day when I'm finished with show business."

A few weeks later he was in Scotland, performing at the Caird Hall in Dundee. By this time he had extended his act to an hour and fifteen minutes. His one ambition this particular night was to see if he could hold the audience's attention for an hour and a half. Everything went well for the first three quarters of the show. By now he had learned to judge the spontaneous reaction of an audience and could feel their enjoyment and participation increasing with his. Then, about a quarter of an hour from the end of the show everything went mad. The teenagers in the front rows of the stalls began screeching for another song. They came out of their seats and on to the stage. They rushed at him for all the world like tigers out of a cage. Their long nails dug through his thin suit. Their stiletto heeled shoes nailed his feet. He tried to get away, but they were all round him. Then two stagehands came to his rescue. They fought their way through the crowd, caught hold of an arm and pulled. At the same time some of the fans grabbed his other arm and tugged even more fiercely.

He said "I was conscious of a searing, stabbing pain in my shoulder and a second later everything went dark. I don't remember anything else until I came round on the dressing room floor, I was in terrible pain but all I can remember saying was they wouldn't let me finish... they wouldn't let me finish."

Then he was on the way to the hospital. His only thoughts, as he lay in bed were that he had failed. He had tried to change from a pop singer to an entertainer and he had failed. All the audience had wanted was an idol they could tear to pieces in a wild orgy of self-abandonment.

Everything was cancelled for the next few weeks, as Tommy recovered.

He went home to his mum feeling that he never wanted to go on a stage again. For three months he refused to do any work. He was advised of the contracts he was breaking. He was told that if he didn't go back to work immediately he would be finished. He turned a completely deaf ear to everyone who came pounding at his door. Then came the turning point. He had to decide whether to could go on, or just disappear from show business altogether.

His Mother helped him regain the confidence he needed.

He told John, "I suppose there are millions of men who believe they've got the best mum in the world. And I suppose I'm just one of them. But you'd have a job convincing me that there is a better one."

He had another row with his managers when they said that they were worried about him having announced his engagement to Ann.

"We had a big party but John never came to it," he told everybody.

'Come On Lets Go' was recorded the following week. It got into the Top Ten in November. Peter Tipthorpe interviewed Tommy for the 'Photoplay' magazine, who told him I did not think he could sing and he thought the girls who scooted into the record shops to buy his discs needed their brains examined. Said Tommy to this (sic) "I don't mind wot you think and I don't mind wot others like you think. Rock 'n' roll is the best thing in years. I enjoy it an' if I can get scratch doin' it all the better. No matter wot anyone says it'll stick around for some time and I 'ope to stick around wiv it. And, if you don't like it – blow man blow. I don't mind squares. I've respect for 'em. I know me career can't last forever. Some time people will get tired of me and my sort of music. But I hate squares who keep on 'aving a crack at rock 'n' roll an' we fellows who sing it. I don't want people to think me life consists of one rock 'n' roll song, I 'ave ambitions to better 'me self. It was sad I failed me medical for National Service. Terrible that was. But I know, I've got a wonky heart, it gets me sometimes as I have dizzy spells, but a bit of rest usually puts it right."

Tommy made his comeback to the stage on 16th June 1958, at a Coventry Theatre, John, Larry and Tommy had a big reunion in the dressing room. Tommy said he was to blame, and John said it was his fault and Larry blamed himself. But when they all shook hands, Tommy knew they would all be pals again.

When the papers found out about Tommy's engagement to Ann it was big headlines.

To keep them happy Ann gave them an interview; "It was love at first sight; I almost fainted with surprise when he asked me out. Of all the people who could go out with Tommy Steele he chose me. When he kissed me for the first time it was like soaring into the clouds at the beginning of a beautiful dream. When Tommy was working away we spoke every day on the phone. When he was home we met every day. We went out like other courting couples but not to the same coffee bars close by, we went out into the country where people didn't know us. We sat in the back rows of picture houses and watched the same films as his fans. If we wanted to go out locally Tommy used to wear a dark wig and I wore no make up so that I looked like an old hag."

On 28th June Tommy made an appearance on TV again in a 'Saturday Spectacular,' hosted by Bob Monkhouse

When the summer season shows finished Tommy went over to America to work on the music for Cinderella, with Rogers and Hammerstein.

On 28th October ' This Is Your Life' Tommy was the surprise guest.

In the November Tommy was called once again to do a Royal Variety Performance - this time in front of the Queen Mother. (Tommy had been a surprise guest and his name did not even appear on the programme)

The Amalgamated Press Ltd got Tommy to do a Disc Party Song Book for the Roxy, a lively, jivey all star love story weekly, in which some of Tommy's famous friends tell stories about Tommy.

That winter, Tommy hit the road for the last time with his rock 'n' roll act.

Riots were reported in Nottingham when police had to cancel two shows as 5000 fans fought over 2500 seats.

When Tommy arrived in Hull he decided to exchange his Mg Magnette Varitone car registered number 655 LME with Paraghon Motors that was just behind his hotel for one of the first automatic cars.

The MG was bought by Mr Jack Kaye, a specialist grocer who had to have the car specially treated to remove the lipstick graffiti. He restored it to its original state. Throughout the life of the car he stated, 'It always was an eye catcher with its two tone blue bodywork, leather seats and walnut dashboard '

On 15th November 1958, Tommy appeared in front of a full house at the Granada Kettering and said, "This is my last concert, let's celebrate." Then he led the audience in a gigantic conga to the tune of 'Water, Water'. He included his new release 'Come On Let's Go' in this extra long 63-minute show and closed with his biggest hit, 'Singin' the Blues'. The fans went wild - he quit the live rock 'n' roll circuit whilst he was at the very top.

In the December Tommy opened at the London Coliseum as Buttons in 'Cinderella'. Rodgers and Hammerstein allowed him to put in the show one of his own songs, 'You and Me' that he sang with Jimmy Edwards. Others in the cast were Yana, Bruce Trent, Kenneth Williams, and Ted Durante playing the baron's stepdaughters. Also in the cast were Betty Marsden and the Bill Shepherd singers.

During the run of the show Tommy celebrated his twenty-second birthday. He took a cake, which had been made for him, down to an old folk's home and shared it with them. The company performed an excerpt from the pantomime for the Light Programme on Christmas Day.

"Tommy drops the rock for pantomime," are the headlines in one of the national papers.

"Think of Tommy Steele and what springs to mind? A rock 'n' roll star with a cheerful cockney personality and a guitar. If that was your answer you were wrong on two counts. When 'Cinderella' opens at the London Coliseum you will see why. It may come as a shock to many of his fans to learn that he has discarded his guitar for the roll as Buttons. There will not be a break in the show for his rock act. Last Christmas, when Tommy played pantomime 'Humpty Dumpty' at Liverpool, there was such a commotion from his fans that he was forced to appeal to them for silence. So it was at Tommy's own suggestion that he should play Buttons as a normal pantomime. He felt that rock 'n' roll suddenly thrust into a Rodgers and Hammerstein score would be out of place and would dampen the effect of this fabulous spectacle. "Fabulous spectacle" is by no means an overstatement for Harold Fielding's presentation. No expense had been spared to make this show in the best tradition of the live theatre. Tommy's co-stars were Yana, Jimmy Edwards and Bruce Trent's impressive voice added for good measure.

The estimated cost of the whole show said Harold Fielding is £100,000; the ballroom scene itself cost £12.500.

In the words of Harold Fielding "We have worked with one end in view - to provide the audience with an exciting adventure. Tommy's portrayal should establish him as one of our foremost stars of musical comedy. As a pantomime 'Cinderella' is unique in many ways. It is the first time that the legendary song-writing team of Rodgers and Hammerstein have ventured into this idiom. It will take full advantage of the gigantic stage at the Coliseum - one of the largest in the world - including the revolving section, and should be a tremendous attraction. A Rodgers and Hammerstein score is in itself a great draw, and 'Cinderella' the first to be heard in London since 'The King And I'. There were fourteen songs in the panto. Tommy got his fair share of singing time. 'A Very Special Day' and 'Marriage Type Love' were both sung alone, but he also sang two duets with Yana (who plays Cinderella) 'When Your Driving Through The Moonlight' and 'A Lovely Night.' 'Marriage Type Love' was featured in the American TV production "Me And Juliet," but had not been heard before by British audiences. The only song, which has previously been heard here, is 'No Other Love' Ronnie Hilton's hit record of 1956. In the show it was sung by Bruce Trent.

The show held special memories for Tommy, because it opened on 18th December - the day after his 22nd birthday!

Tommy had had no really sensational hits in Britain. 'Nairobi' and 'The only Man On the Island' were successes in the early part of the year. But since the unfortunate incident at Dundee he had been out of the charts for a fair spell. However, he came back with a bang with the release of 'Come On, Lets Go - a hit that coincided with a West End opening."

Tommy was asked by his managers to appear on TV in 'The 1959 Show,' and he also made an appearance at the Billy Smart's circus with Jayne Mansfield. Burma, the elephant walked over Tommy and Jayne in the ring as a stunt.

Newspaper reports stated that Tommy was to be a blackmailer in his next film 'Serious Charge.' The film contained songs written by Lionel Bart, but due to other commitments, the part was given to Andrew Ray, with Cliff Richard taking the part of his younger brother. During the film Cliff started putting it about that Britain was starved of rock 'n' roll and that neither Tommy nor Terry Dene had captured the American sound. This made Tommy mad. He knew he was king and nobody was going to take that away from him. Tommy knew for a fact that one company told Cliff he would never make a singer in a thousand years and that Harold

Fielding had told him not to give up his day job. Tommy found out they were doing the filming at Boreham Wood Studios so on one of his days off he went down to see Cliff in his dressing room.

"Hi Cliff" he said. "Filming going. O.K.?"

'Yes,' replied Cliff.

"Have you ever played knuckles?" Tommy asked.

"No!" Said Cliff.

"We used to play it at sea, it was great, would you like me to show you"' said Tommy.

Cliff was a little reluctant, but Tommy showed him any way.

"Look," said Tommy, "It's dead simple. You hold out your hand knuckles to knuckles and I will give you first go'. You have to hit the back of my knuckles with your fist. If you hit my knuckles you get another go until you miss. Then it's my turn."

Tommy let Cliff hit his knuckles once and that was it. When Tommy had finished with him his knuckles were cut to ribbons and he needed makeup on the back of them for the rest of the shooting of the film.

During the run of the pantomime, 'Cinderella,' Tommy's managers were approached by Anglo-Amalgamated for him to make another film, 'Tommy the Toreador'. Tommy was informed that parts of the film would be shot in Andalusia, Spain. He agreed to do it on one condition that Ann went along as well. May, June and July 1959 were taken up with the filming. Tommy played the part of Tommy Tomkins, a British sailor who ends up in Spain with bullfighters and smugglers.

With a guitar under his arm labelled - 'For Mr.' K. Tommy flew out to Russia on the Wednesday after the filming. He was representing the British Youth at the Moscow Film Festival. "... My fan club bought the guitar and asked me to present it to a Russian youth organisation." Tommy told the MM at London Airport. "But I plan to give it to Mr Khrushchev if I get half a chance. This is a tremendous opportunity of seeing Moscow and I have been awake for the past two nights with excitement." Travelling with Tommy was his manager John Kennedy and The British film party was completed by Carole Lesley, Peter Arne and Richard Todd.

Tommy would be introduced to Russian film audiences at all the leading Moscow cinemas they visited, but did not perform unless he was specifically asked to do so.

After visiting Russia he was due to return to London at 1.30 p.m. on Saturday and fly to Dublin later in the afternoon to play for the TV All Stars Football XI against a team selected by playwright Brendan Behan.

'Tommy The Toreador' was his first colour film, and a very tuneful one. This was the movie that gave Tommy his biggest selling single "Little White Bull". This number in the film is a highlight. (Just watch it on video to see how many times Tommy's hair changes styles!) His co-star was the lovely Janet Munro. The comedy came from Sid James, Bernard Cribbens, Ferdy Mayne, Eric Sykes, Kenneth Williams and Noel Purcell. Virgilio Texera, Pepe Nieto, Ferdy Mayne, and Warren Mitchel played some of the other parts in the film. The story and screenplay were by George H. Brown and Patrick Kirwan. The song 'Little White Bull' became famous; and got to number six in the hit parade in the December. All the money the song made went to Children's Cancer Research charity. This was the first time an entertainer had made such a gesture. The writers of Little White Bull were Lionel Bart, Mike Pratt and Tommy Steele (written under his pseudonym, Jimmy Bennett.)

The film was premiered in the West End in November and before the end of the month, Tommy began work on his fourth film 'Light up the Sky,' Tommy played the role of Eric McGaffey. Starring in the film also were Ian Carmichael and Benny Hill. The title of the film in USA was 'Skywatch',

During 1959 Tommy appeared in four television 'Saturday Spectaculars'.

When filming 'Light up the Sky' finished in February 1960, Tommy started making preparations for a tour of Australia. But before he went, he had to make an appearance at a midnight charity show at the London Palladium, meeting the Duke of Edinburgh. At the Songwriter's Guild he was awarded an Ivor Novello Award.

His mum picked it up for him as he was recording his new album 'Get Happy. It had to be completed before he went to Australia.

He went Australia for six weeks with the re-formed Steelemen and a fifteen- piece band fronted by Harry Robinson.

During the tour Tommy made two important decisions about his career in the pop world: His life and his intention to marry Ann at the earliest opportunity.

He knew that if he failed, he wanted her by his side.

He sat down in the hotel and had a heart to heart with John. He told him that he was fed up with being a puppet on the end of a guitar lead. He longed to be just plain old Tommy Hicks, a seaman living his own life. He had had enough of the boom, boom of rock 'n' roll. "I've put everything aside to be a rock 'n' roll singer, including my girlfriend. I wanted to marry Ann before I came here, and when I get home that is the first thing I am going to do. As far as I am concerned human relations are far more important to me than my name at the top of a bill!"

John knew no other world since he had started with Tommy, but they decided to part. Tommy stayed with Larry Parnes, who also managed Marty Wilde and Vince Eager

The second decision he made was to take the lead in a play he had been offered. It meant a big cut in wages but at least he wouldn't have to travel the world.

The play 'She Stoops To Conquer' was based at the Old Vic. The third decision was made when he got to Sydney.

He had lost his voice during the tour and was told by a doctor not to sing or talk for seven days. As soon as he was able to speak he telephoned Ann asking her to be his wife.

Ann said yes at once, and it was reported in the newspapers.

When he returned home from the tour Ann was waiting for him at the airport and from then on they made plans for their wedding.

Fan club post card of Tommy with Ann

# Get Me To The Church On Time!

The newspaper headlines lasted for days. It was reported that Tommy and Ann would get married on 18th June 1960 at the Roman Catholic Church in Soho.

On 8th of June a notice appeared in the 'Times,' The Archbishop of Westminster, Cardinal Godfrey, has granted a special dispensation to allow Mr Tommy Steele to marry Anne Donoghue in London. The wedding could not take place unless a dispensation was granted as Mr Steele is a non-Catholic and Miss Anne Donoghue is a Roman Catholic.'

On 18th June 1960, Tommy and Ann got married at the Church of St. Patrick, Soho London.

He stood at the front of the church quaking in his shoes wondering if Ann eventually would turn up.

After the wedding, he signed the register with a name he had not used for almost four years - Tommy Hicks.

Several newspapers sent reporters and the Pathe News sent a film crew to the wedding, which was shown in cinemas all around the country.

Three of the reports of the show business wedding of the year are as follows -

Police Hold Back 2,000 Yelling Fans

A crowd of more than 2000 packed Soho Square this afternoon when Tommy Steele married Ann Donoughue in the show business wedding of the year. To a background of pop music from portable radios about 90 police; some mounted, kept squealing fans clear of the road.

Tommy got to the church 15 minutes early in a black limousine.

His brother, Colin who was the best man, accompanied him. Tommy wore a dark blue wild silk suit; already crumpled he posed for cameramen on the church steps, giving the thumbs up sign, with both thumbs. And the crowd went mad screeching: 'Tommy, Tommy, Tommy.' They screamed again for Harry Fowler, for Max Bygraves, for Andrew Ray, and for Mr and Mrs Hicks, she with an imposing spray of orchids on her left shoulder of her blue silk dress. Then came the bridesmaids - Tommy's sister Sandra, and Ann's sister Kathleen in peach silk; Sid James and his wife flinched at their ovation; Jimmy Edwards posed whilst his wife dashed straight into the church and John Gregson tried to dodge it altogether.

The bride arrived punctually her face pale and without makeup. Her dress was of slipper satin with a high neckline and waist length sleeves, a closely fitted bodice, and a flaring skirt containing 30 yards of embroidered silk taffeta.

By the time Tommy and his wife left the church the crowd had grown still more. At one point they broke through the police cordon to crowd round the car pushing cameras through the windows to get their own personal snaps of the newly weds. Tommy and his wife were greeted with high-pitched screams of 'We want Tommy' from young girls perched on the railings and walls.

The couple drove to the Savoy Hotel for the reception.

Some fans said their allegiance to Tommy would end after the wedding.

Rita Mower aged 16, of East Ham said; "I have been a fan for years but now he's taken the plunge I will lose interest."

The first fan there at 6.30am, was middle aged Mrs Doreen Chong from nearby Broadwick Street said, "I don't mind if he is married, I still love him."

"Oh, What a Wonderful Wedding." another newspaper wrote "Tommy Steele went through his wedding day the way he goes through life - gay, inhibited and almost carefree. The only solemnity was where it should have been in the church. The rest was laughs and jokes. He shook hands left-handed when he bade me farewell after the celebration. His right hand was sore, limp and bruised from receiving too many hearty handshake congratulations. It was the only thing that was suffering. His marriage was dubbed the show business wedding of the year. On the surface it was. True there were cameras and crowds, but these are all part of the ceremony. Even an intruding microphone is quite normal these days with so many brides wanting to tape their big day. Best man Colin Hicks flew in from Italy just as any other brother would have come from the farthest part of the world for such an occasion if it were possible. Ann's sister, Kathleen, who was the senior bridesmaid wept as the moment came for her to walk down the aisle. The church ceremony, in the parish where Ann lived during the engagement, was remarkably simple. The priest was stating the more than obvious when he remarked that the ballyhoo had been left outside. Tommy and Ann picked the guests themselves. There were the families, large ones, in both cases-supplemented by some of the friends they have made during their show business careers. Leo Pollini and Alan Stuart, two of the Steelemen were there. So were Roland Shaw, Tommy's former recording MD; and Terry Kennedy, the guitarist who went out to Australia with him. Comedians Mike and Bernie Winters, who toured with him for almost his first year, were remembered, Bernie flying back from filming in Ireland for the event. Major Neville Willing, who gave him the booking at the Café de Paris which sealed his early success in 1957; Freddie Carpenter, who produced his London Coliseum pantomime the following year; his co-star in it, Jimmy Edwards; Herbert Smith, who had the idea of making the fantastically successful 'Tommy Steele Story' film, C. J. Latta head of the ABC who showed all his films were all present. More V.I.P. guest who were there were Hugh Mendl his Decca recording manager; Leslie Grade, who books all his ATV shows; actor John Le Mesurier and Alma Cogan, his Blackpool Opera House co-star; Kerr Robertson and Pat Doncaster, record critics; Lord Stoneham, President of Youth Ventures, of which Tommy is a Committee man. Betty Partiger, who has run his fan club for four hectic years, was not forgotten, nor was his manager's secretary Vanessa, and office boy, Michael. Most of the Showbiz XI took the 'field; Chas McDevitt, Glen Mason, Harry Fowler, Andrew Ray, Franklyn Boyd, Jimmy Henney and John Burgess them acting as ushers. Not forgetting: Harold Fielding, the impresario who gave him his first bookings; agent Ian Bevan and managers John Kennedy and Larry Parnes. At the sumptuous Savoy Hotel River Room, the famous and the unknowns all mixed together all with one thing in common - the love for the bride and groom. His little sister, Sandra, caught the mood too; she broke roses off her bridesmaid bouquet and threw them to the waiting crowds outside the hotel. At the reception Lionel Bart was given the job of proposing their health, as it was he who introduced them three years previously. But the real Cockney celebrations came later in the day, when the families moved on to a pub in Eltham."

About the reception one newspaper wrote. "Away from the bright light and the glamour of the show business wedding Tommy and his bride of a few hours Ann Donoughue, really let their hair down. I know I was there. And a right Cockney do it was. All his mates and his aunts and uncles and cousins - and Ann's too turned up for the celebration in the upstairs room of the Carpenter's Arms. I found Tommy in his shirtsleeves with his bride on his knee; laughing and singing all the songs that every Londoner loves to sing. During a quick chorus of 'Knocked 'em in the Old Kent Road' the Cockney kid and his bride led 70 whooping guests around the floor. With a glass of orange squash in his hand he said, "This is the real kind of wedding party for me. It's far better than being amongst all the plush at the Savoy. I'm sorry but we've got no jellied eels", grinned Tommy" 'but never mind lets have a knees up folks!" And the noises of their merriment rang loud and clear along the Eltham High Street, well into the night."

After the wedding Tommy and Ann had a few days away and then they had to find their way to Blackpool, because the week after he was appearing in the 'Big Show of 1960,' at the Opera House.

Trust him to take a wrong turning as they ended up in Wales, seventy miles it took him to find the house they had rented for the season in Bispham.

The address of the property was 11 Madison Avenue, Bispham. On doing some research on the property it turns out that it was used by many of the top stars that were appearing in Blackpool around that time.

"It was supposed to be a secret, the house that Ann and I were renting," he said. "But you can't keep a secret in Blackpool or anywhere else for that matter for very long. The fans found us all right, and I don't blame them. I love them all; they're the greatest people on earth. There isn't a popular performer who'd argue against saying that. The only thing was that they kept on coming to the house and ringing the bell for autographs. So I will tell you what I did. I stuck a note on the door asking the fans to stick their autograph books or anything they wanted signing through the letter box and come round at five o'clock and pick them up. It worked a treat, lets face it a feller has to get some kip sometimes, and I'm a lad who likes his forty winks. I even got to sign the autographs in bed whilst having a cup of tea. Starring with him were Alma Cogan, Eddie Calvert, Freddie Frinton, Sid Millward, Wally Stewart and the nitwits Harber and Dale, The Mathurins, The Cliff Adam's Singers and the Malcolm Goddard Dancers."

Whilst he was up in Blackpool he got a message from Harry Robinson his Australian musical director, to inform him that he had heard a great song in America, and he wanted Tommy to record it.

"Well" Tommy told him. "Its miles from Blackpool to London and it's a bit of a problem for me to get to where I record the records. You can lose some kip that way. You know it takes hours to make record - not just the three minutes it takes to play it."

"Well I can tell you this," said Harry

"The disc company has come up with a good idea. Why don't we bring the recording studios to you?"

And bring one they did - a mobile unit - and they cut the disc 'Happy Go Lucky Blues and The Girl With The Long Black Hair right there in Blackpool. He was glad they didn't get lost on the way like he had done.

"Wow!" he said. "What a journey that was."

The record-breaking Blackpool summer season certainly gave him confidence, but only up to a point. He still had the Old Vic to face and this made his knees knock. One thing that gave him heart to go on was when the famous actress Peggy Mount phoned and said she'd heard he didn't want to play the part of Tony Lumpkin. He said to her that it wasn't that he didn't want, but that he was just scared stiff at the thought.

Then Peggy said, "Well! I'll be truthful with you; I won't do the play unless you are playing Lumpkin."

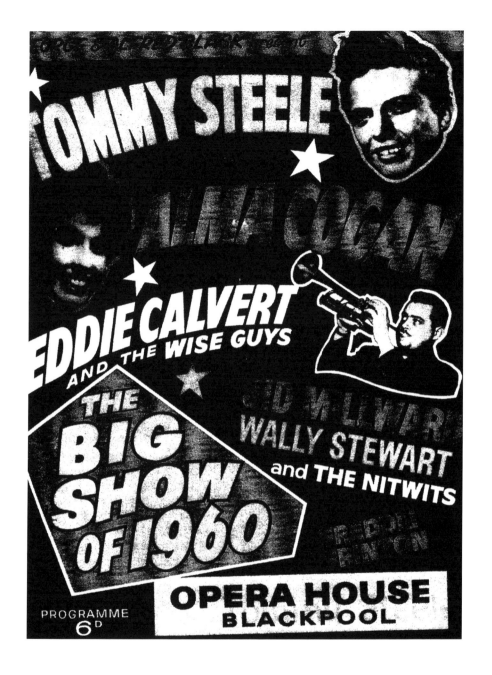

# It's All Happening

During his stay in Blackpool Tommy started learning the words for 'She Stoops To Conquer.' Before the show opened at the Old Vic he appeared in a special midnight matinee with Sir John Gielgud, Anton Dolin and John Gilpin, the funds of which went to the Coventry Theatre Festival,

Tommy appeared in a special 'City of London Week' edition of the BBC Light Programme's 'Commonwealth of Song,' representing Britain.

Tommy was petrified on the first day of the rehearsals for 'She Stoops To Conquer'. Having arrived a little late, he entered into a room to find the Old Vic stars sitting round in a circle. As he came in, - the conversation stopped and everyone was staring at him. Tommy sat down started looking at the script and when it came his turn to read, he spoke each word as if he had forgotten how to read. For a moment there was silence as the all stared at him. They must have thought, "He can't even read, let alone act!" However, after a moment or two they all realised Tommy was joking. Laughed together, the ice was broken.

On 8 November 1960 Tommy had his first night as Tony Lumpkin in 'She Stoops To Conquer and he was presented to the Queen Mother during her visit.

In the first week Tommy learned what the flies were - and they weren't the things you looked at before you went out onto the street. The flies are right above you on the stage. They hold up all the curtains and the scenery. If somebody shouts, "Let go number ten," a man called a fly man, would let go of a great rope, and either the curtains or a lump of scenery would come crashing down. And gaw'd help you if you were underneath it. Another stage term is a blackout. That is when all the stage lights go out. When that happens get off the stage quick or the sceneshifters soon knock you out of the way.

Tommy said, "I am sure that these people have cat's eyes, as they were experts at seeing in the dark. It was like the London Black out."

Talk to Tommy and sooner or later he turns to football. For instance, when I met him at the Old Vic he was almost more exited about the prospects of his transfer from the Show Biz XI to Queens Park Rangers' 'A' team, than his transition from a rock 'n' roll idol to a classic actor.

He says that when he left Britain to tour Australia an appearance in 'She Stoops To Conquer' was the farthest thing from his mind. "Yet here I am in the dressing room previously occupied by the Olivier's, Wolfits and Guinness's, and tickled pink at the whole idea. I've learned so much since I've been here. For me this is the start in rep, and I am just an apprentice. I'm not one for lessons. I've never taken a lesson in my life; because I believe you can gain more from real experience and that what you learn should come from the heart. Each performance is different and teaches me something new about audiences and about myself. I'm enjoying every minute of it and I'd love to come again if they ask me and the play is right."

Well this play is right for Tommy, certainly. His natural instincts and talent fit him admirably for the part and he has won a much wider following as a result. The congratulatory messages and telegrams papering the walls around his make up mirror are proof of this. He regards it as only another part of his plan to graduate to an all round entertainer. "I want to do a bit of each, but only a bit. I don't believe in flogging anything. I might go abroad again. I wouldn't mind returning to Scandinavia. You feel you can easily fly home from there, and I get very home sick when I'm away, from the country I love."

Was Hollywood after him? I asked.

"I have declined three Hollywood offers, said Tommy, "but if they make another one I shall take it. You see I've come to the conclusion that we shall never make a decent film musical here - and my ambition to star in a really good one.' Tommy the Toreador' was the nearest I've ever got to it. We could do it. That's the pity. We've got better dancers than the Americans, and our songwriters are marvellous. The root of the problem is that accountants run our studios. Production costs are whittled right down before even the filming begins - partly because there aren't sufficiently big markets for our musicals overseas. It is a constant fight for class and finesse, and you can't get either without spending money. So unless there is a change I shan't bother."

Before I left him a head popped round the door; "Mr Steele a telephone call for you from a Mr Anthony Newley. Will you speak to him?"

"As I left I was thinking what a shame it would be if Hollywood claimed Tommy - as it has claimed many a promising young British star. Appearing in 'She Stoops to Conquer' at the Old Vic Theatre with Tommy were Peggy Mount, Judi Dench, John Humphry, Valerie Taylor and Gwen Watford."

A Memory from Pat Richardson.

"On November 8, Tommy appeared at the Old Vic Theatre in "She Stoops to Conquer".  That day, Betty a friend of mine received a telephone call from a London newspaper "Reynolds News". They wanted a Tommy Steele fan to accompany one of their reporters to the first night.

You guessed it - I was just in the right place at the right time! That evening the reporter, Jack Lewis, arrived in a smart car to take me to the theatre.

After a bout of star spotting - Anthony Newley being one of them and various other British TV stars (Gwen Watford and Jill Bennett) the play started.

My eyes were for Tommy, although there was a lovely young girl playing Kate Hardcastle named Judi Dench! Tommy had to speak with a Yorkshire accent; Ann had probably helped him as she comes from Yorkshire. I was born in Yorkshire, she said so I could judge whether he got it right!

After the play finished, the reporters were all invited backstage to interview Tommy. That party of people included me, as guest of Jack Lewis.

The dressing room was full and Ann appeared and gave Tommy a really big hug.

I remember how pretty she was and had on a pale blue glittery dress which was just beautiful.  I looked on in wonderment but had the presence of mind to pinch Tommy's cigarette stub from the ashtray (and I still have it today!)  How sad is that?

On the Tuesday of the second week, I went with Betty to Reading Cool Cats Club to meet up with Tommy and Lord Stoneham, who was then chairman of "Youth Ventures" and something Tommy supported. Again, I was in the presence of my idol, in total awe.

The following day, Betty and I went with Mrs. Hicks (Tommy's Mum) to buy some clothes for children in an orphanage. (The Fan Club had donated money for this.)

Now, on 17 November, it says in my diary: "Went to see Tommy again at the Old Vic. He was wonderful. Met him again backstage and he was really friendly.

When 'She Stoops To Conquer' finished, Tommy and Ann had a belated proper honeymoon in the West Indies, South America and New York.

"It gave us a great kick to meet the famous people of show business," he says. "We went to see Camelot with Richard Burton. We met Judy Garland and Anthony Quinn during the rounds of the parties. We had lots of fun and made many new friends. One night we were invited backstage and talked with Sir Laurence Olivier, who was then playing on Broadway in 'Becket'." This wasn't the first time we had met this great actor, for he had worked together in 1959 when he did a 'Night of a Hundred Stars'. Mind you he was stretching it a bit when he says they worked together because there was a scene in which he bumps into him, he turns and says "Don't I know your face?" This line brought the house down. But it does enable him to say that the first time he saw him it was in front of 3,000 people."

When Tommy returned home he appeared in the Festival of London Performance in the presence of Her Majesty Queen Elizabeth II.

In December he made the film 'It's All Happening,' playing the role of Billy Bowles, as an A & R talent co-ordinator. The title of this film in the USA was 'The Dream Maker'.

The world of Rock 'n' roll had come to an end and he started concentrating on doing some writing, painting and sculpturing at his new house on the Thames at Hampton Wick. Ann chose it and he liked it, because if he had a son, "He would be a cockney like me," he said. "I know people think that cockneys are a common lot, but they've got heritage."

Tommy said, "We were Londoners when London was being built. We bought the house before we were married and I reckon two people never bought a house under stranger conditions. Ann was mad to have an inglenook fireplace and we knew someone who actually had one. It was in an old coaching house, which they were willing to sell. Ann drove down to see it at three o'clock in the morning. She crept into the grounds and had a look round. When she came home, she said it was the most beautiful place she had ever seen. It's got a cobbled courtyard; which is lovely. I was playing in pantomime at the time, so I viewed the place at one o'clock in the morning. It certainly was the cat's whiskers. We went down there at a reasonable hour and made the deal and the place was ours. We didn't hurry with the furnishing. While I was at the Old Vic, we were living with just two deck chairs, a TV and a radiogram; oh and a bed. After all, a fella has to get some kip. All the rest of the house was just bare. But gradually we collected some proper furniture, mostly antique. It was all Ann's idea that we had antique furniture. It didn't mean a thing to me then, but now I'm just a real sucker for these pieces. Of course I didn't realise there were such lovely things in the world. But these are just frills, the main thing about a home is that it should be a shelter from the weather and the world; somewhere you can slam the door on all the problems on the outside and be quite relaxed inside.

The next big thing that happened to me was when I got a letter from the poet John Benjamin. He said he would like to come down and have a talk to me, and I said okay. When he arrived he was wearing a straw boater, and under his arm were some large volumes. It was blazing sunshine and I was sitting on the terrace watching the telly. I asked him if he would like a drink and he had a lager. After a while he turned to me and said "You're the nearest thing to the old time music hall that I know. I want you to join a concert for the Queen at the Mansion House during the city festival, doing one of the old Victorian music hall numbers." Well I felt honoured that he should ask me and said yes, and then he went on; "Now we come to another thing, we'd like you to do a scene with Sir John Gielgud."

"Well this frightened the daylight out of me," said Tommy "He wanted me to do a poem called 'Thirty Bob a Week' and told of a clerk meeting with a city gent and telling him exactly how it felt to live on thirty bob. I'll never forget the first time I read and spoke to Sir John. I walked on to the stage. He had just finished his lines and just as I began my first words; he turned his back on the audience so as not to take the edge off my entrance. He looked at me and gave me every ounce of his attention, and I felt it. Once I met his gaze I couldn't pull away and promptly forgot every word I had to say. Thank heavens it was only a rehearsal. There is a terrific amount of tension when you're playing in front of the Queen, of course, but this Mansion House 'do' went well. When it was all over we were asked to go into the anti-room. I'd met the Queen before at the Royal Command Performance, in line with the other people, but on this occasion there were only five of us, John Benjamin, Sir John Gielgud, Billy Danvers, Randolph Sutton and myself. The Queen was standing there with a drink and we all stood around and talked to her. 'It's the second time I've had the pleasure of seeing you this weekend,' she said to me. Astonished I said; Oh, really Ma'am, wondering how? "

The queen nodded. "Yes I saw your television show the other night."

"I didn't half feel pleased that the night she stayed in she should watch me on television!"

'Light Up The Sky' and 'Tommy the Toreador' were listed as two of the year's top moneymaking movies.

Tommy appeared in a medieval type Christmas Show for ITV, and also he appeared as Father Christmas with Dickie Henderson at the London's Savoy Hotel. He got the "Cat's Whisker' award for the most improved all round entertainer and he taped a one-hour show for ATV, which was to be shown at a later date.

On 3 March 1961 his fan club sent out a picture of Tommy, on the back of it he had written these words,- Hello all, I hope you're in for an exciting surprise just as I was.

The 'Daily Herald' caught me with some really intimate and personal questions. Talk about facing the facts! Still: you'll be able to read the answers on Monday in the 'Daily Herald' Cheerio Tommy Steele.

I was so sorry to have missed the newspaper, as I was away for a few days myself.

In April 1961 Tommy was in the Tommy Steele Show at 'The Coventry Theatre,' in the show were Teddy Johnson and Pearl Carr, Jimmy James, The Raindrops, Joe Baker and Jackglas, Desmond Walter Ellis, The Kims and Regine and Andre Berny. The Bedford and Stockton cast were Joe Church, the Five Dallas Boys, Joe Baker and Jack Douglas.

On June 11 1961 Tommy was top of the bill on 'Val Parnell's Sunday Night at the London Palladium'.

In the July of 1961 he recorded his last record to get into the charts at position 30 'The Writing On The Wall'

On July 16 Tommy appeared in two Sunday concerts organised by Harold Fielding at the Opera House Blackpool, the first one at 6.20 pm and another at 8.15pm

On August 13 Tommy appeared in two Sunday concerts organised by Harold Fielding at the Opera House Blackpool, the first one at 6.20 pm and another at 8.15pm

He opened at the Windmill Theatre, Great Yarmouth for a Summer Season. In the cast were the Dillonair Dance Group, Frankie Howard, Jumping Jax, Barry McDonald, The Jaywalkers, Elizabeth and Collins, a knife throwing act, and Miss Sunny Rodgers. Then he got the shock of his life. He was asked to appear in "A Midsummer Night's Dream." But I have no record of him having appearing in it.

On August 20 Tommy appeared in two Sunday concerts organised by Harold Fielding at the Winter Gardens Bournemouth, the first one at 6.20 pm and another at 8.15pm

During the summer season show he appeared in the BBC Light Programme's 'Seaside Night' from the Wellington Theatre, Great Yarmouth.

On December 23 he opened at the Empire Theatre, Liverpool in 'Humpty Dumpty' playing the part of Humpty in the cast were Eve Boswell, Ted Lune and Wyn Calvin, the pantomime closed on Saturday March 3 1962

In the January 1962 Tommy made a 'Palladium' appearance and an appearance on 'Parade of the Pops'.

During the summer of 1962 Tommy appeared in 'Sunday Concerts' at the Blackpool Opera House. He also appeared on 'Thank your Lucky Stars' on TV on June 23.

The always busy Tommy appeared on Bernard Delfonts 'Steele Hour' presentation for ITV Television which was followed by an appearance at the 'Mansion House' before the Queen, reading poetry, singing music hall songs along with John Betjemin, Randolph Sutton, Billy Danvers and Sir John Gielgud.

On Monday 7 May 1962 Tommy managed to play a game of football at Walthamstow Avenue Football Stadium with the 'Showbiz XI. He came to Manchester's 'Belle Vue' for another game of football later in the month and was fined twenty-five pounds for dangerous driving in his Jaguar.

During the year he appeared in a German Concert in aid of the United Nations Welfare Fund.

Tommy and his wife Anne went to Buckingham Palace to have cocktails with the Queen and the Prince Philip. When we got the invitation, Anne immediately said, like most women do, "I haven't got a darned thing to wear," so she rushed out to buy a little black dress.

"Then" said Tommy "I got into a tizzy about whether I should drive my own car or hire one and I decided to hire a taxi and let the driver worry about which gate to go in. As we drove past the blokes in busbies, Ann clutched my hands, and then when we got out and saw all those flunkies wearing white breeches, they didn't half scare me. Then a wonderful thing happened - they gave me the thumbs up sign and cried 'Wotcher Tommy'.

When we were shown into a room, which held famous scientists, and posh people who didn't talk our language, our hearts sank.

Then Prince Philip put his head round the door and beckoned us all into the other room where the Queen was waiting.

Well I can tell you it was a right good do, a far cry from the bread and dripping that we were going to have for our tea back home."

However, there is one thing he knows for certain, no matter how many times he hits the high spots he always goes back every week for his pie and mash in Bermondsey. After that he loves to bury his face in a freshly baked doughnut from another shop nearby. He'll never lose his love of the common places because he feels that that would be the sure death of Tommy Steele.

Tommy appeared at the Queen's Theatre Blackpool for two weeks in 'You'll See Stars,' He played football at Manchester Stalybridge and was mobbed, he was interviewed by the 'Home Service,' appeared in a charity concert at the 'London Palladium,' He filmed 'Quincy's Quest' for TV, wrote at 'Christmas Story' for the 'TV Times' magazine. He also received the 'Cat's Whisker Award' for several British TV shows.

In the early part of 1963 Tommy appeared in 'Sing A Song for Sixpence' on ITV as one of John Betjemin's guest.

Larry informed Tommy that Harold Fielding was looking out for a musical that he could do. When nothing came up, Harold decided to commission a show especially for him. He got hold of David Heneker and Beverley Cross and the result was a musical version of the H. G. Wells novel Kipps.

All Tommy's writing, painting and sculptures were put on hold as he prepared for the opening night of 'Half A Sixpence.' It opened on March 21 1963 at the Cambridge Theatre, after a few days trial a Wimbledon Theatre. John Dexter directed it and his leading lady was Marti Webb, it played 678 performances at the London's Cambridge Theatre and another 512 at New York's Broadhurst Theatre.

About Half a Sixpence, he said, "I am sure this is to be the most important first night in my life." The musical was based on H. G. Well's famous story 'Kipps.' But nothing is ever a sure fire thing in show business. "If it is a flop," he said, "I'm not going to pretend that I won't be disappointed."

It was three years before that he had made the decision to give up rock 'n' roll and to make a new career for himself.

"Sometimes," he said, "I've felt uncertain whether I would succeed and sometimes it's been a bit of a struggle, but at least I had Ann to share it with me. The biggest test yet will be the premier of this musical and we're both keeping our fingers crossed. But the way I see it, the world owes you nothing, and if you do something that doesn't click it's no good going round for days in a deep trench. In this game you're bound to have failures. In fact you've got to fail to succeed sometimes. I don't kid myself; I know one day the day will come when I'm not box office any more. It will be a blow, of course, but until that day comes I'm not going to stop. Anyway, when the time comes, I'm pretty sure Ann and I won't be broke; that's if we go on living the same as we do now. We don't like putting on the Ritz, we just enjoy having our own friends round and these are simple ordinary folks like ourselves. Of course we would like to have a family - we'd like four or five children - wouldn't I get a thrill having one of my sons playing in the football league. But to come back to the present and this musical - another great change in my world. During the out of town trial at Wimbledon all the songs were greeted with enthusiasm but I felt that it lacked a snappy number and at the last minute before we opened at the Cambridge Theatre 'Flash, Bang, Wallop' was put in."

"Half a Sixpence" was written as a starring vehicle for Tommy – the pop star whose meteoric rise had been satirised in Espresso Bongo. The songs from the show 'Half A Sixpence' included the title number; 'She's To Far Above Me' and 'If The Rain's Got To Fall.'

In 1963 Tommy again ran into a spot of bother with the law - speeding at 90 M.P.H. on the Hammersmith flyover, and he had his licence taken off him. He had to use the services of a chauffeur for a year.

A memory from Pat Richardson:

We were lucky to get a front row seat for the first night at the Cambridge Theatre. Front row seats in the gods! The stage looked like a postage stamp, and I can still hear those words.... "C'mon Edwin you 'aven't caught any mice again 'ave you!"

We (Sue and I) after one performance, waited for Tom afterwards at the stage door. Eventually out he came and during our conversation with him, he asked where we were staying. When we told him, he said, "I'll give you a lift."

He had an MG open top sports car, so us two and Tom squeezed into two seats (guess who had to sit astride the gear lever - holding on to Tom for dear life!). That sort of memory never leaves you."

While 'Half A Sixpence' was playing, Heneker was working on another musical for Harold Fielding, this time with the songwriter John Taylor.

This was to be a good old-fashioned Cinderella story that the critics hate but the public adore. It was to star the legendary Anna Neagle and it would make stars of Joe Brown and Derek Nimmo, "Charlie Girl" opened on 15th December 1965 and ran for 2202 performances, out-running "Oklahoma," "South Pacific," "Hello Dolly" and "The Boy Friend."

"Half a Sixpence was an instant success with the London crowd and it only closed so that I could take it to Broadway," Tommy said.

One morning when Tommy was sitting up in bed with his wife Ann having his early morning cuppa and going through the post, there amongst the bills was an envelope with the words across the top 'To the Master of the Household.' "Another soap coupon," he said to Ann, and almost threw it away. But then he decided to open it. When he looked inside you could have knocked him down with a feather. He said, "It was an invitation from the Queen and the Duke of Edinburgh asking him and Ann to a party at Buckingham Palace!"

He had had the honour of meeting the Queen before but he had never been to Buckingham Palace, and if anything, it made him realise how his world had changed.

Tommy said. "But nobody knows better than me that in show business your world can turn upside down overnight. For in the space of seven years I've gone from sausage and mash in Bermondsey to sausage on sticks in Belgravia, from rock 'n' roll to playing at the Old Vic, from living for kicks to living with a wife." Flushed with the success it deserved, he took a scene from 'Half a Sixpence' to the Royal Variety Performance on 4th November 1963.

In the December of 1964, Tommy appeared in a production of 'Richard Whittington Esquire' for Television.

Just before Tommy left England to open up on Broadway his manager Larry Parnes decided he wanted to part company with him. The headlines hit the newspapers: The nine-year association between Tommy and his manager Larry Parnes has ended. Steele is not renewing the managerial contract that terminated recently and he is unlikely to appoint a new one. Parnes and Kennedy were joint managers for five years until 1961 when Parnes became his sole manager. Ian Bevan will continue to act as agent but even that is unlikely to remain when his contract expires.

This left Tommy with Harold Fielding.

On 25 April 1965 he opened at the Broadhurst Theatre, New York.

Appearing with Tommy in this production were Sally Lee, Mercer Mcleod, Jean Cameron, Trescott Ripley. Playing Ann was Polly James.

It quite simply took Broadway by storm, with Tommy being nominated for a Tony Award, and an AMBO.

Tommy recalls the crossing from England to America on the Queen Elizabeth.

"Well there was I lying on my bunk in a first class cabin on M-deck. It was in the dark, about one in the morning. I remember the throb of the engines, the whole feeling, and the smell. Ships have smells, you know. I must have dosed because I woke with a start and began to sweat, I thought: It's all been a dream, this fantastic dream for ten years, it didn't happen. I'm still a seaman. I thought I'd lost everything but do you know, the only thing I felt robbed of was Ann, the rest didn't matter. I had to force myself to get up and switch on the light. It was a risk I had to take but I dreaded taking it. Fear had taken over from reason. It was queer. When I did put on the light, there was the first class cabin with me in it heading for Broadway. I had a terrible day after that. Ann stayed behind so that she could put the covers on the furniture, things like that, and was to follow me out."

On June 6 1965 Tommy and the cast of Half a Sixpence made an appearance on 'Toast of the Town' an American TV series. The greatest thrill of his life was when he met Gene Kelly, who asked him to appear with him in a show called 'New York, New York.' It was shown on the American television on

February 14 1966. This was a film made by American Airways to promote the town. Appearing alongside Tommy and Gene was Woody Allen.

Whilst Tommy was playing 'Half a Sixpence' in New York he was called by Walt Disney to go and have lunch, resulting in him staying on in America to film "The Happiest Millionaire." The "Happiest Millionaire" starred Fred McMurray, Greer Garson, John Davidson, Gladys Cooper and Lesley Ann Warren. It was based on the book 'My Philadelphia Father.' In it Tommy played the part of the Irish butler John Lawless.

On March 28 1966, Tommy made an appearance on 'The Perry Como Show' TV series.

The Happiest Millionaire was the last live action feature to be produced by Walt Disney before his death. It arrived when large-scale musicals were fading in popularity.

Tommy said, "When I went over to America to do 'The Happiest Millionaire' I thought I would sail on the 'Mauritania' instead of flying. I thought it would be a bit of a rest. Instead of that I ran into all my old buddies and felt worse when I got off the boat than when I got on. I was pleased because they didn't think I had changed a bit."

One of his old pals said of him, "For all his money and his fame he is the same little cheeky kid who used to live near the 'Bricklayer's Arm. Right down to dropping his aitches. When Tommy was making the film they were fascinated by his 'Cockney' slang and for a few weeks it was all the rage. People were going round saying things like, "I got Brahms and list last night and fell down the apples, and didn't get me ead down till late this morning."

The Happiest millionaire didn't perform well at the box office as it was hoped. In an attempt to broaden its appeal, the studio shortened it from 155 minutes to 144 and then trimmed it down to 113. The longer versions were in stereo, which were lost for 17 years. Due to a lengthy search through the vaults by the employees, the stereo versions were found. The studios chose the 144-minute version for cassette release. The 159-minute version was only screened once for a charity premiere. In mastering it for tape the studio omitted the original entrance and intermission music, but the remainder of the movie is intact. Richard and Robert Sherman penned the songs for the film.

Tom with Colin, Mum and Dad

# An Interview with Tommy's Mum

A magazine editor had an interview with Tommy's mum stated "I met Tommy's mum just after she got back from her first trip to New York to see her son in the star roll of 'Half A Sixpence' at the Broadhurst Theatre on Broadway. She opened the door wide as she saw me walking up the curving drive to the big house in the quiet residential street in Catford. 'Come in dear' she cried. 'You managed to find us all right?'
Her bright blue eyes exactly like her sons were sparkling with friendliness her smile as wide as Tommy's.
Within minutes I was sitting in a big comfortable chair under a picture of Tommy being presented to the Queen at the Royal Variety Performance.
"I suppose you want to know how our Tommy's getting on over in America.
Well, you'd never believe what a hit he is. They all love him. It's ridiculous really. Every night he brings the house down. All the big stars are pouring in to see him - Sammy Davis Jnr., Gene Kelly, Barbara Streisand, and Anthony Newley. You know dear, Tommy is so thrilled about that, but I never feel I'm with famous people when he introduces them to me. I just like them as people and hope that they've all got someone nice looking after them. Some of them looked so tired sometimes you know. Now I've always brought Tommy up to

take care of himself. He knows how to cook, he doesn't drink, only gallons of orange juice, and he gets a proper rest. Ann, his wife, has carried on the good work and he has never been fitter. You have to be fit in show business; you know dear, its very hard work.

And the pace in America! If you just stop for a minute, all those automobiles hoot at you. They haven't got time to breathe in the city.

When Ann and Tommy met us at the airport, I couldn't get over all the mad hustle and bustle everywhere. They took me out to Radio City to see a film and after that a stage show. It was non-stop entertainment all the time. I've never seen anything like it in my life, and all the shops, cinemas and theatres are open all night. I never got a wink of sleep the two days I was in New York. Tommy took his dad and me everywhere, and I met all the stars of Broadway. There was one thing, which gave me the biggest thrill I ever had. Tommy and Ann were just taking us into the theatre when there, shining right above Broadway in gigantic letters going round and round I saw "Tommy Steele now appearing in Half a Sixpence." I clutched at Tommy and said; now there's something for your camera, son I was so exited. And now I'm even more excited, Paramount has asked him to star in a film of Half a Sixpence. Tommy tells me they hope to start shooting in June, so he'll need to take a holiday before that happens.

You know in London it doesn't matter much what the critics say about a show, people still go and see it, if it's been recommended by a friend - but on Broadway if the critics, as Tommy says, pan a show then its finished. It often closes overnight if the reviews have been really bad. So you can imagine exactly how I felt waiting here at home. He thought he was going to be hell. His dad was already there - he never misses one of Tommy's opening nights, no matter where in the world he is. But I just can't stand the tension. At home the rest of us just sit at home waiting for a phone call. He always phones me after the first nights because he knows I just can't bear the tension. Well, that night I knew everything was all right when I heard him laugh clear across the Atlantic.

We're O.K. mum, they love us. And don't they, you want to hear them.

I couldn't believe it. When I was over there I sat with his dad listening to all the cheers and the applause and thought - this is ridiculous. You see, when Tommy first told me he wanted to turn professional, I was worried. He had a good and steady job as a physical training instructor on the liners and I told him so. I told him it's a decent life, a healthy life with some permanence. I told his manager that if he couldn't fix Tommy a booking during his three weeks leave I just wouldn't hear of it. Well he did, Tommy got a television spot and a part in a show in Sunderland.

I couldn't watch him the first time he was on television. I sat in the next room whilst the rest of the family watched. Tommy's younger brothers, Colin and Roy and his sister Sandra, the youngest member all looked in and I were shaking just listening. Even when I knew everything was all right I just kept on thinking about what was going to happen when it was all over. I just hoped we would be around to cheer him up if he didn't make it, and wondered if it would change him if he did.

That night at New York, I had a little grin to myself, remembering the first day when I realised that our Tommy was a born entertainer.

It was when our Queen was crowned, and the whole street arranged a party. The trestle tables were all laid out, and the flags were flying - all the mums had cooked cakes and cut the sandwiches and it poured and poured with rain. The children were so disappointed, but Tommy soon put a stop to that. Do you know he took them all down to the local hall and he entertained them all day long? He just never stopped. Looking at him then, I thought to myself this child has got something. The children had the time of their lives. Tommy was only thirteen then. But we, his dad and me never thought or dreamed he would go on the professional stage. Tommy went to work on the liners - he's always been mad about the sea. On the liners he used to entertain the passengers in his spare time with a kind of variety act. Then he went down with spinal meningitis and he nearly died during those months in Guy's Hospital. He was home for a while after that but Tommy was not one to give up. I didn't want him to go back to sea, but Tommy had made up his mind, he was going and go he did. I'll tell you one thing, my dear if you want to be a good Mother, learn to keep your mouth shut. It's the only way to bring your children up, to be independent. Tommy didn't realise how worried I was when he first started, but even if he had, he'd have carried on because he wanted to do it. He couldn't have imagined himself, though, in that big posh house where he and Ann are living in Scarsdale, just outside New York. We lived there, dad and I, while we were over there."

How does it feel - all that luxury - after a lifetime in South East London?

"We will enjoy it of course while it lasts, but you can never tell what will happen."

What? Even after two Royal Command Performances and Tommy being the toast of Broadway?

Mrs Hicks laughs. "You know what mums are like, always worrying. You talking about the Royal Command Performances remind me. Do you know what his dad did after the first one? Well, there we were sitting in the stalls with all the celebrities cheering. Well he gets up and says to every body. "That's my son!" I pulled on his sleeve and made him sit down. Dad felt such a fool afterwards, letting himself go like that. But I must admit I had tears in my eyes - it all seemed so wonderful. Tommy was so thrilled about being asked to appear before the Royal family. He'd always longed to meet the Queen. Since then, he has met yet many other members of the Royal family - during the visit of the Princess Margaret to America he was a guest at a party given for them by director Joshua Logan. Mind you, with all this, you can be sure he doesn't get treated any different to the rest of my children when he's at home. They've all got their own talents. It just happens that Tommy's are the sort the rest of the world love to see."

"What do you think is the secret of his being so friendly with everyone and not putting any sides since has become so famous?" asked the reporter. Ah. Well, you don't know Bermondsey, there are all types down there and we were brought up to hit it off with everybody. Around the docks there were good and bad, and our boys learned to pick them out the hard way. I never told them what to do; I just gave them a hint here and there along the way. They didn't go far wrong, and Tommy knows the difference between people famous or not. Tommy still loves Bermondsey, every Christmas he's home he goes down there and goes to the Ship, (the local pub,) and they have a knees up. Everyone has a great time. I usually stay at home and get the dinner ready and it's great to see them all come home looking so happy. There is something about Bermondsey that's really catching. Tommy has not got a big head - he hasn't pushed himself into the caviar class yet. It's still roast rabbit, jellied eels or pie and mash or chips for his favourite dinner. You know, although he's enjoying New York he's still homesick for England. He came home just for a weekend and he didn't want to see anyone but his family. He's no nightclub bird. He likes to see all the children and have a natter with us all. I am sure that's why he is so good in pantomimes. He really loves to hear children laugh.

Tommy and Ann can have most things that money can buy, but they long for a family of their own. But I tell them there's plenty of time yet, but there will be a celebration one day.

You want to see some of the parties we have, Frankie Howard, Jimmy Tarbuck and Alma Cogan came to the last one. They like my cold buffets - just plain and simple food. In my house they are just one of the family. Perhaps that's why people like him so much."

Tommy with his teammates

# He's Sports Crazy

"Saturday is the best day of the week, its sports day, you see", said Tommy during an exclusive interview..
"Ann knows and just lets me get on with it. Shall I tell you what I do every single weekend I'm not working?" His eyes sparkle.
"On Saturday I sleep till eleven. Then I take Kipps, the collie Ann gave me, into the field with a ball. We kick around a bit. He's the best centre half in the world. Then I come home, bath and dress. I put a packet of fags in one pocket and 32\6 in the other. Then I climb into my Excalibur 1927 Mercedes - not an original - and drive off towards Kings Road. Then I park near Alvaro's, walk into the restaurant, leave my Mac with the woman, try to avoid the éclair trolley because I always manage to get cream on my double-breasted, and sit down at the same table. It's laid for fifteen people.  The Mount Street Harriers, we call ourselves. There's Terry Stamp, Tony Newley, Herbie Kretzer and Duggie Heywood (my tailor), and lots of others I only know as Dick or Fred. We have a smashing meal, and a good swear, and tell a few jokes. Then we all throw 22\6 in the middle of the table; pay Duggie, who is the secretary, 10\- and pile off to see Chelsea or Fulham. Fulham for a laugh! Chelsea for a cry! Then I come home, take off my shoes, open up the telly - which is concealed in a bookcase - have a lovely tea and watch 'Match of the Day.
On Sunday morning I drive to the British Oxygen Ground to play football with a 'Johnny Haynes X1' team. After lunch, I have a second game with the 'Showbiz X1."

Tommy was a fine outside right incidentally and when he was a teenager had hopes of being a professional footballer, but he got injured and moved into show business instead.

John Kennedy said in 1957, Tommy is a great football fan, one day we were watching a football game and Tommy started wandering among the artistes who were watching the game with a notebook and pencil, taking names.

"What are you up to?" I asked.

"Just my football team," he said

I spluttered "Football team? What are you talking about?"

"'S' alright, chum. I don't expect you and Larry to play. I don't think you've got enough wind. It's mainly for the Steelemen and blokes like Mike and Bernie Winters."

The team was duly formed and played matches against stagehands and local schools.

Tommy played centre forward and everyone had a good time - until one day it leaked out in the local press where the match was taking place. When we arrived at the pitch we found several hundred girls waiting. Every time Tommy got the ball they cheered. When he lost it they booed the player who took it off him.

We were all enjoying the fun until one girl decided to run on the pitch and try to kiss Tommy. In a flash the rest of the girls joined in. That was the end of the match. Tommy was pursued off the field, sprinting for his life to Larry's car. We drove off just in time, but not before the radio aerial had been broken by one girl trying to stop us.

Jimmy Henney founded the Showbiz X1 in 1958, which regularly raised large sums of money for charity. The team boasted such stars as David Frost, Sean Connery, Ronnie Carroll, Dave King, Jimmy Tarbuck, Des O'Connor and of course our favourite Tommy Steele. Sometimes the team was supplemented with professional footballers such as Danny Blanchflower, Billy Wright and Wally Barnes.

Tommy even turned down an appearance on an ABC religious programme 'The Sunday Break' to play football. His manager Larry Parnes told a paper, "He always plays for the All Star X1 on Sundays - but when the panto at the Coliseum finishes he plans to take a holiday so he won't be playing football for a while".

Terje Dalene of Oslo, Norway, takes up the story,

"Tommy played for the Showbiz X1 from the late fifties until the end of the nineteen sixties. I have books from the 1960s and 70s, which talks about all the big players of the time,

George Best, Bobby and Jackie Charlton Gordon Banks and amongst them is Tommy Steele. Bobby Charlton is called "The White Knight", Gordon Banks, "The Caged Lion," he was the goalkeeper. George Best, is known as, "The Little Matador" and Tommy Steele, "The Professional Amateur." Tommy is also pictured in another book called the "Book of All Sports 1960."The editor said to me; "I want you to write a story about the Show Biz X1 which has been playing football matches all over the country. For a second my legs shook like those of a rock-and roller, for musically, I am the squarest of squares. Further, I like my Soccer played hard and seriously and I thought these players from the night world would hardly be in a fit state to do just that. No longer do I think ... not now that I have seen the Show Biz X1 in action, and have met Jim Henney, the team's founder and organiser, and learned the full story.

Now I am an enthusiastic fan. This is the story, Jim Henney, manager of a music-publishing firm and TV compare, with Pete Murray, also a TV compare, formed the Showbiz XI in 1958. Originally, the idea was to "get the boys in the business into the fresh air for exercise." Stars of radio, TV and stage jumped at the idea and soon a match was arranged with a team from Battersea, on a Wormwood Scrubs playing field. In that match Henney broke a wrist in three places.

We move on. That first team wore ordinary sports shirts; Henney and Murray decided it was not good enough. They decided that if they wore black then they would not have to change to avoid a clash of colours. So black it was and Henney and Murray went to a West End shop that offered a free supply. Whilst in that shop they hit on the idea of calling the team the Show Biz XI. And so it was. And so it is. Next step was to organise training. Queen's Park Rangers, the nearest club to the West End of London, were approached. They were delighted to help. Alex Farmer, the Q.P.R. trainer, was placed at their disposal. He now goes with his "adopted boys" to every game. For, make no mistake, the Show Biz XI are a good football team.

In this book Tommy is amongst all the famous athletes of the time.

The book contains Floyd Patterson and Ingemar Johansson, Stanley Matthews and Rod Laver, On 3 August 1960 at the Bloomfield Road Ground Blackpool Tommy Steele's XI played Stan Mortensen's XI. The referee was Stanley Matthews, probably the most talked about footballer in England.

On Sunday 23 April, 1961 the showbiz X1 played George Swindin's X1 at Alexandra park f.c. ground. Showbiz line-up, Pip Wedge, Jimmy Henney, John Burgess, Billy Wright, Walley Barnes, Peter Thompson, Tommy Steele, Glen Mason, Sean Connery, Alex Forbes, and Dave King. Subs: - Ronnie Carroll, Chas. Mcdevitt, Jackie Gordon.

The opposition were - George Swindin's X1 to be chosen from, Bill Dodgin, Frankie Broome, George Swindin, Laurie Scott, Freddie Cox, Teddy Bates, Ronnie Burgess, Bernard Joy, Ronnie Greenwood, Len Goulden, Bill Nicholson, Alec Stock and Harry Evans."

A memory from Pat Richardson:

"On Sunday, 28 October 1962, Tom had told my friend and I that he was playing football at Belle Vue that day. We, on the other hand, had read that he was playing at Stalybridge, Cheshire, so that's where we went. Tom eventually arrived at half-time (he'd been to Belle Vue!). However, he scored a goal and my diary says, "The crowd went completely mad." They all met up after the game at the Lamb Inn, Hyde.

A Charity Football Match between the Showbiz XI v. Billy Wright's XI was played on Sunday, 25 October 1964 at Bloomfield Park, Palmers Green. Kick-off was at 2.45 p.m. by Susan Maughan in aid of the St. John Ambulance Brigade.

Reading v Show Biz XI was played on Tuesday 13 December 1966 at Elm Park. The Show Biz team included Tommy Steele, Jimmy Tarbuck, Harry Fowler, Danny Blanchflower, Billy Wright, Brian Close, Len Ducquemin, Kenny Lynch, & Jess Conrad. David Coleman's World of Football, 1968 calls Tommy in his article "The Professional Amateur." If Tommy Steele wasn't an entertainer, would he like to make his career in professional football?

"Yes," Tommy says emphatically. "Very much."

He used to train with a First Division club, and now his weekly routine is staggeringly thorough. Every morning of the week he runs half a mile to the recreation ground, jogging and sprinting for a mile, and then he joins a group of mates for a five-a-side game for three-quarters of an hour. On Saturdays he is always watching a match. On Sundays he is always playing in one, as well as some mid-week games.

They're not "friendly" matches on Sundays, he says - "I don't think I've ever played a 'friendly' game. Somewhere between the game in which everyone is totally dedicated and the 'friendly' match, somewhere in the middle is the word competitive."

Tommy tries not to get permanently attached to one team, because he doesn't want to get into a situation where he can't put them aside. He keeps his eye on individual players - like Johnny Giles, whom he saw play one of his first games for Leeds against Fulham. Tommy was doing a radio report for the BBC and feels as if he had a hand in 'discovering' Giles. "The goals" he says "are the really important thing unless you're rooting for any particular side. The thing is to go and see the thought that goes into the mid-field play. "In these days of 4-2-4 and all that sort of thing, the midfield play is the thing for my money, that's really exciting, "the position has become now where the game is tight and hard and you have a lot of chess moves. Once upon a time the long ball down the middle was the ideal thing to strip the defence, the big men in front, and five forwards. Wolves were famous for it, but today it's more chessboard moves, the short sharp passes, the flick back, it's the midfield play, which brings off the goals. It's more confined. "It may be harder, but the game has not got worse. It's got better. I think the players of today would walk all over the players of yesterday. The most important people after the war were forwards. You would rarely read about a centre or a right back that was worth a hundred thousand pounds. And the forwards of yesterday would have a lot of trouble breaking down the defences of today."

Tommy very keenly feels the belated recognition of football by the upper classes. The knighthoods are starting to come to football's way after centuries, he says .. "Soccer I suppose was always looked upon as a crowd game - the difference between it and the Sport of Kings, racing, and cricket. If you went to the Sport of Kings you watched from a tent, sipping champagne and having an occasional flutter with that horrible gentleman at the rails. In cricket it was the case of, shall we go in for tea, and let's have a cosy little chat in the pavilion whilst we watch the occasional over, and oh well done that was a splendid shot. And with Soccer it meant jostling with 50,000 people in an out of the way ground, and shouting at the referee, and being really in the game. I mean, one doesn't cheer from the pavilion at Lords, and one doesn't shout from the paddock at Ascot, but you can shout your bloody head off at a football ground."

Jimmy Hill's Football Book 20th Feb 1970, wrote:-

"Becoming a director could compensate for not being a professional player, said Tommy. " Football has always meant a lot to me. Next to my family, it is the thing I miss most when

I have to go to the States for film work. Usually I manage to take my family with me. But I have yet to find a way to smuggle a top League team across the Atlantic!

When I was a kid I always dreamt of being a professional footballer. I used to spend hours kicking at a ball, a tin can or anything that wouldn't kick back. I scored some magnificent imaginary goals in the back streets of Bermondsey where I spent my childhood. Millwall was my local club, I was born just a few hundred yards from the Den and spent many happy Saturday afternoons on the terraces cheering on the Lions and jeering at the visitors. I am telling you all of this so that you can appreciate how I felt when my name was linked with the Millwall chairmanship. I am still a little bewildered as to how it all started. All I know that within just a few hours of Mickey Purser letting it be known that he might stand down from the Millwall chairmanship; the name of Tommy Steele was being head-lined as the likely successor.

At first I must admit that it was an idea that appealed to me. I felt that becoming a club chairman or director could compensate me for not realising that ambition of playing professional football. Yes, I thought, it would certainly be great to be involved, because my interests in football have always gone deeper than just being a grandstand critic. Anyway I wrote an open letter to Mickey Purser said Tommy, via the Daily Express in which I suggested that perhaps we could get together for the elusive meeting everyone was speculating about. The main point I made in the letter was the fact that I would be more than honoured to become chairman of the club. I added: to Millwall I would try to bring ideas for the betterment of a Saturday at The Den - and not only through its football.

If you and all concerned feel that this would be a plus for the club then I must in fairness mention a big minus. I have never sat on a football club before, so my knowledge of internal politics is nil. But if you, sir, and your fellows can envisage a rather young chairman shouting the odds, perhaps we can have that excusive meeting everyone is speculating about.

You have, no doubt, since read of the later developments so I will not bore you with anymore details. All I wish to stress is that from the start my objectives were to help not to hinder, Millwall I would like to thank Jimmy Hill for the use of his Platform. Now what time is the next train to the London Palladium?"

Tommy stopped playing football when Emma was born in 1969 but the team continued playing.

Jimmy Henney died in September 1998, but the team continued.

On 29th October 2005 they were playing at the County Ground, Swindon in aid of the NSPCC.

Football is not the only sport Tommy played. He now plays golf, which he learned to play in Llandudno. He also likes riding horses and up to quite recently played squash. Not long ago he took up tennis and loves sea fishing when he is on holiday".

Ann, Tommy and Baby Emma

# The Best Has Yet To Come

Tommy returned to England in the September of 1966 to work on the film "Half a Sixpence" at the Paramount \ Areran Studios playing the role of Arthur Kipps which was based on the H G Well's story of Kipps.

On November 14th 1966 Tommy was once again at the Royal Variety Performance attended by the Queen Mother, the Duke and Duchess of Kent and Prince Richard of Gloucester, which was filmed by the BBC and broadcast six days later. After the National Anthem was played the audience settled down for a great night of stars.

Des O'Connor compared the whole show. The first act consisted of the Bachelors, followed by Jack Douglas, Des O'Connor, Gene Pitney and the Piero Brothers. Following this quartet were Morecambe and Wise and Juliette Greco. Next were the English team members holding the World Cup. These were followed by Wayne Newton who was unknown in Great Britain and closing the fist half of the show, Tommy celebrating ten years in show business by singing Little White Bull. Tommy shared the number one dressing room with Matt Monro and Sammy Davis Jr.

On January 25 1967 Tommy made an appearance in a TV documentary 'Come and Get your Money.'

On March 26 Tommy appeared in a TV movie 'The Heart of Show Business.'

The film Half A Sixpence was completed In April 1967. He starred in the film with Julia Foster, Cyril Richard, Penelope Horner, Elaine Taylor, Hilton Edwards, Pamela Brown and James Villiers. The 1967 film is regarded as a classic of its kind.

On December 20 Tommy appeared in a thirty minute TV documentary 'Cinema' for Granada Television.

The following month Tommy went back to the States to start on the filming of 'Finians Rainbow' with Fred Astaire. Tommy played the part of Ogg the Leprechaun. What an occasion that was. He had always wanted to meet Fred. It had been one of his ambitions. The other was to meet Walt Disney. He did meet them both in the space of twelve months. Whist Tommy was in the States he went to 'The World Premiere of Finian's Rainbow, along with his co-star Petula Clarke who played Fred Astaire's daughter 'Sharon' in the film.

On January 31 1968 He made an appearance in America on 'The Joey Bishop Show' an American TV series.

In March 1968 he filmed 'Twelfth Night' for ITV. (This was first shown on the television in 1970.)

In April he was filming 'Where's Jack' in Ireland with Stanley Baker, Fiona Lewis and Alan Badel. Tommy played the part of Jack Sheppard

Sometime during the filming of 'Where's Jack' their baby was conceived.

In 1968, Tommy bought a pillar-box red copy of a 1927 Mercedes. The American company Excalibur, who specialise in making up-to-date working replicas of early jalopies without sparing the cost, built it. It was reported in a Danish newspaper that he paid 74,000 Kroner for his sports car and that he had his initials T.S. on the driver's side and A.S. on the passenger's side.

Tommy had great love of speed. (The Mercedes did 120 m.p.h. flat out.)

After almost three years of studio work he wanted to get back to the stage. Harold Fielding fixed him up with 'The Servant of Two Masters', and from November 1968 till February 1969 he played Truffaldino for a limited season. Appearing with Tommy were Graham Crowden who was the Guardian Elf of fairyland in the 'Tommy Steele Christmas Show' on television in 1960, Edward de Souza, Michele Dotrice, Julia Lockwood, Ronald Radd, Ken Wynne, Clive Francis and Morag Hood. Toby Robertson directed it.

On October 18 1968 Tommy flew over to America to appear again on the 'Joey Bishop Show.'

From the start of their marriage Tommy and Ann wanted a baby. "Because" he said, "we had both come from large families. Our happiness was complete when after nine years of trying, on 27th March 1969 our daughter Emma was born. When I was told that I was a dad, I cried my eyes out.

On July 8 Tommy had to fly out to America to be on the 'David Frost Show' TV talk show

It was reported that Tommy said, "For a year I am going to be with my daughter just as much as I can. I just want to be sure that she knows I'm her dad. And I don't want to miss one single bedtime cuddle. Planning for Emma, watching her grow, being there at bath times, is what life is all about. I am going to take photographs of her every day for Ann and I always figured on having children, but when they didn't come along we waited. We always knew that somebody up there would let us have a kid when the time was right. After all we could afford all the things we could possibly want. Yet for all we had we couldn't own a simple thing like a baby. But if the Lord wouldn't let us have one then we would have each other. There always was and always will be a special bond between us for I cannot bear to be without her. When I work away she comes with me and if she can't, then I don't take the work it's as simple as that. Ann and I have only been separated a few times in our marriage and it has been murder. When she is not with me I feel so utterly lost. I always do when she is not nearby. If anything should happen to her I just couldn't live without her."

During Emma's first year Tommy wrote and filmed "Tommy Steele and Things" for the BBC Omnibus series, just so that he could be with Emma each night.

He photographed her first smile and her first steps. What more could a man want. He moved into a bigger house with a larger garden at Petersham, Surrey.

After having the year off, which he promised himself, He flew once again to America to be on 'The David Frost Show' on December 21. Tommy returned to the stage with 'Dick Whittington' at the London Palladium.

It opened on 23rd December. It had been ten years since he had played in pantomime in London, and it was fun to be back. Appearing with him were Mary Hopkin, Kenneth Connor, Billy Dainty, Ruppert's Bears, Sheila Melvin and David Adams.

Lesie Macdoanay wrote in the London Palladium Souvenir Brochure. The first 'Turn Again, Whittington starring Norman Wisdom, broke all records. This year the pantomime is once again Dick Whittington starring Tommy Steele and Mary Hopkin, and I am proud to say that this will eclipse all records. Bookings, in fact, have been so tremendous that the run has been extended for a further four weeks even before the pantomime has opened.

Fast on the heels of the Palladium season came the chance to appear again in cabaret at Caesars Palace, Las Vegas.

He said to Ann, "Before I accept it I want to try the show out at Blackpool."

During the spring of 1970 he wrote and filmed 'In search of Charlie Chaplin for BBC television.

'The Tommy Steele Show' starring Tommy, Mary Hopkin, Billy Dainty and Eric Brenn at the ABC Theatre, Blackpool was an instant success.

On February 17 1971 Tommy appeared on 'Tonight Show Starring Jonny Carson' an American talk show, and on February 18, 1971 he opened in Las Vegas.

In the dressing room after his sensational opening night he was talking to Harold Fielding and he made the remark "Lets take it to London, Gov." He always referred Harold Fielding Gov. Accepting the challenge of finding a suitable theatre Harold Fielding replied.

"It's a deal, even if I have to take Charlie Girl off after five and a half years. I know 'Meet Me In London' will provide us with eleven of the most exciting weeks in the theatre we have known for a long time. Truly great stage personalities are very rare and I salute one of the greatest it has been my good fortune to know."

When he returned to England in April he did a ten-week season at the Adelphi Theatre, London. The show was called 'Meet Me In London'.

Now that Emma was able to travel with them he went over to Scandinavia where he did some Variety shows at the Tivoli. From there they went on to Stockholm where he appeared in cabaret at Berns.

When he got back to London, he started working on two programmes for the London Weekend Television, 'The Tommy Steele Hour' and 'A Special Tommy Steele'. The latter was entered at the Montreux Festival.

It was back over the pond in 1973 where he appeared in the 'London Palladium Show' at the O'Keefe Centre in Toronto,

Canada. When Tommy appeared at the O'Keefe Centre the packed theatre applauded constantly on the opening night after he sang 'If The Rains Got to Fall' for almost one minute before he could continue. After the show he gave an interview to the packcd house and they were unanimous in their support of Tommy after questioning him for almost ninety minutes.

This was followed by a six-week Tommy Steele variety show at the London Palladium starring Jose Moreno, Joe Church, The New Dollys, The Wychwoods, The Irving Davies Dancers and June Bronhill.

After having a holiday with Emma and Ann, September was spent touring Scandinavia. It was during this tour that he started composing his autobiography in music 'My Life, My Song.' In 1974 Pye Records and the BBC Television recorded it.

Tommy said, "I told you it was all happening.

# My Life My Song

My Life My Song was written and composed by Tommy in 1973 and recorded by Pye in 1974.

In side the album cover Sir John Betjeman wrote these words: "These are the songs of a lover. He is living with hope on the way to eternity, which is not frightening."

Inside the album cover were the words of the songs and accompanying pages a picture painted by Tommy

Stowbrae Ltd owns the copywriters to the lyrics.

.

<u>My life, My song</u>:

When all my breath has gone away, and my views just fade, and all my thoughts of days gone by are gone, There'll still be one last word to say, about this life I've played, life was more than living, more a song.

This is my life my song, I sing it 'cos I'm free, whether I'm right or wrong, it beats my heart it's in my key, this is my life my song, it's written every day, it's my life I sing about, it's me.

I've put my life together, in verses and refrains, there's nothin' in I didn't think upon, books performed in leather, I'll leave to other names, life for me is singing it's a song.

This is my life my song, I sing it 'cos I'm free, whether I'm right or wrong, it beats my heart it's in my key, this is my life my song, it's written every day, it's my life I sing about, it's me, it's me.

## Conceived:

My Mother and my little Dad met somewhere, they didn't care 'bout any other pair, just made it there, I was born within the year, December, I remember my pretty Mother's chest, and it was the best.

Oh love comes early in life, love come – come take my life, life is easily defended, if you've got a life to lead, life is easily expended, and you just don't breathe.

I went to school, played the fool, Didn't learn much, such was my life in my little way, but I'm living it every day, same old way, hey, hey, one thing sure rich or poor, it's likewise, like the wise and witty folk say, pity they, who delay, no way.

Oh love comes early in life, love come – come take my life, life is easily defended, if you've got a life to lead, life is easily expended, and you just don't breathe.


## War:

Run bugger run shout me mum, Show yer bum and hide your eyes, Who gonna look when house is shook, And bomb is dropping from de sky.

Here come de Spitfire, Here come de Messerschmitt, Here come de Hurricane, and de Focke-Wulf

Dash nipper dash - come de crash, House she lying on de ground, if you stay you gonna play, Tishoo, Tishoo all fall down.

Here come de Spitfire, Here come de Messerschmitt, Here come de Hurricane, And de Focke-Wolf

Find a chick take her quick, Have knee treble in de park, I tell you mate it ain't too great, When bombs is dropping in de dark.

But today same old way, Kids buy weapons by de score, Dey ain't real but still I feel, You gotta love a gun to love a war. You gotta love a gun to love a war, You gotta love a gun to love a war.

## Youngest Love:

Only love its time for weeping, deep in me heart is a tear cried for you, in me voice a whisper calling, falling in love with you, come into my arms my darling, tell me that you mean it too, if that's wishful dreaming darlin', I'll dream the dream for two.

Lovely lass me eyes are tearful, fool that I am I can't help the pain, can't you see me, can't you see me, look over here again, on the wall the chalk is fading, made in truest prose I swear, I love you know, will she won't she, take the time to care.

Work:

Leaving School any fool does, That's the rule and it's just 'cos, You gotta pull, gotta pull away, Till they say you get the pay, Till you die
Factory - fact to me is, Naturally - got to be busy bee, And the man in the limousine
Shows how it might have been Till you die, Why! Work work, Work work
Keep alive - in the tenement, Nine to five goes to pay the rent, And the loot from polluted air, Goes to suit the millionaire, Till its die die die, Why why why, Why why why, Die die die, Work work work work, Work work work work
There are no holes in the cemetery, Save the souls of the funny free, You and me got to be a tree, Got to make it got to be, A high high  high, Fly fly fly, No lie lie lie - c'mon and Try try try, Work work work work, work work work work.
Don't let 'em con ya, Lay it on ya, We're the people, The poor poor, Long long, Suffering people, Work.

Adventure:

Steady as she goes Joe straight ahead, steady as she goes Joe take her head, feel her as she reels Joe in her bed, make her answer the helm.
Steady as she goes Joe bring he through, steady as she goes Joe she's for you, you've got a heavy swell and she's come to, make her answer the helm.
Make her answer the helm, it's you that she's sailing for, the weather's prevailing more, she's answering well.
Steady as she goes Joe let her fight, steady as she goes Joe now she's right, she stays and she lays well in the night, make her answer the helm.
Steady as she goes Joe let her fight, steady as she goes Joe now she's right, she stays and she lays well in the night, make her answer the helm.
Steady as she goes Joe in your hand, steady as she goes Joe like you planned, she's wet and she'll get you back to land, make her answer the helm.

Make her answer the helm, it's you that she's sailing for, the weather's prevailing more, she's answering well.

Revolution:

In the middle of the fifties, The beat generation was born, The children refused hand me down music And the revolution was on They all got together, Everyone answered the call, And history will tell forever. The battle for rock 'n' roll
Rock of ages I'm for thee, Was the song of victory, And victory was very sweet, Blue suede shoes were on our feet,
There were seventy-eight revolutions, per minute in those days, More than any South American state the records say, And pretty soon the pace died down to a steady forty-five, Viva Zap! And all that crap, and rock 'n' jazz 'n' jive.
Rock of ages was our thing, 'The king is dead, God save the king', God save The Who and Cathy's Clown, Peggy Sue and Charlie Brown.
Many tried and many reigned, and many ran away, Some just died and some remained to fight another day, And like El Presidente, the leader had a ball, Till one more revolution, took him to the firing wall.
Rock of ages make me strong, I'm the singer not the song.

Ambition:

Want to, I have to, got to be someone but who, this guy – must try, ambition ambition, a wish come true.
No fear, come here. Let me hold you don't you disappear, I swear – I'll be there, ambition ambition, I wish, I care.
A dream doesn't mean it can happen, so say the prophets of gloom, hope isn't there to be sat on, back I need room.
Somehow, be now, now you're here with me I see how, I'm helpless – it's still yes, ambition ambition, a wish come true.
But should I fail, is it lonely, is it cold, I'm told it's sad, it can't be bad, this need it's only. The only need I've ever had, and what of life, what of living, must they go their separate way, what of love and what of giving, I can't say, I can't say.
Take me, make me, I've forsaken all don't break me, this time, just mine, ambition ambition a wish sublime.
Empty, I'm empty, make me full it's cruel to tempt me, lead me, feed me, ambition ambition, oh can't you see.

Lonely one lonely one- try to sleep, sleep must come, come the morn I'll carry on, But till the dawn no more song to sing, just bring me the silence of my mind, my mind.

Wilderness:
Lullaby, lullaby baby bye bye, go fly 'way no more day, lullaby lullaby lee you can see trees, orange pink and grey, in the fluffy sky you'll fly, I can help you go, little so and so.
Lullaby, lullaby, lullaby baby bye bye, go fly 'way no more day, lullaby lullaby lie you can try, hear me when I say, you don't have to hide, inside, take it kinda slow, little so and so.
Lullaby don't you cry little lullaby.

Marriage:

You, you are love, I, I am up above the clouds, and the clouds are high, and there is no sound, save the whisper of the wind when you're around.
You, you're the one, warm, like the summer sun, but the sun can't kiss, and the sun can't cry, you, you are my miss and I'll love you till I die.
Pay the piper and he'll play the tune of love, but you have to know the words, to see what he's a-playing of, and it takes time to learn the song, but we'll pay the piper well, so he'll let us sing along, pay the piper and he'll play his loving song.
Come, come with me, sing sing the melody, it will be strong, and evergreen, come love sing the song come join the dream.
Pay the piper and he'll play the tune of love, but you have to know the words, to see what he's a-playing of, and it takes time to learn the song, but we'll pay the piper well, so he'll let us sing along, pay the piper and he'll play his loving song.

Fatherhood:

Blue skies 'n' butterflies, bees 'n' trees 'n' piggy sties, five bar gates and fields of green, and beavers building in a stream.
And I'm with you, and you're with me, and that makes two, and your mummy makes three, hee, hee, hee.
Summer sunshine, silly showers, lambs 'neath oaks and folks with flowers, people laughing, kiddies crying, someone somewhere sadly sighing.
And I'm with you, and you're with me, and that makes two, and your mummy makes three, hee, hee, hee.

The butterfly has had its day, its colours carefully stowed away, for him the summer's done alas, but not for us my love my lass.

And I'm with you, and you're with me, and that makes two, and your mummy makes three, hee, hee, hee.

There's autumn, winter, spring to come, and this is summer our first one.

Hope:

Deep in the jungle the old folk tell a story, of people dying – where they all go, there in the village they know the story very well, it tell you people – you gotta go.

They say look in the night sky, they say look in the night sky, they say look in the night, pick out a star, and there you are, This life can't last forever, this life can't last forever, this life can't last, can't last, pick out a star and there you are, pick out a star and there you are.

In every mud hut, the families one by one look out, they pick the bright star, they gonna be, in every man's life he knows that all the good he does. Will make his star shine, will make him free.

They say look in the night sky, they say look in the night sky, they say look in the night, pick out a star, and there you are, This life can't last forever, this life can't last forever, this life can't last, can't last, pick out a star and there you are, pick out a star and there you are.

There in the story there in he story there is hope for every one, it tells the people who gonna go, up in the dark sky a star is waitin' there for you, you keep it shining you make it glow.

They say look in the night sky, they say look in the night sky, they say look in the night, pick out a star, and there you are, This life can't last forever, this life can't last forever, this life can't last, can't last, pick out a star and there you are, pick out a star and there you are.

# Tommy's Stage Manager Gets Killed

In May 1974 Tommy heard some awful news. His personal stage director, Mr Edwin Thornley, the man behind many of his hit shows, was found stabbed to death on Hungerford Bridge, which spans the River Thames at Charing Cross. He decided there and then to offer an immediate reward of one thousand pounds for any information on who could have done such a thing. In due time a man named Robert Walker was captured and jailed for the murder of Mr Thornley. The trial took place at the Old Bailey.

One day, whist Tommy was watching television; he saw the film 'Hans Andersen.' Having spent so much time in that country he decided, he wanted to be in it, Harold Fielding had the idea to stage the musical based on the music using Loesser's songs. Sam Goldwyn owned the rights and he vetoed the idea. Just before his death in 1973 he relented. The result was 'Hans Andersen' the stage show. Appearing with Tommy in this production were Sally Ann Howes, Anthony Valentine, Bob Todd, Lila Kaye, John Baskcomb and Geoffrey Toone.

Things did not go right during the rehearsals and for the first time in his life he blew his top with everybody. Just forty-eight hours before the opening night they practised the scene where the stagecoach is supposed to turn into a mighty sailing ship. It was always going wrong, and it never worked out. He was unhappy with the songs and he had an altercation with his musical director Alyn Ainsworth.

Sick of trying to get the music right and standing around, decided he'd had enough and walked out, taking his orchestra with him.

Tommy blamed the stage staff and they blamed somebody else. They practised it for another three hours and eventually Tommy asked Harold Fielding to cancel the show. It could not have happened at a worst moment. On the Sunday they were to make a cast recording. He told Harold Fielding that he was not doing the recording because it would be far better if they spent the time getting the show right.

He told him there were at least sixteen things, which needed adjusting, and if they were not adjusted, the show would not open. (Not only was Tommy annoyed, but also so was the record producer Norman Newell.)

The studio had been booked and Norman Newell started making arrangements for the understudy, Barry Hopkins, to cut the disc. But now it was Barry Hopkins turn to protest. He had been told that he would not be required on the Sunday and had made other arrangements. At home, Alyn Ainsworth sat down at his piano, and there on the music stand was an unfinished arrangement of one of the shows numbers 'Jenny Kissed Me.' Any bitterness which had happened between him and Tommy were soon forgotten and the next morning the music was on the bandstands. (But Alyn stayed at home.)

Tommy had had a good sleep after he had spoken to Harold Fielding and soon after he set off to the recording studios. The recording session went without a hitch. The most difficult number 'The Kings New Clothes' was recorded in one take.

Tommy talks about children.

"When a child comes along you can kiss goodbye to the life you once knew, you find your self changing your hours, your thoughts, your holidays, everything. The old life is gone for good. And another great life starts.

Emma's five and a half now. I'll be taking her with me to the matinees when my new show Hans Christian Andersen opens at the London Palladium.

She's decided to be my dresser. She went to the theatre recently and saw a friend of mine being dressed and suddenly she said:

'Does that lady always dress her?'

'Yes' I said.

'Is it very difficult?' she asked.

'Not really, it depends on how many dresses you've got to wear on stage.'

"Will you be wearing a lot of dresses?"

"No, I'll be wearing a suit," I said.

"D'you mean your trousers and under trousers?"

"Yes" I said.

"Well," she said. 'I pick them for you every day, anyway"

"That's true" I said.

"And I've seen your bum, so, I'm going to be your dresser" she said.

"She wants 10p a week for doing it and she wants to be able to walk with me to the wings as every dresser does. Knowing her she'll follow me on. She comes into the bedroom in the mornings when I'm half a sleep and demands to know, whether I've drunk my tea?

I say "I Have"

She looks into the cup and bosses me, 'you haven't even touched it yet! You'd better get up now; I'll go to your wardrobe and pick your things!'

"Once she got out a swimming costume for me because it was raining."

We have stories every night before she goes to bed, and lots of next mornings as she calls them and she wants a different one every night.

I prefer to make up the stories myself. There always has to be a little girl called Emma in them. I can tell her some of Hans Andersen's but not the scary ones like the 'Red Shoes' where the only way to stop the feet from dancing is to get the woodsman to chop off her feet. No Way!

Her games are very inventive, one day she decided to be a nurse, I was in bed and she came in with a friend of hers, she started with a stethoscope on my back that a doctor friend had given her.

"I know what the trouble is turning me over and began pouring a full bottle of make-up remover all over my stomach, it was freezing. They wrapped me in the duvet. I went along with it for about five minutes then I jumped out of bed and ran a hot bath. You can't growl at them, they don't mean to be naughty. Discipline is mostly done through her Mother; I suppose I'm there to be a threat – wait till your dad gets home - I don't know what sort of woman Emma will grow up to be. But I'm determined she is to grow up with a very loving background. I would like to believe Emma will have the level headedness of her Mother so that she won't be put off by any sudden turn ups.

I'd like her to have strength from me, plus a combination of our love together, that's not a bad thing to go out into the world with – if you haven't got that then you've got nothing - that is what life is all about."

'Hans Christian Andersen' opened on Tommy's thirty-eighth birthday 17th December 1974, at the London Palladium and that night he received a standing ovation. Tommy was asked to write something for the programme. Not knowing what to write, Ann suggested that he write about his paintings.

He described how he painted with verve and simplicity saying; "I have a great feeling for colour. My best works I feel are on sporting themes, particularly football. I am not a good portraitist but I delight in painting my wife Ann and my daughter Emma and a few close friends. I achieve likenesses which are not immediately recognisable physically but which to those who know the subject are a perfect likeness psychologically. My pictures start off as doodles, and then they become drawings. Then I decide if it will be a painting or a sculpture. Once it is completed I take great joy in showing the pieces to the people. I do not sell the pieces. I give them to my friends and family."

'Hans Andersen' was only supposed to run over the Christmas season, but it continued until the following November. He was told by the management, "It took more in box office receipts than any other Palladium show before it."

On 26th September 1974, Tommy was invited to a Foyle's Literary Luncheon at the Dorchester, to honour the publication of his 'Autobiography in music' entitled 'My Life My Song' that was due out on the 27th.

From 1st of October until 15th of October he exhibited his paintings of 'My Life, My Song' at the Christopher Wade Gallery in London.

On 24th October 1975 he was at the new Rotherhithe Civic Centre with his dad, who unveiled his statue 'The Bermondsey boy.

'He explained what the statue represented. 'It is a boy in a hurry, with his head down clutching a book. It is a work with a personal feel, he's rushing through life, determined to get there, get somewhere, but he hangs on to the knowledge he picks up on the way. A bit like me I suppose."

On 26th October 1975 he opened the Rotherhithe Civic Centre.

On December 14th 'Woman's Own published 'The Tommy Steele Songbook with favourites from his new great new show 'Hans Andersen.'

When Tommy finished at the London Palladium he decided to take the show on a tour of the provinces, but first there were a couple of changes he wanted to make. He rang Harold Fielding to ask him if he minded if he put them in.

"Well, if you're going to change things in the show, why don't you direct the show yourself," he asked him. And so he did.

'Hans Andersen came to the Manchester Palace Theatre on 15th December 1975. Appearing in the tour were Bob Todd, Lila Kaye, Colette Gleeson, Geoffrey Toone, Robert Bridges and Patrick McIntyre who was a dancer in Tommy's film 'Half A Sixpence.' After the Manchester Palace it went on to the 'Birmingham Hippodrome where it played from February 21st to March 20th inclusive. From there it travelled to the Bristol Hippodrome where it played from March 26th to April 24th 1976 inclusive.

The sole representatives for Tommy Steele at that time were Talent Artists Ltd. 13 Bruton Street WI.

# A Change of Direction

After the show, 'Hans Andersen' finished he was glad of a rest, then he started writing a production for Thames Television. It was called 'Tommy Steele and a Show'. In September it was shown on Television. It was such a success that it was used as the British entry at the Montreux Festival. It was also nominated in the USA for an Emmy award.

Then he stopped doing everything to concentrate on his squash playing.

The reason was that he had been entered in the Rank Xerox Pro-Celebrity Squash Challenge Meeting. He was playing against John Cleese;

"I brought him to his knees by beating him 9-2, 9-0 and 9-1," said Tommy.

An interview for the Reveille came out on 15th October 1976.

Jack Pleasant wrote this for the magazine.

Tommy's pushing 40 - and still going great!

"The news certainly made me feel old; Tommy Steele is 40 next birthday". Not that it worries Tommy, who said, "If life begins at 40, then I don't know what I've had so far. I saw my doctor the other day and he said I'm fitter now than I've ever been. I'm the same weight as I was when I was 19 and my heart is better than it was then."

"What do you remember about your first appearance at the Sunderland Empire in 1956?" asked Jack

"Remember? I certainly do. I'll never forget it. I was so scared I stood in the wings trembling and then came the horrible words, "You're on boy." I was ever so nervous. I kept on jumping about to stop myself from shaking. Fortunately it was all a great success - so much so that I kept the jumping about in my act."

"I hear you have a soft spot for the Reveille and what was the most wonderful event in all that time?" asked Jack.

"I do, you ran my life story in those early days. It was a great series and it must have helped my career. Looking back over the last jam-packed twenty years, I have to choose as the most wonderful event something that happened outside show business, and that was the birth of my daughter. Ann was thirty-six hours in labour, and I was there right up to the time when she had to have a caesarean section.

They wouldn't let me stay for the operation. But really, that shared experience was marvellous. Husbands who stand outside smoking in the waiting room and eventually peep at the baby through a glass screen are mad. You should be in there rubbing her back and sharing it all. I was so moved I wrote a poem about the childbirth for Annie the next day."

Here is the poem for the new arrival written by Tommy Steele;

My Gawd, she cried
I could have died
When I took my chance
And peeped inside
I couldn't see the misses there
She was sort of hidden
By the towels on the chair
The doctors was washing his hands by the bed
And the midwife was shouting
Sort of losing her head
She called my Mabel a lazy mare
And told her to push and pull here and there
And what with that and the children next door
And the boiling water all over the floor
And the gas goes out when they wanted some more
I tell you this much, mate, and plain,
I'll never go through childbirth again.

After the birth of Emma, Tommy decided on another Change of Direction.

Tommy quotes, "Show business successes. Well I've loved 'em all, "Half a Sixpence," which also became a Broadway hit, Finian's Rainbow, cabaret in Las Vegas, Hans Andersen. I loved them all. But of course I've had my downs too. In 1960, I got the idea that to learn more about show business. I'd go to Australia to conquer new audiences. I was very lonely and didn't go down well at all down under. It was most possibly the unhappiest time of my life. A case of 'Too bad Blue.' There was one good thing about it though. I missed Ann so much - we were engaged at that time - that I married her as soon as I got home. One of the best moves I made. I have been a very lucky fellow really. For instance one of my big breaks was being booked to appear at the famous Café de Paris in London. The first night was televised and my mum and dad were there. What happened, just as I started to sing, the mike packed up. It could have been a nightmare. But I managed to chat to the audience while it was being repaired and I believe that this predicament somehow made the audience warm to me. I felt they were all on my side. I got off to a terrific start and the management wanted me to stay for another four weeks, at double the money. The secret is that I have never let success go to my head!"

He was in 1976, still down to earth, seeing a lot of his parents and even going back to his boyhood area to eat his pie and mash and jellied eels.

"Three days later on my birthday," he said, "I was back at The London Palladium with the re-jigged Hans Andersen, with me acting as director. Harold Fielding rang me up to ask how much of the show I had changed.

I told him, "Not much - only about seventy per cent."

"Only Seventy per cent of the production - why so much?" he asked.

"Well," I told him, "Now the show is more magical!"

"Whilst he was on the phone I told him to look out for something simpler to do, as being a director and acting in the show is very demanding."

When Hans Andersen came to a close, Harold Fielding rang him.

"How do you fancy being in a Gilbert and Sullivan production?" he asked.

Tommy told him "I've always wanted to play in one of those productions, particularly Jack Point in Yeomen of the Guard."

"Well now's your chance, Harold said."The Festival of the city of London would like you to take part in 'Yeoman of the Guard' at the Tower of London."

But first he had a seven city tour of the country with the Tommy Steele Anniversary Show it opened at the Theatre Royal, Nottingham on the 19th October 1976. With him on the tour were Lennie Bennett, Johnny Hart, The Cool Breeze, The Mosaics, His Orchestra and Chorus line. From Nottingham he went to Coventry Theatre, His Majesty's Theatre and ending at the Manchester Palace Theatre.

Then he had a break spending some time with his wife Anne and baby Emma in a rented a cottage in Torbay, Devon

He opened at The Festival Theatre, Paignton on July 15th 1977 with 'The Tommy Steele Show,' appearing with him were Lennie Bennett, The Cool Breeze, The Mosaics, Michael Allport and Jennifer. The season finished on September 24[th.]

In 1977 Nigel Hunter wrote on the 'Focus on Tommy Steele 2 LP Record Set":- " The phrase 'all round entertainer' has now become the subject of such scorn and hilarity in popular music because of the considerable numbers of pop idols who have declared solemnly that this was their ultimate ambition shortly before disappearing into total and often well-deserved oblivion. Peter Sellers did a wickedly funny send-up of such an idol on his first LP, and many believed the source of his inspiration was Tommy. There seems to be no specific record of Tommy ever uttering this well worn phrase, but whether he did or didn't is immaterial because he has become an all round entertainer beyond dispute in the best and truest sense of description in an easy style which is all his own.

For Tommy things happened rapidly, very rapidly but unlike his contemporises he has stayed the course with outstanding success, developing and expanding as an artist and winning a generation of devoted fans, as well as retaining the allegiance of the original ones."

Then it was into rehearsals for 'The Yeomen Of The Guard' a Gilbert and Sullivan musical in the Moat of H M Tower of London. It played from 17th July to 12th August 1978, Tommy played Jack Point. It was recorded for television by ATV and transmitted on 23rd December.

He was at his Mother's house for his fortieth birthday December 17th with Ann and his daughter Emma.

They had, during the evening, been talking about the war years. Just before he was due to leave, his Mother said to his dad, "Why don't you show Tommy your picture?"

Tommy looked puzzled and asked, "What picture?"

"The one your dad keeps in the back of the wardrobe," said his mum.

There was he forty years of age and he didn't know his dad had a picture in the wardrobe.

"Get it out and show him," said his mum.

His dad went up the stairs and came back with a picture frame wrapped in old newspaper and tied with some string.

"What is it?" asked Tommy, struggling to untie the string.

"Just take the paper off and have a look," said his mum.

He got the paper off and looked at the picture.

There was his dad in a dinner suit, dickey bow, holding a big cigar in his hand. He was sitting with two other men in a swanky restaurant.

"What is this?" asked Tommy.

"Well do you want me to explain?" said his dad.

"I certainly do", said Tommy.

"You'd better sit yourselves back down - this could take a while," said his dad.

Tommy and his family sat back down, whilst his dad explained the picture and how it came to be taken.

"During the war, at least once a week, I was picked up by a government car and taken to a secret location where I would sit and talk for a few hours about the race tracks and the work that I did on them. After I had talked, I got back in the car and was brought home."

"What for?" asked Tommy.

"Well" said his dad, "I was stopped one day while doing my job at the track by a couple of fellows, and they said, I looked exactly like Winston Churchill, and would I do a job for them. They gave me the suit and dickey and some cigars and told me to be ready on a certain day and they would pick me up. Well they did. As far as I know, I was a decoy for the great man himself. I was told I must never say anything to anybody about what I was doing, and to this day I never have. The picture was given to me after the war finished and it has been stuck in the back of the wardrobe ever since".

This set the seed in Tommy's mind to write his book on espionage.

'The Final Run' - which went into the top ten best sellers list.

In January 1979 Tommy was awarded an OBE in the New Years Honours list, a just reward for someone as patriotic as he is, for he genuinely loves Britain and would never consider living anywhere else.

"When the invitation came to go to the palace to get my OBE in March in an interview he stated:-

"You're only allowed to take two people to the Palace and my wife Annie and daughter Emma were wonderful about it – especially Emma. I said to Annie:-

"What do you think? I'd love to take my mum and dad"

Annie said:

"Well, I've been to the Palace before and I think it would be lovely for Mum."

Then we had to approach Emma. She's as patriotic as I am, as excited about the Queen I said to her one night:- You know I've got to go to the Palace to receive an award. And you know you're only allowed to take two people, and Mummy would like Nana to go in her place. And what do you think about Poppie? "Oh they must go together."

"No hesitation, no look of disappointment. I nearly cried on the spot, that she could be such a lovely little girl."

So my Mum and Dad went with me to the Palace, afterwards we went to Fortnum's for tea.

At home he got to grips with 'Quincy's Quest' for Thames Television. It had been broadcast on Thursday November 29th 1962 before a specially invited audience. This new Christmas musical, 'Quincy', was shown on TV on 20th December 1979; it was made into a TV film for the American audience.

On September 22 1979 Tommy made an appearance on the BBC 'Parkinson' TV series for Granada Television.

On December 22$^{nd}$ 1979 spoke about moving into show business. "When I came into show business I loved it so much I wanted to stay doing what I was doing. So I had to improve, to be as good as the people who were doing it then. I knew it was going to take a lot of work and it did, and still does. Show business has a lot of heart, a lot of creativity but it also has a lot of technology and you have to keep ahead, merely to keep up."

He never learned to dance, never had an acting lesson, and he's not a great singer you enjoy him because you are guaranteed to get a 'buzz out of Tommy – which is all he asks. "I learned how to project my voice to the back of the auditorium by someone shouting 'Speak up, we can't here you.' I don't dance, I'm given a routine and I make sure you don't see me do it until I've worked on it for a month.. I'm a very hard working copy-cat. I'm still learning. I'll never stop."

"It all started with travelling players, moving round the countryside, and that's what I am, a travelling player, always on the move, trying to entertain. There have been casualties along the way. I've done things I wish I hadn't. Mistakes hurt, however small. In retrospect the things I regret are the things I know, and if I'm honest, I would not do again. There was a pantomime I did once. It was an embarrassing production. I knew it was bad. I was ashamed of myself in it. I really thought I could rely on *me;* you can't rely on you in this business. I left too much to chance, going into battle without ammunition. I hated every performance, every day feeling depressed at what I had to go through that evening." Straight after that I did a completely different season in the West End. Another disaster but, thankfully, I came out of it with a lot of experience"

He knows why he made the mistake?

He said "I had just made four movies for Hollywood and I was on location with Alan Badel, an actor I admired, and he said to me: "You're not very happy doing this sort of thing are you? And I said; No! I get bored by it, there is so much waiting around.

He said: "You're a man of the theatre ... my advice is get back to it as soon as you can."

"I took the advice too literally and accepted the first thing I was offered, and was not up to it. I've learned to stand back and think. We're a family that believes regrouping. We pull back, that way you avoid a panic situation, work on the mistakes."

"Years ago I decided to restrict my performances to those I feel confident in. There are always long gaps between happenings. I'm always three years ahead. 'An Evening With Tommy Steele' started over three years ago, six months of planning, then the set designing and dressing, the music arranged, casting, rehearsals, then playing in the theatres, most people don't hear about this but the show is taken all over the country – polishing off the rough edges – until it is ready to bring to the West End."

Out of five or six things offered to me I' ll only attempt to do one or two. By attempt I mean spend more time investigating whether there's anything there for me or not."

"I won't take any work that takes me away for long spells from Annie, Emma and the family. The longest I go away for is three weeks, not a day more than that."

"Annie and I go out once or twice a week for dinner, but she doesn't like pie and mash, or jellied eels like I do."

Then he started work on his one-man summer show 'An Evening With Tommy Steele,' it went on at the 'Blackpool ABC Theatre' and it ran from 30th July until 14th September.

'An Evening with Tommy Steele' opened at the Prince of Wales Theatre, London on Thursday, 11th October 1979 for a limited season of twelve weeks. It finally came to a close on 29th November 1980, after running for sixty weeks, 456 performances. Having captivated London with 'An Evening

With Tommy Steele,' he decided to take it on tour. The tour started at Manchester's Apollo Theatre on 14th April 1981 and ended in Bristol on 24th May. He never did any shows on Sundays though. Sundays were the special day for his family reunions.

In 1981 he painted the 'Entertainer.' It was used as the backdrop for his One Man Show at the Prince Of Wales Theatre and is now in the possession of the Theatre Museum in Covent Garden.

In November 1981 the BBC showed 'Tommy Steele: A Handful of Songs' A television special tribute celebrating Tommy Steele's 25 years in show business. Then it was back to directing and acting in the tour of 'Hans Andersen' around the provinces. The tour lasted from 14th September 1981 until 16th January 1982.

Tim Heald of the Sunday Telegraph wrote

"At 44, Tommy was as energetic as he was when he was nineteen – still dancing and singing. He is now writing and directing his own shows. Tommy is celebrating his twenty-five years in show business by taking Hans Andersen on tour. It's a long way from the young deckhand who became a rock star at nineteen. Today he is a family entertainer, a sort of male successor to Gracie Fields. One of the few times when he was tongue-tied was the day he received his OBE in the New Years Honours List back in 1979.

Behind the door marked 'canteen' at the Mayfair Gym, Marylebone (where he rehearsed for Hans Andersen) Tommy sits on the closed lid of a piano, surrounded by a group of actors in an attentive semi-circle.

"Super" says Tommy looking as if he means it. There in his right hand was an 'Astley Major' cigar and a small book of scribbled notes in the other.

"Lovely, your characterisations are perfect!"

He grins revealing his very white, rather prominent teeth.

"Now, just relax."

He manages to look both alert and relaxed at the same time.

It takes effort to look like that.

He never touches alcohol and consumes prodigious quantities of cod-liver-oil tablets. ("If you think they are doing you good, then they are doing you good!" his doctor told him.)

He does drink lots of coffee and over lunch is apt to treat himself to an extra sausage for 'afters'. When he is not rehearsing or performing - both remarkable strenuous activities in his case - he runs for four miles every morning with three fast 440 metres in the middle. Stripped for a shower reveals a fairly modest chest and arms, but extraordinary strong muscled legs with not a hint of fat anywhere.

"I am taking the show on an arduous tour of Oxford, Leeds, Liverpool and Southampton," says Tommy.

Harold Fielding bought the stage rights especially for me.

The show ran for a year at the Palladium first of all.

There really wasn't any story in the film; it was just a series of vignettes. Beverly Cross and I wrote the stage story but every time it is revised I write it on my own. I first directed it in 1977 and this year I'm doing it again, singing dancing, directing and playing the lead!

All go, innit," he laughs as he hurries from the running through some lines with his principles in the canteen, to rehearsing songs with the chorus, and then going through a dance routine down stairs.

The energy and the enthusiasm seem quite unforced. Downstairs still clutching his cigar and papers, he capers through the energetic rendering of 'The Kings New Clothes.' He singles out one of the little girls and tells her not to look down at the floor when she speaks her lines, "Otherwise your mum's not gonna see your face and I'm gonna get some letters."

At least she does as she is told and afterwards gives every appearance as if she is enjoying it. Just after they break for lunch Harold Fielding arrives with the designer to discuss the set.

Harold Fielding is a dapper elderly gentleman; he is wearing a dark brown suit with a pink shirt and tie.

Tommy calls him 'The Guv.'

The Guv's wife, Maisie, has come along too, and takes an active part in the discussions.

"We don't have any children", explains Mr Fielding. "The shows are our babies and we love and cherish them as if they were".

He glances at Tommy and smiles paternally. For a quarter of a century he has loved and cherished him, too.

"There has never been a written contract between us, millions have been made, millions entertained, but still never a signature. His word is his bond. In all that time he has the same team looking after him; impresario, agent, lawyer and accountant, it seems to have paid off. I have seen others earn fortunes and fritter them away, but not Tommy. Today he has a beautiful period mansion in Ham."

"Good place for an actor to live, isn't it"? Says Tommy. "Ham!"

Harold Fielding gives a chuckle and continues, "Which you can clearly see from the Thames and which is a regular part of the guides patter on boat trips to Hampton Court. He also has a house in Marbella. He has been happily married for over twenty years, and has a daughter of twelve to whom he is devoted. Above all, he still has the energy and the enthusiasm. The boy is extraordinary. He's multi-talented. And one day will be one of the world's great directors. The confidence he has is pervasive and catching. You name it, and he does it. This year he had a painting hung in the Royal Academy Summer Exhibition. He is going to try a novel next year. Failure is not something to which he is accustomed. He was top of the bill at nineteen you know!"

Did Tommy Steele think that his transition from deckhand to rock star, and from Hicks to Steele, in about three weeks at all remarkable?

"No," he says, "I can remember saying to the Guv, "Top of the bill - do I go on last? Everything that came along I thought was the norm, I always have. I'll tell you why I've been successful and others haven't. It's because I went somewhere they didn't want to go. Most rock stars went on being rock stars but in many ways I never enjoyed it."

Harold Fielding remembers him telephoning from Dundee saying, "He'd been mobbed. He hated it. And the record business was anathema to him."

"I go out of that purely by design", says Tommy.

"Finding the idea, writing the song, singing it, and recording it, I have enjoyed immensely. But then the fun of it is gone. If you are a star you have to go round flogging the record. I only ever had one number one hit record that was 'Singin' The Blues' then I decided to concentrate my talent elsewhere. I did films, did plays, and appeared on television and musicals."

Harold Fielding chips in, "He is the perfect professional, in the olden days he could be a bit wild, and he once came in to see me on a pair of crutches because he didn't want to go on that evening. It was pure fictional but I forgave him. He was hot headed but there was gold there! When this show finishes I have plans for a new spectacular!"

Tommy's book, 'Quincy' was published on 26th October 1981 by William Heinemann in hardback, and by Pan Books in paperback.

Tommy by this time had now been in show business for twenty-five years and the BBC transmitted a tribute to him 'A Handful Of Songs'

The 'Hans Andersen' show took in Oxford, Liverpool, Coventry, Leeds and Southampton and then he started making preparations to take it over to Australia.

Tommy said that 1982 was a very bad year for him.

First his dad had died in 1977.

Tommy said, "He was 76 and he'd only been to the hospital once in his life. The young doctor told me that my dad would only have a short time to live. I'd brought some chocolate almonds and standing by his bed giving them to him he said 'Oh chocolate almonds, they're my favourites.' At that moment I felt so angry with him. For all those years I never knew he liked them. Think of all the chocolate almonds I could have given him years before!"

The day his Father died Tommy was due on stage that night - and being from a hard-grafting working class background, he didn't consider cancelling. I comforted my Mother, who told me to go to work."

He died of Cancer. And then in 1982 his mum died.

From, 'The Press and Journal':

"Before going to Australia to do 'The Tommy Steele Show' Tommy and Ann and went to see his Mums specialist for a prognosis,"

In Australia Tommy recalls. "The phone rang and the doctor said, 'She's taken to her bed.' I flew home that night. When I walked into her room I had the shock of my life and at that moment I think she knew she was dying."

"She died of Lung Cancer. She did not live to see her 64th birthday."

Before they both died, he would pack Ann and Emma into the car and drive them over for Sunday lunch. He was blessed with two lovely parents and was glad that they stayed with him through most of his adulthood.

"They were privy to my success," he said, "and I was able to make things happen for them, which is a great joy. Those happy Sundays were just great; memories like those will last forever. My parents had a totally loving marriage, they were devoted to each other and that togetherness and love was my saviour."

He always knew that if he made a mistake he could always go home to them, as there was always a cuddle and a caress rather than a reprimand. That's what we have always tried to give our daughter, a strong and an understanding love. When all the children left home, the house at Catford was too big for his mum to manage, so he bought them a bungalow at Bingley. It was a good job that he had Ann and his daughter to support him when his mum and dad died. But his life had to go on."

"Our marriage," he says "works because we're best friends. That's the key to a successful relationship. You have to be friends as well as lovers. When we are apart we speak every day on the telephone."

He had Christmas at home that year with his family. It was a sad time not sharing it with his mum and dad.

During the summer he took a holiday.

This gave him and Ann a nice bit of leisure time in which to enjoy the domestic life. "And we do this in a very simple way," he said.

"In fact Ann says that as far as food is concerned, a person earning ten pounds a week would eat as well as we do."

In August and September 1982 he was in Stockholm and Gothenburg, after which he returned to London.

On 3rd of December 1982 Tommy was in Liverpool for the unavailing of his statue 'Eleanor Rigby' 'a tribute to the 'Beatles' it was dedicated to "All the lonely people..." Tommy quoted "Hidden inside the sculpture is a four leaf clover for luck; a page from the bible for spiritual help; a sonnet for lovers; an adventure book for excitement; and a pair of football boots for action: half a sixpence and a copy of the Liverpool Echo. I put them all inside the statue so she would be full of magical properties. I give Eleanor to Liverpool with

164

an open heart and many thanks for my happy times in the city. Later in the day both he and Ann switched on the Christmas lights. On Thursday, 7th October 2004 the Liverpool City Council put out an immediate press release. 'Eleanor Rigby Won't Be Lonely Any More!'

The lonely figure of Eleanor Rigby has been a feature of Stanley Street for many years but she's moving and about to get some company! While works continue for the Met Quarter shopping complex, the statue is moving to Harrington Street, behind B.H.S. And the four Beatles 'thrones', currently standing at the top of Harrington Street, are being moved along so she can sit in the middle with plenty of room for people to sit all around her. Eleanor certainly has a fitting temporary home as the Cavern Quarter has been transformed with brand new high quality paving and new lighting. Councillor Mike Storey, Leader of Liverpool City Council said: "Eleanor Rigby has become an important part of the Liverpool street scene so I am very pleased that she will be still on display - even in a temporary home while work goes on at the Met Quarter.

On the 4th December 1982 Tommy and Ann made there way back to London and the preparations for the London Palladium production of 'Singin' In The Rain' were started at once. He asked Roy Castle to take one of the main parts. After speaking to him for almost an hour Roy decided to do the part. He said that the part of Cosmo Brown in the film had been his favourite part, but on the other hand was he too old to do it?

"No," replied Tommy.

"Singin' In The Rain" opened on 30th June 1983 and just over two years later, after running for a massive 894 performances, it came to a close.

"Singin' In the Rain' nearly didn't open, for it was hit by vandals on the eve of the opening when seven of the most elaborate costumes for the Ziegfeld Follies routine were slashed. The dressmakers who had spent six months making the costumes were called in and they repaired them an hour before they were required on stage.

In the afternoon Roy Castle was practising one of the exhaustive dance routines - missed the mat, on which he had to land, and very badly strained his ankle, and suffered two cracked ribs in the bargain. From in front of the fire curtain he could hear the audience taking their seats. He limped back to his dressing room and ice packs were put on the swellings.

Emotions of sympathy began to show on Tommy's face.

At that time there was no understudy to take Roy's part.

Roy told Tommy not to worry, he would be alright.

The opening night went ahead as planned.

From the programme of the 1983 first ever production of "Singin' In The Rain" - at the London Palladium.

"It is the story of the movie making in the 20s at the time when Hollywood switched from making silent to talkies. Much of the action takes place in the studios of Monumental Pictures. The title song 'Singin' In The Rain' was already a 'golden oldie' before it gave a name to the Gene Kelley/Donald O'Connor movie in 1952. The song was written in 1929 by Arthur Freed and Nacio Herb Brown, and featured in Hollywood's first 'all talking, all dancing' musical film, 'The Hollywood Review.' It had made two other screen appearances before Gene Kelly got hold of it. Judy Garland sang it in 'Little Nelly Kelly' and 'Universal' featured it in 'Hi, Beautiful.' It's been in two more films since Kelly, and the betting is it has still more films to come. Freed and Brown wrote most of the other songs in the film, which was not surprising considering that Freed was the producer of the film and by that time was one of the most powerful men on the MGM lot.

# Tommy and The Guv.

In the fickle world of theatre, few professional associations have lasted so long, or been as successful, as that between impresario Harold Fielding and entertainer Tommy Steele that has endured for more than a quarter of a century. It began in 1956 when Fielding, at that time best known as a classical concert promoter, surprised his colleagues by engaging the rock 'n' roll sensation of the moment, and presenting him in a provincial variety tour.

It was not long before he brought him to London in a rock show at the Dominion Theatre. In those days, Steele's appearances were greeted by adoring female fans with the screaming frenzy, which later became associated with the Beatles. Worshipping teenager's hungry for a glimpse of their new idol besieged Fielding's staid offices in Haymarket - Tommy's tours throughout Britain drew packed houses. So did his tours in Europe, South Africa and Australia. But both Tommy and Fielding had more enduring goals in mind.

In 1958, Fielding acquired the rights to base a stage show on Rodgers and Hammerstein's television score for Cinderella, The lavish production which opened at the Coliseum on 17th December (Tommy's birthday, and the launching date for many subsequent Fielding/Steele projects) was an overwhelming success and opened the doors for both men.

For Tommy it meant the beginning of a theatrical career, which did not depend on the whims of teenage fans.

For Fielding it meant the end of concert promotion and the start of a career as producer of large-scale musicals.

Both careers have prospered, perhaps beyond their wildest dreams, and each in his way is now at the top of the theatrical tree. Over the years, Tommy has worked with other producers and Fielding has worked with other famous stars, but both have achieved their best working with each other. For several years after Cinderella, Fielding searched for a musical that Tommy could play in the West End and hopefully take to Broadway.

Eventually he commissioned David Henecker and Beverley Cross to write one and the result was 'Half a Sixpence' - the musical version of H. G. Wells' Kipps.

The character of Arthur Kipps suited Tommy to the proverbial T. It was a hit in London, it was a hit on Broadway, and it became a worldwide hit as a major film. Tommy was the star of all three, and 'Half a Sixpence' made him an international name.

For several years he was based in America - filming with Walt Disney, dancing with Fred Astaire, playing in Las Vegas - but a return to the London stage was inevitable.

In 1974 Fielding secured the rights to another great musical score, Frank Loesser's songs from the film 'Hans Christian Andersen.' Tommy collaborated with Beverley Cross in writing a new stage book. The result was a record-breaking triumph at the London Palladium where it ran for almost a year and was revived for a second season in 1977.

This show brought a third name into the Fielding/Steele partnership - that of the London Palladium. There seems to be some special magic about the combination of Tommy Steele in a Harold Fielding production at the Palladium, and it is no coincidence that the bare announcement of these three facts with the title of the show brought an all-time record advance booking for 'Singin' in the Rain. 'Tommy has joined the select list of great Palladium stars, and this time he is director as well as star. Fielding's trust in him is such that he gave an open-ended budget that went well over the seven-figure mark before the curtain rose on the first night.

Both men have a lavish taste in stage spectacle. For 'Singin' in the Rain' they have stretched the facilities of the Palladium to the ninth degree.

Hidden from the audience's view - above the stage, below the stage, beside the stage, behind the stage, wherever the ingenious mechanists could find an inch of room - is a bewildering array of machinery.

There are lifts, hoists, winches, computer boards, pumps (yes pumps! don't forget the show's title) and electronic gadgetry of all shapes and sizes.

Costumes have been made with an extravagance, which recalls the days of such spectacular showmen as C. B. Cochran and Florenz Ziegfeld. Huge sets move in and out in bewildering array, yet more important than this entire spectacle is the performance itself.

For That, Fielding says, 'Trust in Tommy'. And Tommy says, 'Trust the Gov'nor'. After twenty-seven years, they have every reason to trust each other".

What the press said....

"...magnificently costumed, as spectacular as Ziegfeld, breathtakingly choreographed, and mounted with exuberant panache..."

"...Singin' in the Rain has brought the big lavish musical back to the West End with a vengeance. It is the most ambitious theatrical project attempted in this country. If ever there was a show to rescue the West End from its current rainy season, this has to be the one that will blow away the clouds with its lavish sets, superb Hollywood costumes and glittering Busby Berkeley dance routines.

The sunshine is the story itself and the spectacular way in which it has been brought to life on the stage. Musically, the show is magical".

"... Tommy Steele's is a lovely performance ... here is a player haloed by a curious radiance whenever he steps onto a stage. This occasion is a triumph for him".

"...An incomparable string of familiar melodies which the audience only has to hear in the overture to applaud ... a spectacle worthy of a night away from the TV.

... a cornucopia of visual and musical delights".

"... Cheers and torrential applause".

"... It has "hit" written all over it".

"... The sets are lavish, the costumes stunning, the dance routines rival Broadway in its heyday ...A splash hit".

"... A family spectacular inconceivable achievement ... Singing in the Rain not only proves that a screen success can be brought to the stage but that Tommy Steele can challenge the success of Gene Kelly. What is more he succeeds ... this is entertainment on a grand scale ... See it".

"... If you're in London and you have to choose only one show, then I'd advise Tommy Steele in Singin' in the Rain. For production, direction, lighting, laughter and sound, go and take a look and see how it should be done".

"...What makes this show ideal entertainment are its flamboyant sets and its technical wizardry. The on the Palladium stage is a full-size steam train, chugging across the prairie into an ambush by Indians. There's a gleaming Rolls Royce and huge revolving art deco staircases, 18 hang the expense scenes and a king's ransom in 1920's costumes clothing flocks of leggy chorus girls. For sheer extravagance it hasn't been matched in London for a long while".

In an interview in 2005 Tommy tells how hard it was to do the show, explaining that, "Roy Castle had to have oxygen in the wings just to keep going." Tommy stated that, "He was alright because he played a lot of squash at that time".

Six months after "Singin' In The Rain" opened, Jack Pleasant of the Weekend Magazine interviewed Tommy.

"The eyes still sparkle. The coloured hair may be a bit darker now, but there's no sign of it thinning. The bubbling zest for life is obviously just as keen as it was when he was a guitar-strumming teenager.

"Wotcha mate" says a beaming Tommy Steele, bounding from the plush sofa in his dressing room to shake my hands.

"Seen the show? Terrific, ain't it?

The critics were less enthusiastic about it when it opened at the Palladium in June but it has been playing to packed houses since then. It's been doing so well there are people standing at most of the performances. It'll run for at least two years here, and then we'll probably tour the country with it. The chances are that I'll direct another production of the musical in America".

It's yet another feather in the boater of the versatile Steele who, as well as managing to stay at the top of the entertainment business for more than a quarter of a century, has also managed to cram in success as a sculptor, painter and novelist and represent his county, Surrey, at squash.

Tommy will be forty-eight in December - just a couple of years away from his half a century. I venture to ask, is fifty a milestone he views with dread?

"Far from it," says Tommy. It's all in the mind."

He must be one of the fittest forty-seven year olds around. At 10 stone 7lb., he reckons he's at his ideal weight.

"I play four hard games of squash every week, but it's really just for pleasure nowadays, this show has such a pace it gives me all the exercise I need. Every day I take one multi vitamin pill, five wheat germ tablets, five cod liver oil capsules, a lecithin pill and fibre on my foods. It's not so startling. Give your car the right petrol and oil and have it regularly serviced and it will perform properly.

Your body is exactly the same." Tommy reckons his favourite meal is roast chicken and mushrooms or steak and chips - when he can't get his beloved jellied eels, or pie and mash of his Cockney childhood.

"What do you think about marriage?" Said Jack.

"The secret of a happy marriage is having the luck to find the right person so that special chemistry between you never fades. Emma is our great delight, of course. We'd been married ten years and we were beginning to wonder if we'd ever have a child when she came along".

What is his weekend routine? Said Jack.

"Having not got to bed until about three a.m. on Saturday I get up around eleven. I have a cup of coffee and a piece of toast and then go to my squash club to meet my mates and watch the lunchtime soccer previews on the TV. I get to the theatre about one and have a half an hour workout on stage and a chat with the company. After the afternoon performance, I have a massage in my dressing room and then a sleep.

When I wake up, I'll perhaps have another cup of coffee and a chocolate biscuit and then start preparing for the evenings show. I never leave the theatre until 11 p.m. but when I get home Ann is always up to give me my main meal of the day. I only have a lie in on Sundays if Emma isn't taking part in a show-jumping event. When she is I get up about nine and Ann and I drive her with one of her ponies in a horse box to wherever it's taking place. Emma has two ponies – Leo and Revvie and I was told she's a potential champion. She's certainly won a lot of rosettes. We'll usually just grab a sandwich during the day and make up for it with a nice meal when we get home. Perhaps it doesn't sound too exciting, but it suits me. I'm a great home lover.

Our house is a beautiful 17th century building in red brick that was in a terrible state when we bought it. We are lucky to have another house at Marbella."

What about the future? Asked Jack.

"'Singin' In The Rain' is taking up almost all of my time at the moment.

I've simply not had time for painting or sculpture. My first novel, a thriller called 'The Final Run' did well and the publishers have asked me to do another one.

But I re-wrote 'The Final Run' manuscript seven times before I was happy with it and I wouldn't fancy going through all that again. It was published on 14th March 1983, by Collins and soon entered the best sellers list. A few months later it was published in paperback by Fontana.

What were his most treasured possessions beside his wife and daughter?

"Two battered hats. Two great thrills of my life were the occasions I danced with my long time idols, Fred Astaire and Gene Kelly. Afterwards they swapped hats with me. Kelly's was a straw boater and Astaire's a soft cap. I really treasure those hats - they're memories of two people I admire most, and that's not a lot of old hat."

In September 1983 Tommy had another interview with a newspaper this time they wrote, "Tommy bound of the stage into the wings at the London Palladium and, proffering an infectious toothy grin and the perennially tousled boyish charm, accompanied me back to his dressing room. It is five minutes short of ten o'clock. Everybody is pleased. It has been a good show, with a responsive audience, and the star has given it the works.

But he has paid the price.

He is drenched in perspiration, exhausted, leaden-footed. He is like a man who has just run a fifty-mile marathon. Everything he had inside him before the show, all the whiz-bang reserves of energy and the incessant compulsion to please, is now spent, distributed in so many tiny parcels to each person lucky enough to have been "out-front" a few minutes earlier. It is an astonishing sight. He had just danced and sung and tumbled his way through the spectacular 'Singin In The Rain' stage musical in London.

From the same side-on vantage point, in the wings, I have seen only one other man-of-the-theatre gives his all in so powerful, so uncompromising and so total manner: ballet dancer Rudolf Nureyev.

They have so much in common; each is an avowed perfectionist, giving so much of themselves during a performance that they virtually tear themselves to pieces, heart from limb, not to say body and soul.

Each is supreme in his chosen field, each a millionaire. Is it any wonder?

They differ in only one fundamental respect. Whereas Rudi has been happily married since the age of sixteen to classical ballet, Tommy has remained, by and large, an unabashed bigamist: married to former dancer Ann Donoghue and to show business of which he has stayed at the top for more than a quarter of a century.

He describes his first professional love, the stage, quite simply as 'my magnificent obsession' and he talks lovingly of Ann as a valuable friend and confidant and a very good reason for being alive.

"Without her," he says, "My career wouldn't be what it is today. She is fifty per cent of my whole success. With the love that she gives, with the help she offers, that strength is there whenever I feel myself floundering. Her influence on my life during rehearsals is total."

"Ann is a very good judge of what or wrong, and we talk about all these things a lot at home."

When 'Singin' in the Rain' finished at the Palladium he had a long summer holiday during which he wrote the music 'A Portrait Of Pablo.'

On 6th November 1985 conducted it at the Barbican with the London Symphony Orchestra in the presence of the Duchess of Kent.

He had almost a year off whilst he wrote his second novel 'To Paint A Tiger' and a children's saga 'The Broad Sword Of Bokaria.'

On 13th September 1986, he conducted the Aarhus Symphony Orchestra in a performance of 'A Portrait Of Pablo' at the Aarhus Hall, Denmark.

And then it was back on tour again with 'Singin' in The Rain.'

On 29th September he was in Bristol, from there he went to Birmingham and on 6th April 1987 was at the Shijuku Koma Theatre in Japan.

Harold Fielding tells the story of their visit to Japan.

"In the spring of 1987, amidst the beauty of the Japanese cherry-blossom season, Tom and I took the 81 tons of this production's scenery and costumes in an American cargo jet to Tokyo, plus 71 cast, musicians and crew, all to play just 35 performances in English, at the Koma Theatre in the very centre of the city's exciting nightlife district, Shinjuku. It was a huge success; we, and the fabulous audiences, "had a ball". We had some fun loading all the scenery into the theatre, the train had to be hoisted though a hole in the back wall and, because of the very narrow streets we had to take all the scenery through the front doors and store it temporarily on the seats in the auditorium itself."

Having had the summer off, his next appearance was in 'Tommy Steele in Concert' on 12th September at the Royal Festival Hall. It was transmitted on Radio 2 on 14th September. Then he took in a tour of the provinces, with 'An Evening With Tommy Steele,' which took in the towns of Sunderland, Hull, Eastbourne and Norwich.

In 1987 Tommy also appeared on 'Test of Faith' a BBC TV documentary.

In April 1988, he was off on his travels again - this time to Denmark, where he conducted the Odense Symphony Orchestra and Choir in a performance of 'An Elderly Persons Guide to Rock' and 'A Portrait Of Pablo' at the Odense Konserthus, Denmark.

On 10th April he was back on tour in England with 'Tommy Steele in Cabaret' with his dancers. They went to Windsor, Usk and Birmingham, and then he took a well-earned rest. But there is no rest for the wicked for he was asked at short notice, to fly out to Copenhagen to be a guest artiste in the final programme of the Danish programme 'Superchance'. He sang 'A Handful Of Songs', 'Bridge over Troubled Water', 'Beautiful Noise' and 'Half a Sixpence'. It was held at the Bella Centret and relayed from there by Danish Television to the whole of the country.

On 1st April 1989, he returned to the Manchester Palace with 'Singin' In The Rain': appearing with him were Sarah Payne, Bunny May, Roy Sone and Danielle Carson After a three months engagement he was in the Spanish Open Squash Championships.

On 13th of June he opened once more at the London Palladium with 'Singin' in The Rain'. The run was extended for another three months.

During the summer Tommy learned that his one time manager, Larry Parnes, had died at the age of fifty-nine. He knew he had been ill for some time for he had contracted meningitis some ten years earlier. He was to say, "It is always a shock when a good friend dies."

# Another New Musical

In 1990, Tommy travelled over to New York to work on another new musical he was planning to direct. He worked on the script and the music with the American composer Julie Styne. It was based on the Billy Wilder film, which starred Tony Curtis, Jack Lemmon and Marilyn Monroe. The show was called 'Some Like It Hot.'

Rehearsals started in 1991, after which it was taken on a tour of the provinces.

'Some like it Hot' came to the Manchester Opera House on 13th August until 21st September. Appearing with him were Billy Boyle, Royce Mills and Mandy Perryment.

On February 28 1992 Tommy made an appearance on 'The Aspel and Company' TV series talking about 'Some Like It Hot' for the London Weekend TV.

'Some like it Hot opened at the 'Prince Edward Theatre London on 2nd March 1992 and ended on 20th June 1992.

From 18th December 1992 until 16th January 1993, his daughter Emma was playing 'Cinderella' at the Devonshire Park Theatre, Eastbourne.

1993 was a year of creation and writing for Tommy.

Tommy was at the Festival Hall in London conducting his new piece 'Rock Suite' and then he completed another novel called 'Four Faces for Ada' and a musical based on the life of Billy Cotton. He did a sculpture which had been commissioned by the Rugby Football Union and which was erected at Twickenham. After that he went back over to Denmark where he was awarded the prestigious ' Hans Andersen Award' in recognition of his portrayal of the Danish author and poet.

In 1994, whilst he was in conversation with a friend over what type of format his next show should be, it was suggested to him that they do one night of 'Half a Sixpence,' one night of 'Singing In The Rain,' one night of 'Some Like it Hot' and two nights of his other shows.

He told his friend that it was not possible. But it set the scene for 'What A Show!

In the meantime, he directed the Paul Nicholas production of 'Singin' in The Rain', which later toured the country, with great success.

In 1994 'What A Show' toured the provinces appearing with him were, Ruth Anderson, Bernadene, Nicola Garretty, Paul Harrison, Fiona Jaynes, Richard Joseph, Mark Petitt, Specer Stafford and Christian Williams.

On 8th November 1995 Tommy held an exhibition of his paintings and sculptures at Foster and Reeds London

'What A Show' came to a close in London at the Prince of Wales Theatre on 6th January 1996 - and even before it ended he was thinking of his next show.

During 1996 though, he had lots of functions to attend, this being his forty years in show business. One of the functions during the year was one for his fan club at the Richmond Park Hotel.

Daily Mail, Saturday, March 22, 1997 wrote:

Home that's a Steele at £10million.

Montrose House: Is up for sale up to £10m, and the elegant interior of Tommy Steele's home were pictured."

"Once his fortune was Half a Sixpence, but now he could make up to £10million by selling his mansion where he has lived for almost 30 years.

The Cockney stage and film star wants to return to South London – although in somewhat grander surroundings than those of his childhood. He has been viewing a riverside penthouse flat in Lambeth, close to the Bermondsey streets where he grew up. Millionaire Steele said he and his wife Ann decided to put the 14-room Montrose House in Richmond, Surrey, up for sale after their daughter Emma moved out last year.

Tommy Steele recalled: "I loved this house. I used to pass it on the way to work. I'd look at it and wonder who lived there? When we bought it was in a state, but now it has a heated swimming pool, a summerhouse and a squash court where I exercise regularly. I have happy memories in this house and if we could leave here and put the happiness in a box and take it with us then we would be very lucky people".

Ian Stewart of the estate agency said: "This must be the most magnificent house in the area for its sheer scale and stateliness and is worth between £5 and £10m in today's market".

In March, April and May 1998 Tommy was touring the country with 'Tommy Steele in Concert.'

Then he had a well-earned rest before he moved into his new home in the old MI 6 building.

During this year Harold Fielding had a series of strokes and had to move into a nursing home.

In 1999 Tommy did shows at two venues in England - one at St Austell at the New Cornwall Coliseum on Friday 14th May, as a part of the Daphne du Maurier Festival and another at Oxford at the 'Old Fire Station Theatre, of 'Charlie Chaplin - The Musical.'

Then it was off on a tour of Scandinavia.

On August 26 Tommy appeared on BingoLotto a Swedish TV game show and on 6th November he was at the Alborg Congress Hall in Denmark.

On 10th November Tommy met up again with the competition winner Hanna from Alborg. She was happy to meet him again 42 years after their first meeting. She is now a grandmother and still a big Steele fan with a big S.

The year 2000 saw Tommy in America for nine months.

On 29th October 2000 Tommy appeared at the Concert Hall in Oslo, it was not a full house, (unfortunately because of bad advertising.)

'Vastmanlands Lans Tidning,' a Swedish newspaper wrote in their 2nd November, 2000 edition,

Rock On With Steele

"The rock idol of the fifties, Tommy Steele is back on stage in Vesteras concert hall, Vesteras, tonight. In the fifties all girls fainted just by the sight of him. In the end of the fifties there was a big competition between Tommy Steele and Elvis Presley. Both came from working class, became very popular and rose to fame within a very short time.

When Tommy visited Sweden there was mass hysteria, girls fainted and in Stockholm on September 9, 1957 there was even a riot, Tommy visited Sweden twice within seven months. His films gathered more people than the Elvis films."

There were 4500 people in the Eskilstuna Sports hall when Tommy made the stage show there on 21st April 1958.

'Vastmanlands Lans Tidning,' 3 November 2000 wrote: - "It was top world-class entertainment last night when rock legend and musical artist Tommy Steele made a great show in the Vesteras concert hall. It is fantastic to see such a complete artist and entertainer that he has turned out to be. His magical way of telling things between songs captures the audience. You can feel you can sit there forever and just listen to him. Look what style he has got."

Tommy appeared in Concert with his own orchestra for one week at the Tivoli Gardens, Copenhagen on the 16 July 2001. In the first half of the show he sang, 'Song and Dance man', 'Handful of Songs' 'Let Me Entertain You,' 'Half a Sixpence', 'Bridge Over Troubled Water', 'The King's New Clothes', 'Ugly duckling' and 'Superbird'.

The second half was made up of rock 'n' roll numbers: -

'Johnny 'B' Goode', 'Promist Land,' a Chuck Berry number. 'Sweet Caroline,' 'Water, Water,' 'Teddy Bear', 'Hound Dog', 'Blue Suede Shoes', 'Hand Jive,' 'Butterfingers,' 'Hero' (to Ann) 'When You Gotta Go'. After a standing ovation he returned to the stage and sung 'Waterloo', after another standing ovation he returned to the stage and said, "We may as well stay here all night!" Then he sang 'How are things in Glocamora, chatted about his films. Did 'River Dance' and finished with 'Handful of Songs'.  The show that night went on for a good two and half hours. The morning after the show a Swedish magazine, 'Harlequin', asked female reader whom they dream and fantasy about? The replies were as follows: - 1. Brad Pitt, 2. Sean Connery, 3. Richard Gere, 4. Mel Gibson, 5 Bruce Willis, 6. Kevin Costner, 7. Arnold Schwarzenegger, 8. Tommy Steele, 9. Steven Seagal and 10. Tom Selleck.

 As you can see, Tommy Steele has still got a hot name with the Swedish females, but where has Elvis Gone?

On the 27th September 2003 at the age of 85 the person who made it all happen for Tommy died. That person was his friend and mentor Harold Fielding. He died in a private nursing home at Kingston-upon-Thames where he had lived after a series of strokes in 1998. Harold Fielding's contribution to the Blackpool's summer season's entertainment spanned 40 unbroken years – attracting more than three million people – until he bowed out due to personal reasons.

There was a service of Celebration for the life and work of Harold Fielding at St. George Church, Hanover Square, London. A tribute was given by Tommy and read at the service by Jonjo O'Neill who also sung 'Flash Bang Wallop' from 'Half a Sixpence'.

# I've Had A Ball

In 2003 Tommy was telephoned by Bill Kenwright to do a tour of the provinces with 'Scrooge The Musical.' Tommy jumped at the chance to do it.

A newspaper sent along a reporter to do an interview with Tommy when he was in Liverpool, in which he speaks about his Mother.

"His remarkable rise from a poverty-stricken childhood to musical star of smash hits made Tommy Steele a millionaire, but, the loss of his Mother brought about a crisis of faith that still haunts him."

"Tommy Steele is once again on tour and is currently at the Empire Theatre in Liverpool. He is starring in the musical Scrooge and his wife and daughter, Emma, drove from London to spend Christmas Day with him. He plays the miserable old skinflint Scrooge who by the end of the show has seen the error of his ways. He sings "I'll begin again" and in the spectacular finale, Tommy and the entire company belt out "Thank You Very Much." When the crippled Tiny Tim hugs the reformed, repentant Scrooge, there is not a dry eye in the house.

It is a musical for all ages. The curtain call clapping is so prolonged that Tommy has to tell the audience "I love you all, Have a Happy New Year, now go home."

All through the musical he is rarely off the stage and, though he's playing an elderly chap, has the supple nimbleness of a young man.

Looking back over the years he's done movies, Shakespeare, musicals, one-man shows, and television spectaculars. The teenyboppers who screamed for him when he belted out "Rock With The Caveman" are now grannies bringing their grandchildren to see him.

He's 67 now, but looks unbelievably unchanged from the irrepressible young Tommy with the toothy smile and so unruly mop of blond hair.

He always gives the impression of being easy going and laid back, but he is a tough businessman, fanatically self-disciplined, a perfectionist and as lithe as he was at the age of nineteen.

Tommy told me. "I did Half A Sixpence in Hollywood and I put on a lot of weight.

I was only thirty and I realised that a certain way of eating had to be my life. I thought it's not a diet, but regimentation for ever."

When Tommy is on tour he stays in the best hotels but he always takes his own microwave and cooks almost every meal for himself in his room. In fact this week you may see him sometimes bounding around Marks and Spencer buying some microwave suppers. Occasionally he breaks with tradition and we meet after the show at a wonderful fish restaurant where Tommy has ordered lobster for both of us in advance. I have a glass of wine but he only drinks water.

When he comes off the stage at the end of an evening he's high on euphoria. Many of his contemporaries took drugs or became alcoholics, but he's never even been tempted to do them.

He's a Londoner from a loving southeast London family and now lives not far from where he grew up. He's sold the mansion he had in Petersham, near Richmond Park, Surrey, and has bought a riverside penthouse in the famous block where Jeffrey Archer lives. It's called Peninsula Heights.

"I wanted to live there since 1968, when I was doing a film with the actor Stanley Baker called "Where's Jack? I went up to see him in the flat on the eighth floor, which is the one that I've bought. I looked at the view and said, "I'd like to live here." He said. "Well you can't because the building is mostly offices for the MI6."

It took Tommy nearly thirty years, but he got his wish, and when he stands on his terrace he can look down river and see the area of Bermondsey where he lived as a child.

"It's like I've come back home. I said to Annie. It's taken me fifty years to move fifty yards."  My mum would have been absolutely thrilled.

On Millennium Eve, we went on the terrace and watched the fireworks all down the river like we were children again. I had pie and mash brought in with haggis, Pease pudding and brown ale for some mates.

When I'm home, I still drive back to Bermondsey on Thursday for pie and mash in The Blue Anchor Lane. I park round the corner and leave the boot up with the jack out, which is an old Bermondsey trick. The wardens think you're having trouble with the tyres so you don't get a parking ticket. When I was working in the West End I got a pair of legs from the props department. I'd park the car, throw the torso underneath it so the legs were sticking out, and it looked as though a fella was working under the car. I got away with it for years".

He was born Thomas Hicks and spent much of his childhood on the move.

His family were always being bombed out and his first public performances were singing in the air-raid shelters, where Londoners spent most of their nights as enemy planes screeched overhead. Eventually they moved into Frean Street and his Mother got a job in the Peak Frean biscuit factory. The terraced houses, with their back yards and outdoor lavatories, have long since been flattened. Expensive developments and warehouse conversions are gradually taking over the area, where as a boy, Tommy played football in the street.

Tommy says. "Those places now cost a fortune to live in. Those wonderful old buildings that used to be rat infested. We played on the wharf side of the docks, diving in and out of the Thames. You'd dive in the water at London Bridge and the swim with the tide past Tower Bridge, and catch a net that was tied under the southeastern arch and pull yourself up. It was a very old, thick boat net and it was called swimming net. If you missed the net you went down river to Tilbury into the mouth of the Thames.

About six or seven boys died doing it and you weren't supposed to try it till you were sixteen. Then when you were older you went in at Waterloo so you had two bridges to go under. It was frightening and you had to be a really strong swimmer, but it was a good kind of scare and when you had

183

done it, you felt like Superman. Those long ago days remain piercingly clear in your mind".

Wealth and fame have never detached him from his roots and his redoubtable Mother?

"She did office cleaning from 4 a.m. till 7.30 a.m. and then she came home and got us ready for school. Then, at 8.30 she went to the Peak Frean factory and worked all day. At the factory she was allowed to buy bags of broken biscuits for two bob. I was the eldest surviving child because my mum had seven children and lost three. One boy died of cancer; one of double pneumonia and whooping cough and the other was killed in a black out in the blitz. So my Mother went through a lot.

There were two sides to her character - she was the combination of an angel and a sergeant major. She was a lovely lady and I still feel she's with me. I talk to her every night before I go on stage. I say, "Here I go, mum, here I go." She was the driving force of the partnership with my dad but I don't think that my dad contributed a hell of a lot to the family. He'd come back after the races with whatever he'd managed to make, but it was never a fixed wage, which is why my Mother had to have three jobs. On top of everything else that she did, she also did school dinners. We were never destitute or never the poorest of the poor, and she would not go into debt.

In those days there was a man called a tallyman, who'd come to the door and you could borrow money from him, but my Mother never did.

She always used to say to me, "Son, in all your life, never borrow for luxuries."

It was an era when many Londoners went hop picking in Kent during the summer. They lived in sheds and despite the hard work, thought of it as a kind of a holiday. But my Mother always refused to go.

She said. The boys always come back with nits and the girls come back expecting children." She always put a few pennies a week away into what was known as a holiday fund and a Christmas fund at the factory.

So at the end of the year, she'd have twelve shillings to take us all to Southend for the day. We'd go on the train or the bus and that was your holiday but, boy, you had a good time. We'd have a paddle in the sea and go to a cafe for Spam and chips, then we'd have Camp coffee with hot milk and that was heaven".

Tommy's Mother lived to see her son's fame and he bought her a bungalow in Kent, but she died of cancer.

"Then" says Tommy bleakly, "I lost my faith because it was a terrible way to go.

The best way is to get knocked over or have a heart attack, but that bloody thing takes time. When my Mother went, that was it for me. I said to God, I can understand you taking her, that's your right, but why give her so much agony?

It's bad enough losing her, but why did you have to hurt her at the same time? I thought of all the years she had worked so hard and what she'd done for the family, but then she had to go through that. There's no holy man in the world who can talk me out of my belief that there has to be a bit of compassion in an Almighty. That's my hang-up. It's my loss because, when I lost my faith. I lost a great comfort. You lose out on hope really, but it doesn't mean you can't do good while you're alive. The nicest thing about being an atheist is that when you do a good deed, it's not because you're hoping for repayment at the end".

Changing the subject, the reporter turns to Ann his wife.

"Well it all started like this. My first booking was at The Sunderland Empire on the 5th November 1956, and the headlines blazed, 'Young sailor becomes overnight show business sensation'. Most people thought I'd have a brief taste of fame and nobody, including me, suspected that I'd end up as one of Britain's legendary stars.

At that time I'd never had a girlfriend, but weeks later I met Annie and we've been together ever since. I hadn't been out on a date till then. Wherever I went, I took my mum. I can't believe what footballers get up to now. Roasting, do they call it? It's bad enough that it happens, but to put a name to it is disgraceful.

Annie's stage name was Annette Donati and she worked at the Windmill as a dancer.

She always emphasises. I was a dancer. I was not a stripper. I was playing the Chiswick Empire for a week when Lionel Bart came round.

He said I've brought this girl with me because she knows of a great party in Soho tonight. Well I'd just done two shows because it was twice nightly and I was exhausted. Also, I had a third performance - getting out of the theatre alive was a nightmare. There were always about 2,000 children at the stage door, so we had a device like a fire engine or a police car to trick them and get me away. That night, Lionel Bart came with a wagon full of paint. He gets me in the back with this dancer from the Windmill who doesn't strip, and we hit Soho.

We were all stinking of paint by this time, looking for the party, and she points to a street and says, "It's down there." Well this is Annie for the rest of our lives because she doesn't know the way anywhere but she always thinks she does. At two a.m., we were still looking for the party. When we did find the house we discovered the party was the following week, so we decided to go to Soho's famous all-night coffee bar, the Sabrina. According to Annie I threw a tantrum and she snapped, "Don't be so spoiled." She's from Yorkshire and this Northern accent telling me off didn't go down to well. We sat there looking daggers at each other, but then Lionel left and it turned out that we both liked the same television commercials. She made me laugh, singing all the jingles in a Northern accent. I was in fits and I've been with her from that day to this.

Annie comes from a Yorkshire show business family and had been a dancer in London since she was sixteen. Her father Eric was a singer known professionally as Enrico Donati and her sister was a human cannonball in the circus. They were Roman Catholics which caused problems. We had to get a special dispensation from the priest to be married and we could not be married at the high altar. I had to have instruction in the faith and we had to promise that our daughter would be brought up in the Catholic religion. We got married at St Patrick's in Soho Square, but never lived or slept together beforehand.

We had a white wedding and, even though we'd been together for four years, it was a true white wedding. At the time Annie had just taken the lead in 'Expresso Bongo' opposite Paul Scofield, but I wanted her to give up work. If I was making a movie, I'd be away for twelve weeks or I'd be on tour. Being separated was no way to begin a marriage.

Annie always tells every body "I retired at the height of my profession."

We wanted a large family but the babies never arrived and we began to think that we were destined to be childless.

My mum said to Annie. "Don't drive yourselves mad, love. If it's meant to happen, it will."

We were so happy together, but there was the feeling that if we were to have a child it would be God given.

Emma came along nine years after we were married and she is wonderful, a great kid and a bundle of laughs, just like her

Mother. After Emma was born, Annie had two miscarriages, so we didn't try any more. But after each miscarriage she had Emma to go home to and cuddle, so that was the saving grace. We are a loving, close-knit trio, but having a father like me can make it difficult for a girl to find a chap who seems good enough.

Lots of people say jokingly, "She's after somebody like you."

She's never found a boy and said "this is the one."

She teaches Palates and yoga and she comes home with the most fantastic looking fellas. They're always handsome, considerate, kind and not destitute.

I'll say to Annie. "I think this is the one." but four months later, it's all over."

When Tommy talks about his wife and daughter, his face lights up.

"Annie and I have been together now for nearly fifty years. Love is a wonderful word, but you don't go through life so long together unless you really like each other and you're mates. When things go wrong, you can take it on the chin and carry on together. You don't say, "Well that's your problem." Annie knows every inch of me, and between us there are no secrets".

Tommy may no longer pray, but he is hugely grateful for his family, his talents and his good fortune. If he makes a wish on New Years Eve, I suspect it will be for Emma to find Mr Perfect and for things to go as they are.

Tommy says, "I've had a lovely, lovely life. Listen, if it all stops tomorrow, I have had a ball. I really have."

In 2004, Melvin Endsley died. He had written 'Singin' The Blues' and 'Knee Deep In The Blues', songs that had taken Tommy into the hit parade.

After a long summer rest, Tommy took 'Scrooge' to the Manchester Palace Theatre. Appearing with Tommy were Barry Howard as Jacob Marley who played the same role with Anthony Newley, Robin Armstrong, Harry Dickman making his fifth appearance in Scrooge, having understudied the title role for the late Anthony Newley and Abigail Jaye who was later to play the leading roles in future productions of Scrooge and Dr. Dolittle. On this occasion William Stuart and Graham Roberts played 'Tiny Tim'.

The Manchester Evening News gave 'Scrooge' a very good critique.

'Steele is still the super-trouper' by Kevin Bourke.

"Just a few days ago, Tommy Steele celebrated his 68th birthday. Yet he's still out there, singing and dancing for all he's worth in the Christmas smash 'Scrooge' at the Palace Theatre.

Of course, he's an old showbiz trouper in the best sense, but why does he keep on going, when he surely could have retired long since?

"The funny thing is, not only am I always doing a show on my birthday, but there are usually two performances that day as well. It works out, too, that every Christmas Eve I'm doing two shows, every Boxing Day I'm doing two shows, every New Years Eve I'm doing two shows, every New Years Day I'm doing two shows. So, I never celebrate everything at the same time as anyone else! Every year, on Christmas Day when I was sitting around being a dad, I'd be thinking I must remember that I've got a matinee to do tomorrow! And I've got to make sure I don't over do it, or go to bed too late!"

So does he ever think that enough is enough?

"All the time! I told them all I was going to do this year was a tour of one-nighters in Scandinavia. That was all right, but then they say 'Oh you just do a few nights' and the next thing you know you've got a full schedule. But no more, this is really it! You just don't want to be in the same show, eight times a week forever. I don't mind doing this because I know it is a great show and I know I enjoy doing it, because I also know that I haven't got another four months of doing it round the corner! "

So why, nearly half a century after his first hit, is he still packing them in? 'The kind of audience who come to see Scrooge is from eight to eighty, so you've got the higher Echelon of age group, who remember the rock 'n' roll days. Then as you go down the age scale, there are the films, the television spectaculars, and the musicals – things like 'Half a Sixpence.' In the olden days you never saw the towns you were appearing in, the only thing you saw was the inside of a van that took you to the theatres. You were bungled in and bungled out of that van".

But by 1960, he turned his back on the rock 'n roll, and he went on stage for the first time as an actor and he liked that better, he wanted to do some more. He said.

"Well I've done it all. I've been a movie star, composer, conductor director and novelist, a sculptor and a painter and if I get the chance I would love to do another film but before I do, when this show ends I'm going to take a holiday".

During the run of the 'Scrooge' Tommy was asked to appear on the Royal Variety Performance to close the show. He was also asked to unveil the 'Blue plaque' awarded to him by the people of Bermondsey.

In the November of 2004 Tommy appeared at The Royal Variety Performance once again, it was filmed by the BBC and shown on December 15.

'Scrooge The Musical' ran from 7th December 2004 in Manchester coming to a close on 15th of January 2005.

When he arrived home from Manchester, he and Ann departed to the States for a well-earned rest.

Tommy came back to London to appear on 'Children in Need' and on the 9th June 2005, to unveil a 'Plaque' in the Cinderella bar of London Palladium, marking his record breaking 1,767 performances at the Palladium.

What's On Stage News. "Sixties legend Tommy Steele unveiled in his honour a plaque at the London Palladium. The plaque commemorates the fact that Steele has performed more times there than any other actor at the famous West End Theatre.

Fittingly, Steele returns to the same stage this autumn to take the title role in 'Scrooge' A pop chart-topper in the 1950s, Steele went on to become one of Britain's best known all-round entertainers, In 1963, he had a hit in the West End with the musical 'Half A Sixpence', which he later starred in on Broadway and in 1967 Hollywood film version. During a long and varied career, Steele has also featured in films such as 'Finians Rainbow', 'The Happiest Millionaire' and 'The Tommy Steele Story'; appeared regularly on television, not least in his popular variety show, 'The Tommy Steele Hour' and release some 20 records on stage, many of Steele's biggest successes have taken place at the London Palladium where, having set a record for headlining more performances than any other artist, a plaque will be unveiled on Thursday 9th June 2005. Prior to 'Scrooge, his productions at the theatre have included 'Hans Christian Andersen', The London Palladium Show,' 'Dick Whittington' and 'Singing in the Rain.' The last, directed by as well as starring Steele, ran for 894 performances."

Two days after the presentation Tommy flew out of the country again. This time he went to Spain to have a rest before he started the rehearsals for 'Scrooge.' in the autumn."

# I'll Never Retire

In 2005 Garry Bushell wrote about Tommy in The People newspaper, "Tommy Steele is sixty nine this year, but no-one seems to have told him. The man has the energy of a thousand milkmen. His blue eyes sparkle with mischief, his smile melts away the years and he's busy, busy, busy. It's hard to believe that this is the original pop idol - a man who had his first hit two years before Cliff Richard and who next year chalks up his 50th anniversary in showbiz.

"You're looking at one lucky bastard," chuckles Tommy with the satisfaction of a man who has fame, fortune, happiness and nothing to prove to anyone. Yet like all great entertainers, he admits he still needs that fix of performance and applause. And that's why later this month he goes back to the London Palladium to play Scrooge in an adaptation of Dickens' A Christmas Carol - a return to the role he played on a nationwide tour in 2003. Then he'll be back with more tour dates and may even return to Hollywood. Cult director Quentin Tarantino, famed for gore-fests such as Pulp Fiction and Reservoir Dogs, wants to make a movie with him.

"I keep expecting to receive a bullet through the post," Tommy laughs.

It's a schedule that would daunt performers half his age, but Tommy is a fit as a butcher's dog and enthusiastically likens the challenge of playing Dickens' loveable skinflint to preparing to run a marathon.

"It's a terrific score and a really honest adaptation," he says in that soft, familiar voice that's as South London as the Old Kent Road.

"This crusty old sod goes round being 'orrible to people and frightening the horses. But he's a loveable old rogue and we know he'll find redemption and be Tommy Steele at the end.

"I don't think I'm anything like Scrooge," he grins.

"But ask my daughter Emma and she'll tell you different.

"I do put old salad into sandwiches rather than sling it and I hang on to milk until it turns into cheese. But anyone who grew up with rationing and austerity is going to hate waste."

Tommy's upbringing was as Dickensian as it gets. He was born Thomas Hicks in working-class Bermondsey on December 17, 1936, just a short jog from the plush Thameside flat where he now lives. Money was always tight. Tommy was one of seven kids, but two of his brothers and his baby sister died in infancy. He spent three and a half years in hospital as a kid, suffering from an enzyme deficiency and spinal meningitis. A nurse introduced him to the novels of Robert Louis Stevenson and Dickens. "I read voraciously." His Dad, Thomas, was a racetrack tout. "He had no education, but he could work out your winnings from a five horse accumulator in his head."

Mum Bet cleaned houses before working shifts at a biscuit factory and serving school dinners in her lunch break. Tommy fell in love with the Palladium as a child. "We could never afford to go, but I'd look at the posters outside and work out what the acts did."Then in 1946, my parents took me there as a treat. Everything plush, marble and gold and red, there were chandeliers and uniforms with buttons, right there in the middle of the austerity of London. I thought: I want to do this! But back then you had to be born in a trunk to get into showbiz."

So he left school at 15, joined the Merchant Navy and discovered rock'n'roll music in New York. Back home on shore leave, Tommy wandered in to the opening night of Soho's 2is coffee bar and stunned the assembled beatniks with a rendition of Blue Suede Shoes. Six months later he was at No1 with his second hit single, at a time when you had to sell 250,000 records a week to get into the Top Three. He had the X Factor all right. By Christmas 1957, Tommy had notched up seven hits and was in panto in Liverpool. Harold Fielding, the West End producer, sent Tommy to New York to spend a week with Rodgers & Hammerstein going through the score for Cinderella which opened at the Coliseum the following year. "This was the world I wanted to be part of since I was a kid. I wanted orchestras, musicals, theatres." So Tommy turned his back on rock'n'roll.

He did Shakespeare at the Old Vic, learnt to tap-dance and recorded novelty songs like Little White Bull. Elvis became a god. Tommy chose variety.

Tommy Steele, OBE, went on to star in films like Half A Sixpence in 1967.

He was a sensation on Broadway and wowed the crowds for two seasons at Caesars Palace in Vegas. He published a novel and exhibited his paintings at the Royal Academy. Never afraid to break rules, Tommy got engaged to dancer Annie when he was 20. They married four years later at a time when eligible male stars weren't supposed to, yet 20,000 fans turned out to wish them well. They're still together now,

Despite the odd stormy patch, and have a 35-year-old daughter, Emma, who teaches yoga. Tommy beams: "I've been lucky in everything. I have a wife who is patient, understanding and witty. "She'd say my best quality was listening, and my worst, not listening..."

He's got a lot more than half a sixpence now, with his own yacht and a second home on the beach in Barbados, but he hasn't got fancy tastes. Tommy drives a green Mini Cooper and bought his current London home because it was near a pie and mash shop - "It's been closed down now, it's a bloody disgrace."

He's got an iPad, but it's still in the box. Tommy doesn't watch much TV, apart from the History Channel.

"Shows like The X Factor don't interest me," he says. "Some poor sod who thinks he can sing, but can't, goes on there and proves it and they give him a roasting?

"That's not a talent show; it's like Jerry Springer with music."

He loves live entertainment. "Ewan McGregor is wonderful in Guys And Dolls. And Ken Dodd is the best comic in the world. I've seen all the big names, but I've never been attacked the way Dodd attacks and I've never seen an audience surrender like they do to him." He dislikes politicians with a vengeance. "But it takes a lot to get me going," he says." When you've been under a bloody Heinkel bomber for about four hours it takes a lot to upset you."

Steele shows no sign of corrosion. How has he stayed so young? "Never diet," he says. "Never use the word. Diet has the connotation that it's not going to be for long. It's three or four weeks of purgatory followed by three days of euphoria, followed by continual bloody purgatory. "You don't need a diet, you need a way of life, and when you have that all the pressure goes." His regime is simple: Eat and drink what you like in moderation. And exercise.

"Let's say you like four pints of beer a night and you know it's too much," he says. "Well say to yourself: If I can make a deal with my body that I can have two pints a night then that's going to be me, not for four weeks but forever.

"If I like chips with my steak, maybe I have twenty four. But if I could have ten chips for the rest of my life and be healthier then that's got to be better. "It's a way of eating that is moderate, but it's not Spartan. You're not missing out, you're cutting down. You'll be healthier, fitter."

His only concession to age is that he's stopped playing squash every day. "Now I play tennis instead," he says "I'll have a two-hour game later. It's really invigorating."

Tommy even does a three-hour concert act with a 70-piece orchestra and choir when he feels like it. "It's like having a meal. It's lovely, but it's a Chinese meal. A couple of months later, you want to do it again. But then someone offers you a 10-course dinner - a musical like Scrooge.

"And I think 'Do I really want to go into a major musical again? '"

It takes a lot of work, a lot of thought. But when the script and score are this good, there was no way to get out of it."

The show will mean Tommy has headlined the Palladium more times than any other star - and a plaque was put up at the venue last month to mark the feat.

He flashes that grin, as wide and bright as a Pearly King's jacket.

"I've been lucky all my life," he says. "I've wealth and my 'ealth and I'm as happy as a sand boy. I know my Mother put an angel on my shoulder.

"And you know what the best thing about being Tommy Steele is?

In my mind and my heart I'm still a kid. I feel wonderful! I don't wanna go. I really don't."

On 24th October 2005 Nicola Christie of the Observer wrote;

He's about to kick off as Scrooge at the London Palladium, having already delivered a record 1,767 performances at the theatre over the years, but 68-year-old Tommy Steele can only think of one thing: getting the part originally played by James Stewart in an upcoming musical based on the film It's a

Wonderful Life. The musical is currently being work shopped with a view to putting it on in the West End, and Steele is determined to land the lead role.

"Will you ask them if they will send a copy of the libretto and everything to the Palladium?" he says. "Oh but they'll say we're not interested, we want a younger man, and then they'll ask me to play Clarence the angel. Tell them I'm not playing Clarence - I want James Stewart!"

A memory from Pat Richardson:

On Thursday, 27 October 2005, I set off for Watford to meet up with my friend Val. She had kindly offered to accommodate me for the few days I was to spend in London with her. That evening we just sat talking and generally putting the world to right and listening, at the same time, to Tommy Steele recordings!

The following day (Friday) we travelled into London and met up with a friend who we had arranged to see, had a walk down Carnaby Street and then back to the Palladium in time to see Tom arrive.

We had a few words with him - he looked relaxed and chatted to other people who had been waiting. How many 'Stars' would spend time with fans as Tom does?

We went into the Palladium and had a look at the Plaque honouring Tom's 1,767 performances at the London Palladium.

Then we got to our seats and waited...........................

Of course, we have both seen Scrooge umpteen times on tour - but the London Palladium is special and there was a sense of eagerness around.

As soon as the opening scenes were over and it was Tom's turn to come on, there was a wild reception for him! Without describing every scene, I will just say that the show was wonderful, there was a great audience - and Tom - well, what can you say about this guy? He gives 1000% every time and you cannot help leaving the theatre with a broad smile across your face!

The following day was Saturday and we had booked for the evening performance only. BUT when you are in London around lunchtime and within earshot of the Palladium - you have to go and see if there are tickets for the matinee! There were! We were in L row and saw the show from an entirely different angle (the first half anyway).

Always we had front row seats (for reasons I won't go into!) Whilst sitting in our seats, we spotted two seats on the front row (near the side) which had not been filled - so at the interval we were down there - and so watched the second half from our favourite position!

After a lovely meal, we were again at the Palladium! We went into the bar area first, as we were a little early, and who should be in there but Shane Ritchie! As he will be touring soon with "Scrooge," I could only assume that he had come to see how it should be done!!

The show was again wonderful - what else is there to say about it really.

Tom is where he belongs, doing what he obviously enjoys immensely and giving his audience exactly what they want! Tom left the theatre fairly quickly after the show and as he got into a cab, I said, "Don't miss "Match of the Day!" - he usually watches this on Saturday nights.

A smile and then he was away..........

The audience's obvious love of the man and the standing ovations after each and every performance of Scrooge are a testament to the phenomenal talent that is Tommy Steele.

What more can I say - we'll be there in January for more!

On New Years Eve 2005 Tommy got all the backstage staff and the cast of Scrooge to come on to the stage, he had the house lights turned on and everybody sang Auld Lang Syne together. What a wonderful ending to an old year. Tommy admitted that the producer Bob Thomson had wrapped his knuckles, warning him never to laugh or wink at the audience but to stay in character until the curtain call.

"You see" said Bill Kenwright, "Tommy's spent a lifetime working hard to get people to like him so he found playing the miserly Scrooge difficult at first.

On 18th May 2006 an exhibition was officially opened at Powys land Museum celebrating Tommy fifty years in show business with Tommy's approval.

On 7th September 2006, his autobiography came out, the title of which is 'Bermondsey Boy: Memories of a Forgotten World' ~ Tommy Steele. Published by Michael Joseph Ltd. Hardcover. Synopsis of the book. Surrounded by docks and sitting on the Southeast of the Thames 1930's Bermondsey was a thriving place. And it was here that Thomas Hicks was born. It wasn't until much later that this Bermondsey boy would become known as Tommy Steele. Saturdays as a young boy were spent gazing at the colourful posters for the Palladium, or wandering up Tower Bridge Road to Joyce's Pie Shop for pie and mash. He brings to life with extraordinary vividness what it was like to live through the devastation of the Blitz - having to run to the shelter naked in the middle of the night wondering as each bomb crashed down, which street had taken a hit. His beloved father Darbo was a tipster who worked the crowds at the races by day, and by night was a doorman at The Nest, an infamous watering hole for entertainers and his Mother Betty, was a part-time tin basher at Feavers box factory. The Hicks household was full of love and laughter but also struck by tragedy with the loss of three children.

Aged fifteen, Tommy joined the merchant navy and it was here he began singing and performing for his fellow seamen and his natural ability as an entertainer soon made him a favourite. Whenever he was ashore in the States, Tommy would listen to the latest music and soon became hooked on the rock unroll movement that was taking America by storm. From Tommy's humble beginnings, to life at sea and finally a life as a performer, "Bermondsey Boy" is a colourful charming and deeply engaging memoir from a much-loved entertainer.

News as at 15th August 2006: A serialisation of the book in the Daily Mail at the end of August/early September and Tommy is scheduled to appear as a guest on 'This Morning' (ITV1) and Radio 2's Steve Wright programme on 7th September.

In 2005 whilst Tommy was playing In Scrooge he had an interview with Leslie Bricuss and he asked him to revive Dr Dolittle and Tommy said to him; "if it is anything like the film or the previous stage production, he didn't want to know.

On September 17 2007 Tommy was on the TV talk show This Morning talking about his up and coming performance in Dr. Dolittle., because Bricuss came back with changes of which Tommy approved and after months of rehearsals it opened at the Churchill Theatre in Bromley on the 27th September 2007 before going on a tour of the country. From October 8th to 20th Tommy was at Wolverhampton Grand Theatre from there it travelled to Wimbledon, then The Manchester Palace followed by The Sunderland Empire.

The year ended with Tommy at the 'Liverpool Empire, where Tommy was interviewed by Chris High for Liverpool BBC Live.

Tommy told him," I still get nervous before every performance. The worst time is when you are standing in the wings waiting for your first cue and you can hear the audience. It's at that time I'd be thrilled if someone tapped me on the shoulder and said there's no show tonight for whatever reason. Of course, when you hit the spotlight, that disappears and you're in the most wonderful place in the world. That happens every night and it's what I thrive on."

So what does Tommy have lined up over the coming months?

"I'll be doing Dolittle throughout next year, once you get hold of a really good show, you don't want to let it go if you can help it," he said.

2008 saw Tommy once again touring in Dr Dolittle first it went to King's Theatre Glasgow then Blackpool on Tuesday February 12th followed by Leeds Grand Theatre, then The Bristol Hippodrome followed by Cardiff New Theatre and then The New Victoria Theatre Woking, and The Birmingham Hippodrome and finally came to a close at the Lyceum, Sheffield on 26th July.

He had to pull out of Dr Dolittle for a couple of weeks on July 8th due to an abscess on one of his teeth and his understudy had to take over the role.

Tommy wrote to his fans:

'Well Dr Dolittle is on his way to a rest and I am doing Ditto! I know some of you got the chance to see it and I am chuffed to think you all took the trouble. Here's to the next time folks, Tommy'

Tommy returned to the stage with Scrooge at the Birmingham Hippodrome on 20th October 2008 for two weeks, from there it went on to The Alhambra Theatre Bradford, Manchester Palace, The New Theatre Hull, The Liverpool Empire, where he gave me a message for the fan club which read:

'Dear all, here it is - Christmas again and here am I – Hair to my buttocks and ever rehearsing the snarl. So from Ebbie and Me Happy Xmas and lots of good cheer and just a little Humbug. Luv Tommy.'

From the Liverpool Empire he went on to the Mayflower at Southampton, The Theatre Royal Plymouth.

On September 24 2009 Tommy made an appearance on 'The One Show, talking about Scrooge.

Scrooge finishing its run at The Demonforth Hall Leicester on 10th January 2010

After a long holiday abroad he was on the 'One Show' again on August 17 talking about taking the show over to Ireland.

Tommy opened in Scrooge on December 7th 2010 at the Grand Canal Theatre, Dublin the season finished on 2nd January 2011.

After having summer away he opened at the Lowry Salford in Scrooge on 12th December 2011 coming to a close on January 7th 2012.

On December 16, 2011 Tommy had an interview with 'Northern Life magazine.

Reproduced courtesy of Editor Karen Shaw

"Does this man's talent know no bounds? He is a performer, writer, sculptor, painter, actor, singer songwriter, composer, conductor, and that he has achieved success in every field including the charm department. On the 5th November 2011 Tommy celebrated his fifty five years treading the boards, and his up-coming 2011/2012 tour will mark Tommy's sixth time playing the title role in the all singing all dancing musical extravaganza 'Scrooge. He has played the role of Scrooge five times previously and in his own words there's no difference in the new production apart this time in his own words "he's six years younger, it's the best part I've ever played in the greatest musical ever"

I managed to catch up to Tommy when the weather was blowing a gale on the banks of the 'Manchester Ship Canal' where the large tankers sailed into the heart of the city. He jokes look out there on the horizon you can see the Armada and Drake is waiting for him to join him. Tommy still has a love of the sea since joining the navy at the tender age of fifteen.

The Lowry is a great theatres, the last time I was up in this neck of the woods was in the seventies when I came to meet the great painter L. S. Lowry. I had performed with another fifty dancers in a dance piece called 'Same Size Boots' where we brought a Lowry painting to life. I had a video of the piece, in those days videos were a rarity and had to carry it up on the train in a massive suitcase. I met him and showed him the dance, there he was sat in front of the TV, and he watched it and asked him afterwards "Well, what did you I said, "Would you like to see it again?"

"Oh, yes" he replied," would they mind?"

I love his work. His work was just like him, very gentle with a great love of the North. As I was leaving afterwards, he said "Do you think they'll remember me?"

Tommy himself is no stranger to the art world, he has had a painting displayed at the Royal Academy and one of his major sculptures is Eleanor Rigby, which he created in 1982 and gave to the city of Liverpool as a tribute to the Beatles. He also did a life-size sculpture of Charlie Chaplin to be delivered to himself at the theatre in Leicester Square. The label read 'Tommy Steele, Leicester Square'. "The lorry driver just dropped it off – in Leicester Square! The police arrested the statue and I had to go and sign for it at the police station. I swear it's the truth," he laughs.

How does he think the current recession will affect theatre going?

"I believe that when there's austerity around, especially in Great Britain, people have to find an oasis of light. There has to be something out there that takes them away from that worry.

Sometimes, it may be a drink at the pub and sometimes it's going to the pictures or to the theatre. You've got to have somewhere to go, where you can forget it all and if we're (the Performers) not there, what's there? A good night out at the theatre can inspire you, the next day you can chat to your mates about it and it can take two or three days to get over it! Isn't it wonderful? Audiences are exactly the same. People cry everywhere, people laugh everywhere and all applaud.

I'm definitely not someone who is negative.

I'm the opposite.

Always chase your dreams.

It's not an easy business to be in but it is a wonderful business to be in.

"I remember," said Tommy "an old tightrope walker who'd just lost half his family in an accident they had on a high wire without a net. He was sitting in his caravan and they were doing this television interview about his life. He was in his seventies. I remember the announcer saying to him, 'What makes you keep doing it'? and he said' To live is to be on the wire and the rest …is waiting.'

And that's really what show business is, you just love it so much you keep waiting to do it again. I'll never retire, just die, that's when I'll stop! As soon as I get on the stage and the spotlight hits me I wouldn't want to be anywhere else."

 On January 3 2012 Tommy made an appeared on 'The Story of Musicals.' a TV series documentary

On June 10 2012 Tommy made an appearance on 'The Royal History of Pop.' a TV documentary

Bill Kenwright talking about Scrooge said, "When we opened in Manchester eight years ago it broke all box office records as we did when we took it to the London Palladium, now were back in the North West this time at 'The Lowry, Salford and I can't wait to see it in it's new home. At this time of the year, what more can you want than Tiny Tim wishing a Merry Christmas to one and all!"

On October 13th 2012 he returned for a limited season at his favourite theatre the London Palladium in a Bill Kenwright presentation of Scrooge it was due to end the run on 5th Jan 2013 but it was extended until the 13th due to popular demand.

On 6th November 2012, Tommy gave the 'Daily Express an interview: at which he quoted "I'm 75 and my Palladium comeback shows that I'll never retire, you can't play Arthur Kipp's when your almost 76 years of age. I'd like to. But I can't!"

In another article in 2005 for the Daily Express Tommy summed up his career and what would happen if it ended tomorrow: I'd say 'Thanks a lot, I've had a ball."

Unbelievable, Tommy was doing Scrooge in 2013 AGAIN!!!! Ending in January 2014.

Last night of Scrooge at Llandudno

An article from the North Wales Pioneer written by Suzanne Jorden reproduced with permission.

Tommy is no stranger to playing a tight fisted, money-minded businessman, but that hasn't put off him off from reprising his role as Ebenezer Scrooge for an eighth time. Steele, whose stage musicals include Half A Sixpence and Singing' in the Rain will return to Venue Cymru's stage to star in Bill Kenwright's production of Scrooge, based on Dickens'

Christmas Carol tale. The 76-year-old has performed the part of Scrooge on and off for 10 years and in 2005, was honoured by the London Palladium for the most headlining performances. Speaking in an interview with the North Wales Pioneer, Mr Steele admitted that although he would never tire of the role, playing a character so disliked was difficult. He said: "I find it hard, so I try and be over the top.

He's not cruel, he's naughty.

"I'm glad people can accept me as this cruddy old person. The audience have to believe. He is nasty but then you go back to his childhood and you think 'poor little sod'. Every step is a road to the Damascus; it's four or five roads until he finally arrives." Mr Steele credited audiences in helping him get into character. "On stage you feel like action man - the audience are the ones that you have to attack. Their reaction brings you up to the next scene and then the next. "I'm happy to return to Llandudno. I love the coastline; I could spend all day walking up and down." Scrooge is at Venue Cymru from Monday, January 6 until Saturday, January 11.

In April 2013 Tommy was made patron of the Rotherhithe and Bermondsey Local History Society. The Chairman, Michael Daniels, said, Tommy was born and bred in these parts and has often spoke of his affection for the neighbourhood in which he started out, he grew up in Frean Street, off St. James' Road, and the Dickens Estate in Jamaica Road where his Blue Plaque now sits He is an amazingly multi talented individual ho has been a household name for as long as I can remember, and I am delighted he has agreed to become our first ever patron.

Later on in the year Tommy awarded six ageing servicemen with medals including the United Kingdom Merchant Navy Veteran Badge and the Royal Navy Armed Forces Badge before an audience of more than two hundred people, at Tower Hamlets charity's 170th anniversary.

But what has happened to the rest of Tommy's family?

John Kennedy took on his brother Colin in the autumn of 1957. The ever ambitious, Kennedy began negotiating film contracts and arranging foreign tours in the hope of breaking the boy abroad. He remained undeveloped although he did make a number of records. (See Discography) In the same month that Tommy got engaged to Ann, the Colin Hicks' contract was terminated. He went in the antiques business. In 2006 he was a pub landlord. In 2013 he started doing some rock 'n' roll concerts with his Cabin Boys.

Tommy's sister Sandra married the Company Director Peter Russell and had a wonderful life but unfortunately this was cut short in 2004, when she died of Colon Cancer at the age of 55.

Roy never went into show business in 2006; he was a bus tour organiser.

For 2015 Tommy will be appearing in a new musical "The Glen Miller Story at several venues up and down the country.

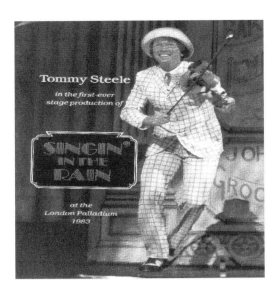

# Singin In The Rain

Tommy bound of the stage into the wings and proffering an infectious, toothy grin and the perennially tousled, boyish charm, accompanies me back to his dressing room. It is five minutes short of ten pm. everybody is pleased. It has been a good show, with a responsive audience, and the star has given it the works.

But he has paid the price.

He is drenched in perspiration, exhausted, leaden footed. He is like a man who has just run a fifty-mile marathon.

Everything he had inside him before the show, all the whiz-bang reserves of energy and the incessant compulsion to please, is now spent, distributed in so many tiny parcels to each person lucky enough to have been 'out front' a few minutes earlier. It is an astonishing sight. Tommy has just danced and sung and tumbled his way through the spectacular musical.

From the same side on vantage point, in the wings, I have seen only one other man of the theatre give his all in so powerful, so uncompromising and so total a manner: ballet dancer Rudolf Nureyev. They have so much in common, Tommy and Rudi, and no wonder they're such great pals. They even look alike! Each is avowed perfectionists, giving so much of themselves during a performance that they virtually tear themselves to pieces, heart from limb, not to say from soul. Each is supreme in his chosen field. Each a millionaire, is it any wonder? They differ in only one fundamental respect. Whereas Rudi has been happily married, since the age of sixteen, to classical ballet, Tommy has remained by and large, an unabashed bigamist: married to former dancer Ann Donoughue and to show business of which he has stayed at the top for more than a quarter of a century.

He describes his first professional love, the stage, quite simply as "my magnificent obsession". And he talks so lovingly of Ann as "a valued friend and confidante and a very good reason for being alive". "Without her", he says, "My career wouldn't be what it is today. She is probably a good fifty per cent of my whole success. With the love that she gives, with the help she offers.... well, that strength is there whenever I feel myself floundering. "Her influence on my life during rehearsals is total," he adds. "Ann is my greatest, most hateful, most welcome critic. I hate it when she finds things wrong, and I'm thankful that 9.9 times out of 10 she is dead right." "I wouldn't be the person I am if I hadn't met and married Ann. "I think when you meet a partner, and decide to stay together, you inherit certain qualities and certain disabilities from each other - and then you become, as it were, another person. I'd like to think, where I'm concerned, it's for the good: and, in Ann's case the same. Ann, he believes firmly, was the backbone of his strength during the making of one of the stage version of one of the all-time great screen musicals, which cost £1 million to produce and which gave Tommy the once-in-a-lifetime opportunity to tackle a role immortalised by his idol, Gene Kelly. Tommy was both the star and the director. Even though he had to compete with eighteen spectacular scene-changes, including the draining of six hundred gallons of water from the stage in five and a half minutes after the show stopping title song. Tommy's chirpy personality still somehow dominates what must now rank as the West End's most lavish musicals.

"When the producer, Harold Fielding, offered me the part, I couldn't believe it.," recalls the boy from Bermondsey who escaped the back streets of South London to become an international star. He gives that toothy grin again. "No, I wasn't inhibited by it. I still believe, and always have done, that it's a song and dance-man's Hamlet. "I'm never inhibited by playing a famous role, he emphasises."I never want to know how other people played it, or, if I do know, I never, ever put myself in that same category anyway. I couldn't possibly say to myself, I'm going to be compared with Gene Kelly, because you simply can't be compared with somebody as great as that.

You've got to say to the audience, 'look this is a great story, a great score and a great show. I'm playing in it with all these other great people and we're doing it live on the stage, and this is our version.

"You have to accept it for that. If you come in and see somebody playing Richard III and start saying, 'Oh, well, he doesn't play it like Olivier,' no one is ever going to play Richard III again. You can't go through life being inhibited like that."

From the very beginning, in fact, Tommy had Gene Kelly's blessing to do the musical. The two entertainers first met in 1965, when Tommy was appearing on Broadway in 'Half a Sixpence.'

He said: "I looked up into my dressing room mirror - and there he was, my idol, standing there. He said simply, 'Hello, smiler, Welcome to the club! And I knew I was at a high point in my life.

"A year later, I and Gene worked together in a television show broadcast live from Broadway.

In preparation for the show, the Hollywood screen star offered to give me dancing lessons - just two of them, and a pianist, alone in a dusty hall for a month.

"He taught me to tap, and so much more. We talked over coffee about things: and we talked about 'Singin In The Rain.' Little did I realise then that one day I'd be the first person ever to take Kelly's part in the same show on the stage.

"Rehearsing for the show was a labour of love. I used to go home absolutely elated; I couldn't wait to get up the next morning. The entire cast was hand chosen by myself, and it's the happiest company I have ever worked with, completely free of arguments and cliques.

"Ann still can't believe that there were no problems during rehearsals.

People say I'm a perfectionist, and I do like to get things right. But that doesn't mean that I make life difficult for the cast.

"Ann's a very good judge of what's right or wrong, and we talk about all these things a lot at home. I'm not one of these showbiz folk who say that the minute they walk off the stage and through their front door they never 'talk shop.' I talk shop endlessly at home. I love it. I can't stop talking about it! "It's a sort of safety valve, letting off your little bit of steam. You've got to have somebody to talk to in this business, otherwise you'd go mad. And if you kept it inside yourself all the time, you'd have no court of appeal, and I think you've got to have court of appeal. "But occasionally the court of appeal does not have the desired result. The only thing, which causes rows in the Steele household, in fact, is when Ann offers her critical judgement on a project close to my heart. I'm not very good, I'm afraid, at taking criticism from Ann," he confesses, his voice coming from a steaming shower cubical. "Oh, I'm terrible. If she gives me strong criticism, I'll spit tacks and go into a short of shell. "But I'm not a sulker; I think that is a weakness. My first reaction is to defend myself; to say what she is suggesting is wrong. Then gradually I start to think about it, and realise that my initial anger was unjustified and that she is more likely to be right.

"Mind you," he goes on, "when I talk about an argument, I'm talking about a quick flare-up over a cup of coffee, it's over by the time the cup is empty. We don't have lasting arguments. "We met at the Chiswick Empire in late 1956, Ann possessed a great sense of humour, and kept me in stitches, she impersonated a well known television commercial, and I think that's when I fell in love with her. I was completely bowled over by her zany personality, and a few months after we were engaged. But it was four years later before we eventually married.

"I never proposed, you know. I never said to her "Will you marry me?

My desire to marry her came out indirectly in a conversation. I sort of found myself saying 'look that's the kind of house we'll have. Do you reckon you'd be happy if we lived in a place like that...? "We both just sort of assumed that we were going to get married. I'd find myself saying. 'What will you be doing in June? Do you fancy getting married then?"

They've been married for twenty-three years and they still hold hands.

"Not a day goes by when I don't remember that I love her," he says, not caring two hoots if he sounds a dewy-eyed sentimentalist. "Sometimes I think our friends think about Annie and I are dull because we like being together."Do you know what our marriage is based on? It's based on friendship - total dependence on friendship, knowing that we talk to each other and respect each other. And, he is quick to add, "We love each other. I don't mean the passionate side of love -

which of course we have; I mean that we are each other's best friends.

On the wall of his dressing room is a framed photograph of his daughter, Emma. "One of my joys", says Tommy. "Its nice that I've been able to give my family a nice comfortable standard of living in a nice big place which means it needs running repairs from time to time - and I'm absolutely useless as a handyman. I've tried, believe me, but I can't even knock a nail in without it bending. "And painting, decorating, gardening? Forget it! I was once asked to clear some weeds from a border and ended up ruining it: I pulled everything out that looked like a weed and they were all the blooming flowers! "Now I'm just trusted to cut the lawn. I'm all right at that. I know what grass is." "My favourite meals are stuffed hearts. I like roast rabbit, roast beef and roast lamb. I like bread and butter pudding, lemon pancakes and steamed pudding with treacle." "I only eat sweets when I'm in a heavy show, like this one, it's great because I can have two sweets a week. Such luxury!" "At the moment I don't really eat all day, sometimes I will have an egg. I may have a hot pie or a chocolate biscuit. But when I get home I'll eat anything I can lay my hands on."

On the table is a knitted mascot, which Emma gave to him. Wherever he goes that mascot goes with him. And Emma is his pride and joy. "I came into this business for a bit of fun and excitement, but I found out I was in the most exciting thing I walked in to, then I wanted to be an all round entertainer, I wanted that. I was told the only way to do that was to start again." "I decided there and then that I wanted to diversify. And I have been doing it ever since. I remember the greatest criticism my father ever gave me, the first time I saw him angry, the first time he ever disliked something I did. It was at a show at the 'Adelphi', called 'Meet Me In London' and up to the first night we had nothing but problems. "The first night the leading lady walked out of the show, which meant that all the way through the three hour show there were big holes where she should have come on, and wasn't coming on; and there were no understudies. So they were throwing things in just to fill the gaps. I was a bungle of nerves. I shouted and I screamed to get some life into the proceedings. And when I went on, the audience were really angry: The curtain had gone up three quarters of an hour late. I garbled through the dialogue, sang all the songs at twice the tempo and did everything I could do that was wrong. At the end of the show my father popped his head round the door to my dressing room and said: 'You aught to be thoroughly ashamed of yourself, I'm going home.' "And I tell you, from that day to this, I've never rushed a show. I'd never allow a first night to do that to me again. The first night of 'Singin in the Rain' was the first time I'd ever had a three-tier standing ovation, it was a great accolade it really brought a tear to my eye. Everything I do I do for the people, the audience. I never do anything and say, "I don't care if they don't like it, I am going to do it." I believe players should be entertainers and not educationalists." Pinned to the frame of his dressing table mirror is a quote from Gene Kelly it reads 'I've been lucky ... it's entirely up to the public and there is nothing you can do about it.' What could be truer?

# What reviews

Just a few of the reviews Tommy's shows have received over the years:

Cinderella

Coliseum 1958
"...the most sumptuous and beautiful Cinderella that I should think London has ever seen. Felix Barker Evening News

She Stoops To Conquer

Old Vic 1960
"... Tommy Steele's Lumpkin mesmerises the audience" Derek Johnson New Musical Express
"... A most likeable Lumpkin beneath the capers - a tower of strength"

Birthday Show

1961 Coventry Theatre
"On stage Tommy presents 40 minutes of the most polished entertainment you're likely to see in a variety theatre. He sings and dances - he is an all round entertainer".

United Nations Charity Concert Germany 1962
"... He received a standing ovation from a capacity audience after his act".

Half a Sixpence

Cambridge Theatre, London 1963
"Cor, what a bloomin triumph for Tommy Steele. His first West End musical - and it's a hit, hit, hit".

Half a Sixpence

Broadhurst Theatre, New York 1965
'A Big Blooming Musical Hit' McClain Journal
'A fully delightful evening. Tommy Steele shines as Broadway's new star. Leonard Lyons
"Steele is a delight, of a kind that does not exist on the American stage." Newsweek
"A song and dance man who's masterly is currently unsurpassed by any other performer in the field". New York Times

One-Man Show

Caesar's Palace, Las Vegas 1971.
"Tommy Steele is a theatrical experience. As a talent he is, in the truest sense of the word, incomparable". Joe Delaney, Las Vegas Sun, "He has the charm, versatility and vitality of a young Danny Kaye. He's a marvellous one-man show". The Hollywood Reporter
"Versatile Cockney Tommy Steele is an overwhelming success. He's an overflowing treasure chest of talent" Frank H Lieverman, Herald Examiner

An Evening with Tommy Steele

Prince of Wales Theatre, London 1979
"Stainless Steele bright as ever". Daily Express
"Enough energy to keep four or five nuclear power plants going" Sunday Mirror
"A beguiling, often dazzling entertainment, mixing nostalgia with new songs and routines. Whatever you do, try not to miss it" Peter Clayton, Sunday Telegraph
Singin' In The Rain

London Palladium 1983

"Tommy Steele's is a lovely performance ... here is a player haloed by a curious radiance whenever he steps onto a stage. The occasion is a triumph for him" Francis King, Sunday Telegraph

"Director-star puts together a show of no expense spared, no holds barred fun, complete with old-fashioned style, sparkle and suggestiveness".

Some Like It Hot

National Tour 1991

"... The driving force behind-the-scenes and centre stage is Tommy Steele whose love affair with the British public continues to be steadfast as ever. He gives them what ... they want. A spectacle of the highest quality, laughs, a blinding central performance, disciplined, high-stepping chorus numbers, shoot-outs, luxurious sets and sparkling costumes". Southern Evening Echo

Scrooge

Tours 2003, 2004, 2005, 2006.
"...Sheer Magic " BBC Radio
"Tommy Steals The Show" "You couldn't ask for more" Leicester Mercury
..Steele is a sensation, a true musical legend" Evening News

Dr Dolittle

Tours 2007, 2008.
"Beautifully staged, well produced, well directed and powerfully performed Mr Steele proves his star quality still exists even fifty years since he first started on the stage".
"Tommy Steele still wows an audience". Tony Flood, The Guardian "With an Oscar winning score, and spectacular sets it is the perfect treat for all the family. "
"An absolute delightful show, with Mr Steele singing all the best songs." The Wimbledon Reporter.

## Scrooge

Tours 2009 2010 2011 2012 2013 2014
" ...Superb. That's the only way to describe Tommy Steele.
He and the cast deserved every bit of the standing ovations
they received" Evening Telegraph.

# The people who have been associated with Tommy

Jack Fallon

Many will remember Tommy mentioning his stint as 'Chick Hicks' with Jack Fallon and his sons of the saddle.

Jack Fallon sadly died in 2006 and this synopsis of his life might interest you.

Jack Fallon played a prominent role in British jazz and popular music, as both musician and agent. He was among the early pioneers of modern jazz, but equally at home in many styles, including light orchestral and country-and-western music. He is perhaps unique in having played with both Duke Ellington and the Beatles.

Patrick "Jack" Fallon was born in London, Ontario, on October 13 1915 and played the violin in his family band from an early age. At 20 he took up the double bass, which became his main instrument, although he continued to practise the violin and also learned the trumpet. He played with the Civic Symphony Orchestra in his hometown and with Frank Crowley's dance band. On the outbreak of war, Fallon joined the Royal Canadian Air Force and was sent to Britain as a member of an RCAF band, the Streamliners, with which he played trumpet on parade and bass at concerts and dances. He had become so well known and accepted among local musicians that no one was surprised when he decided to stay on after the war and pursue a British career. He was briefly a member of Ted Heath's orchestra in 1946, before embarking on the round of touring and nightclub residencies, which constituted the freelance musician's life in the post-war period. In this capacity he worked with such top bandleaders of the day as Harry Parry, Tito Burns and the young George Shearing, with whom he recorded in 1948. In the same year Duke Ellington visited Britain, to play at the London Palladium and make a brief tour.

Union restrictions prevented his full orchestra from appearing, and Ellington brought with him only his vocalist, Kay Davis, and trumpeter-entertainer Ray Nance. Fallon assembled and led the trio, which accompanied them throughout their stay. Later that year he also accompanied the French gipsy guitar virtuoso Django Reinhardt on tour. Fallon was among the earliest players in Britain to grapple with the new and technically challenging style of jazz known as bebop, or simply bop, then being introduced in the United States by Charlie Parker, Dizzy Gillespie and others. He can be heard on some of the very first British recorded attempts, by groups such as the Esquire All-Star Sextet (1948) and the Steve Race Bop Group (1949). At the same time, Fallon was leading the Sons Of The Saddle, a cowboy-style group which played for Riders Of The Range, the BBC Light Programme's hugely popular "musical drama of the West", five series of which ran between 1949 and 1953.

Such American musical stars as did appear in Britain tended to be either pianists or singers. They usually required rhythm accompaniment, and Fallon was among the first to be called. In 1953 he played for the pianist-composer Mary Lou Williams and the vocalist Sarah Vaughan and for Lena Horne in 1955. He became particularly associated with the folk singer Josh White, a great favourite with British audiences throughout the 1950s, especially for his Sunday afternoon radio series featuring spirituals, The Glory Road.

In 1952 Fallon set up his own agency, Cana Variety, which booked entertainers of all kinds, from Noel Coward to the Rolling Stones, successfully responding to changes in public taste. The Beatles were among his clients in their early days.

The 1950s was the decade in which British jazz came of age, and Fallon was often at the centre of developments. He played bass on the first recording by Joe Harriott, the great Jamaican saxophonist, in 1954, and with such leading modern British players as Don Rendell, Tony Kinsey, Tommy Whittle, Ronnie Scott and Tubby Hayes.

He led his own In Town Tonight Sextet in 1954-55 and was often a member of Kenny Baker's Dozen in the long-running radio series Let's Settle For Music. Even so, he still found time to exercise his skill in country- and-western music by recording, and occasionally touring, with Johnny Duncan and his Blue Grass Boys. He played on their 1957 hit single Last Train To San Fernando. In his backing group at that time was the up and coming Tommy Hicks later to be known as Tommy Steele.

Fallon's agency work curtailed his active music making during the 1960s, although he continued to play, adding electric bass guitar to his repertoire of instruments. In 1968 he played violin in Don't Pass Me By, a track on the Beatles' "White Album".

In the 1970s he formed a long-standing partnership with the pianist Lennie Felix, whose wide-ranging and unidiomatic style suited Fallon's eclectic tastes to perfection. In 1983 he joined the trumpeter Digby Fairweather's intimate chamber-jazz group, Velvet, played regularly with the clarinettist Wally Fawkes's Crouch End All-Stars, and could be seen and heard regularly accompanying the now plentiful supply of American jazz stars.

In 1994 Fallon recorded with the American cornetist Dick Sudhalter, but gradually wound down his activities later in the decade. Last year, when he reached 90, he marked his final retirement from active music making by selling his double bass.

Lionel Bart

Lionel Bart died in 1999. He was aged sixty-eight. "How did a simple Cockney from the East End of London manage to become a household name on the musical and pop scene? Talent, hard work, a lot of luck - all this helps, of course, to make one's name known. But Lionel Bart is a name that sticks in the mind; would Lionel Begleiter have been a name on everyone's lips in the same way?

Under the name Bart the man that was later to make an indelible mark on the British pop scene, was born on 1st August 1930. A boy from an impoverished background had to learn a trade, so Lionel became a silk-screen printer. The 50s saw the development of a phenomenon that has since become one of the most dominant elements of society as a whole; pop music in all its commercial aspects. Since the jazz era at the turn of the century all pop music trends had started in America and been taken over by British musicians.

As the 50s progressed London was held more and more firmly in the newest craze from America. But the British version of rock 'n' roll was a very watered down affair compared to the American original, which had started with the immortal Elvis.

British rock 'n' roll musicians simply copied what came over from America at that time, and the result was a flood of lukewarm imitations without any real character of their own.

A young English Man called Thomas Hicks change all that. His first concerts were totally chaotic, disorganised and primitive not for nothing was his first group called the 'Cavemen.' But one member of his band turned out to have a felicitous gift for writing hits, one of the most sensational being 'Rock with the Caveman:'

Lionel Bart, who had since joined Tommy's band and had discovered his talent for composing - writing his own lyrics as well! One hit followed another, including not only noisy rock 'n' roll numbers but also cheerful songs for the whole family, one of them being the naively cheery 'Little White Bull.'

Hits followed for other stars like Cliff Richard's 'Livin Doll' and Anthony Newley 'Do You Mind.' At last English pop music had found its own individual style. One aspect of this new style of pop music which was typically and traditionally English was its connection with the English music hall, the earliest concerts given by Tommy and his Cavemen were in fact short appearances in variety in the old music hall tradition; fire eaters, conjurers, dancing girls, stand up comics and rock 'n' roll in between. This had two significant effects; not only were the musicians confronted with, literally, a variety of show business possibilities, but the professionalism of the other acts had a beneficial effect on their own presentation.

Lionel had grown up with the music hall. It was the typical entertainment of the big city working classes at that time; television was in its infancy, conventional theatre was too high brow and beyond the means of simple working class people, but the music hall, with its rough and ready humour and its manifold attractions, spoke to ordinary people in their own language. All this reflected in Lionel Bart's songs.

This passion for the music halls led to his first stage successes in 1959 with 'Lock Up Your Daughters' and 'Fings Ain't Wot They Used To Be.' But his greatest musical success, and one of the most popular of all time, was 'Oliver', which had its premiere in London on 30th June 1960 and ran for an unprecedented 2618 performances. Nearly all the songs from the show became hits; lively numbers such as the title number 'Oliver!' 'Food Glorious Food' and Consider Yourself', plus tender lyrical songs like 'Where Is Love?' Who Will Buy?' Fagin's witty philosophy of life in 'You've Got To Pick A Pocket Or Two' and 'I'm Reviewing The Situation' and Nancy's 'As Long As He Needs Me.'

Lionel Bart never managed to equal the success of 'Oliver'. But he enjoyed international fame when it was made into a film. But soon he became the victim of his own philanthropic nature, he could not resist a hard luck story, and much of his prosperity dwindled away as he put too much faith in too many untrustworthy business ventures.

By the late 60s these business speculations combined with excesses of alcohol and drugs, had forced him to retire from the public eye. He remained in retreat from the press and public until the end of the 80s, by which time he had managed to overcome his private problems and made a comeback.

From 1989 he started writing advertising jingles.

Up to the time of his death he remained one of the most colourful and interesting figures on the British music scenes. His contribution to pop and the theatre will ensure him a foremost place in the annals of music and theatre history."

Mike Pratt

Mike Pratt was best known for his role as Jeff Randall in the late 60s ITV detective series Randall and Hopkirk (Deceased) alongside Kenneth Cope and Annette Andre. Pratt also wrote episode two of the series titled "A Disturbing Case." He also appeared in TV series such as No Hiding Place, The Saint, Gideon's Way, Z-Cars, Danger Man, Out of the Unknown, Redcap, The Baron, Man in a Suitcase, The Champions, Callan, UFO, The Expert, Hadleigh, Jason King, Arthur of the Britons, Softly, Softly: Taskforce, Crown Court, Father Brown, Oil Strike North and The Adventures of Black Beauty, in which he had a semi-regular role. His last television role was in the BBC drama series The Brothers as airline pilot Don Stacy. He joined the Royal Shakespeare Company in 1966, appearing on stage throughout the rest of the 60s and the early 70s. A successful songwriter, Pratt collaborated with Lionel Bart on many of Tommy Steele's early hits in the late 50s and early 60s. To enable Steele to start to film his life story, co-writers Steele, Bart and Pratt, wrote twelve songs in seven days. A Pratt collaboration, "A Handful of Songs", originally a hit for Tommy Steele in 1957, became the theme tune to a long-running Granada Television children's programme of the same name in the late 70s.In his early career, Pratt worked in advertising, while also taking some part-time acting roles, until in the mid-fifties he took a sabbatical quitting his office job. He drove around Europe in an old-style London taxi with three friends, including Lionel Bart. On returning to England, he earned a living playing jazz and skiffle in London clubs. Pratt has many friends that were musicians hence music was his life until his acting career took off in the 60s. In the 50s, he jammed with The Vipers Skiffle Group at the 2 I's club in London with his friend Tommy Steele. Pratt can be seen jamming skiffle on a 50s Pathé News clip with other musicians of the era including members of The Shadows. Pratt died from lung cancer in July 1976. In August of that year, a show was staged at the Aldwych Theatre in London in his memory. The cast included Glenda Jackson, Kenneth Haigh and John Le Mesurier.


John Kennedy

Here is a re-run of the article from a national newspaper 4th August 2004.
'The first man to rock the nation'
Any kind of white powder on the tables was either sugar or dandruff. Nobody knew much about cocaine yet. It was around. But not at the Two I's on Old Compton Street, Soho. The place was only ever full of cigarette smoke and the smell of instant coffee. A night out was almost healthy.
Teenagers hung around, listened to music, drank coffee and wandered home late but never got stabbed.
The Two I's came out as one of the best places on earth. And this particular night, the street was being washed down by the scream of a loud guitar exploding through the open door.
John Kennedy, Heathrow freelance photographer and curious about the noise, pushed his way off the hot, crowded pavement and squeezed himself on to a stool by the bar. The night became distinguished.
Write it down, September 14, 1956. It was the one when rock 'n' roll began in England. Kennedy had no more of an ear for music than a tree. What he knew about, and knew a lot, was

style and promotion and a teenage kid they could look on as a hero. So he didn't look at the blond youth dancing and singing on the stage too much. He stared first at the faces of all the girls at the tables with their drinks and cigarettes.

It was layer after layer of adulation.

Now he turned to the lively kid banging out some new Elvis number.

Presley was only heard here on record shows and jukeboxes.

Paul Lincoln owned the Two I's. He was a pro wrestler who called himself Dr Death.

Paul moved around the wall looking at the great business. Kennedy tried to talk to him through the noise. "Who's the singer?" he shouted in his ear.

"Tommy Hicks" Paul replied.

Not much went on at Heathrow for a good photographer to get excited about. There was a Pan Am 101 flight from New York that flew film stars. After that, almost nothing. Kennedy spent a lot of time thinking about a switch from newspapers to show business. At least show business was more fun.

This boy on stage at the Two I's would be the push he needed.

"You want to go into serious show business?" Kennedy asked him when they met after his set.

He said he was only on leave as a steward on Cunard ocean liners.

He had two weeks to go. If Kennedy could show him a deal in that time then, sure, he would like to become a star. And that's how Tommy Steele started.

In six months he was a solid gold sensation.

Kennedy did the talking. He wheeled and dealed, snagged a record contract and found another unknown to write songs.

This one was Lionel Bart.

Down the line he wrote 'Oliver' one of the greatest musicals ever.

There hadn't been a man like Kennedy before. Show business was part of the Establishment.

Now there was this tall, slim, handsome guy strutting around cutting deals in the offices of people who wouldn't take a phone call from him before. He was the first one of that kind of agent/manager and afterwards they came along like rain.

Steele made £1,000 a week on stage. Then there were royalties. It was fabulous money.

Kennedy had a partner now, Larry Parnes, a rich investor and night clubber. He brought in some business plans.

Tommy was performing at the Cafe d'Paris straight after Noel Coward.

He was an industry with movie contracts and international recording deals.

Kennedy prospered. He bought Jaguars and had his suits cut in Seville Row. The newspapers put the rise of rock down to him. Tommy was out front pushing it. John Kennedy was the magician in the wings. Life became a roar. He liked the jewellery of the good times. So it was out of a bed-sit into Dorothy Foxon's great and fabled drinking club next to Harrods and into a penthouse on Half Moon Street, Mayfair. Nothing in between. He gambled, sat there at four in the morning opposite Sammy Davis Jnr. in Dorothy's betting three queens against two pairs. There wasn't a second of the day that wasn't touched by fun and glamour.

Rock 'n' roll was down to him and Tommy. History has to rate the two of them as the people who brought it from America. One million cigarettes and late nights drove John Kennedy to the California desert 20 years ago so he could breathe the hot, dry air and help his chest. It was a restless time.

With a new partner he opened a market for outdoor air conditioning. It sounded crazy but it worked. But that didn't challenge him. He was an artist at heart; a photographer and a painter. And one day around the swimming pool of his house he said he was going to be a sculptor.

You don't know anything about it, his friend told him.

"I'll learn and be good at it," he said with his booming confidence.

He did and he was. His artistry is all over the south-western states, right there in the entrance halls of banks and in special places in wealthy people's homes.

Rock 'n' roll, sculpturing, semi-pro gambler, and industrial entrepreneur - it's hard to put much more into one lifetime.

So there was a lot to remember of him when people gathered in the chapel of Palm Springs Mortuary for his funeral last week. On the street the temperature got to 110 degrees. That was also a hot night outside the Two I's, Soho, long ago. The night Kennedy had a little bit of inspiration and a youth revolution began and it genuinely changed the culture of the whole country. On around 23rd July 2004, John Kennedy died. He was 73 years of age.

## Larry Parnes

Larry Parnes left school at 16 and he worked briefly for his family's clothing business. By the age of 18 he was running his own women's clothing shops in Romford, Essex. His family had helped with the finance to purchase three shops but only one proved to be successful and he got into debt.

One evening a friend took him into La Caverne, a bar in Romilly Street in the West End of London. At the end of the evening Larry Parnes intervened in a heated argument between the two owners of the bar and discovered that the two could not work together. He offered to buy one of them out.

In fact he had no money but one of the owners was so keen to get out of the business that he sold his share for £500 to be paid in instalments.

Theatrical agents and producers frequented the bar.

Larry Parnes had been teetotal but took to drinking whisky. After a whisky-drinking contest he discovered that he had been persuaded to invest in a play entitled The House of Shame.

The play toured during 1955 and was making a loss until John Kennedy was recruited as its publicist.

The name was changed to Women of the Streets and two female actors were persuaded to stand outside the theatre dressed as prostitutes during the interval. They were arrested, and after the national press picked up the story the play took off and eventually broke even.

Larry Parnes bumped into John Kennedy again in The Sabrina, a coffee bar in Soho and was persuaded to go to see the singer Tommy Steele perform in the Stork Room in Regent's Street. After the performance Larry and John Kennedy became his managers and a contract was signed in September 1956.

Tommy Hicks adopted the stage name Tommy Steele and became Britain's first rock and roll celebrity and went on to become an all-round entertainer and star of several musicals.

Larry Parnes scoured the coffee bars and dance halls for another star, and Lionel Bart informed him of Reg Smith (née Patterson) who was performing at the Condor Club above The Sabrina coffee bar. In fact Larry Parnes missed his performance but went round to his house and signed him up on the basis of Lionel Bart's testimonial.

He was given the name Marty Wilde and had a string of UK hits.

Larry Parnes developed a network of contacts including the A&R managers Hugh Mendl, Dick Rowe, and Jack Baverstock. The television producer Jack Good was also keen to benefit from the flow of new teenage talent provided by Larry Parnes. Songwriters like Lionel Bart provided original material.

Larry Parnes turned down Cliff Richard after an audition.

In 1958 he took on the management of Roy Taylor and gave him the name Vince Eager, but he failed to have any hits, he dropped him, although he became a household name through a regular starring role on the BBC's programme Drumbeat.

In September 1958 Ron Wycherly walked into Marty Wilde's dressing room at the Essoldo Cinema, Birkenhead, and asked to play a few songs.

Larry Parnes was impressed and signed him on.

He was given the stage name Billy Fury and he became one of the most important figures in the British rock and roll scene.

He also managed a number of other young hopefuls with varying degrees of success. These included, Dickie Pride (Richard Knellar), Duffy Power (Ray Howard), Johnny Gentle (John Askew), Sally Kelly, Terry Dene, Nelson Keene, Peter Wynne, and Georgie Fame (Clive Powell).

His approach was to choose pretty young people and groom them to make them attractive to other teenagers. He often changed their names, and he wanted to give the gifted guitarist Joe Brown the name Elmer Twitch but he refused.

The BBC television programme Panorama included a feature on Larry Parnes as a 'beat svengali' and referred to his 'stable of stars'.

In 1960 the press gave him the nickname Mr Parnes, Shillings and Pence.

He managed the group called 'The Viscounts' which included Gordon Mills who was later to manage Tom Jones. Larry briefly co-managed the Tornadoes with Joe Meek who had formed them but was too busy with his studio work to pay them much attention. Larry missed two opportunities to manage the Beatles. At a time when they were called the Silver Beatles he used them to back his singer Johnny Gentle on a tour of Scotland in 1960. He was also given the opportunity to sign them up as their sole promoter in 1962 but he declined.

His influence in the world of pop music came to an end in the mid 1960s when a new style of manager gained ground. These included Brian Epstein of the Beatles and Andrew Oldham of the Rolling Stones.

In 1967 he announced that he had outgrown the world of pop and would be devoting himself to the theatre.

In 1968 he put on Fortune and Men's Eyes, a play about homosexuality in a Canadian prison, but he lost £5000 on the venture.

In 1972 he bought a twelve - year lease of the Cambridge Theatre and he put on the musicals such as Charlie Girl and Chicago.

He retired after developing meningitis in 1981. Larry Parnes died in 1989 after a long illness.

Harold Lewis Fielding

Harold Lewis Fielding was born at Woking, Surrey on 4th December 1916.

When he was ten years of age his Mother wanted him to take up piano lessons, but he rebelled and took up the violin instead. He went to Paris to study under Joseph Syigeti. At the age of twelve he started touring the country being billed as 'England's Boy Wonder Violinist.'

A group called 'Diva Tetrazzni' supported him in his act.

When the impresario who managed him died, he took over the management of the tour.

In his early twenties the stress of organising and playing took its toll and he developed stage fright, and stopped performing.

In 1942, he began to arrange performances for other artists under the concert impresario Harold Holt. He married Maisie Joyce Skivens at Chiswick Parish Church.

When Harold Holt died he wanted to take over the company but he was turned down.

He left the company and with one hundred pounds capital started up on his own.

In 1945, he introduced a series of Sunday concerts at the Blackpool Opera House. They were called 'Music For Millions' and they were to last for thirty years.

The singers who appeared in the early Blackpool concerts were Richard Tauber, Gigli, Paul Robeson, Gracie Fields and Jessie Matthews.

As a producer he was more interested in entertaining the public than making money.

He started putting on 'summer' shows at eight other seaside towns.

These lasted until 1983, when he finished putting on summer shows, for personal reasons. His contribution to Blackpool's summer season's entertainment spanned forty years, which attracted more than three million people to the Opera House. First Leisure Corporation, the owners at that time, said "We are very sorry to lose such a dear friend, who has become known by generations for his value for money shows with top line artistes.

In the forties he brought stars such as Donald Peers, Sophie Tucker and Duke Ellington. Whilst in the fifties he brought over to England Tony Bennett. He pioneered the coach party trade but preferred the trains because they carried more people. He was one of the very first impresarios to advertise on television."

For a while he managed Sir Thomas Beecham and the Royal Philharmonic Orchestra.

He stated "... his main ambition in life was to make the West End of London another Broadway" and to some extent he succeeded.

Harold Fielding knew what his audiences wanted and his patrons knew that they would enjoy the shows he put on. Unlike most producers he would back his judgement with his own money rather than rely on investors.

This gave him creative control and all the profits, but it also meant that he would have to stand the losses as well.

As a producer he was the shining star of his era.

When Frank Sinatra made his first visit to Britain in 1950 at the Palladium Harold Fielding persuaded him to do a Sunday night concert at Blackpool.

He also persuaded other stars to do the same.

Stars such as Danny Kaye and Judy Garland were only too pleased to co-operate in his schemes.

He liked to be known as the 'Gov'nor'.

He would stand no nonsense or changes without permission. When Dusty Springfield put some amplifiers on the stage, he was far from happy.

When she refused to remove them he told her she would never work for him again, and she never did. Over the years he brought to London the Hollywood legends such as Van Johnson and Ginger Rogers.

In 1955, he presented at the Festival Hall, Jose Greco and his company.

In 1956 he took on Tommy Steele. It was a partnership that was to last until 1990 without a contract ever being signed.

In 1957, along with a fellow producer, Harold Davidson, he organised Count Basie's first British tour. In the same year Rogers and Hammerstein II wrote a television version of 'Cinderella' with Julie Andrews as the star. Over one hundred and seven million people watched it across America.

Harold Fielding acquired the rights to put it on the stage in London. It opened on the 18th December 1958 with Tommy Steele taking the part of 'Buttons' - a part that was omitted in the American Version. Tommy even got permission to use one of his own compositions in the production. It was sung with another of the stars of the production, Jimmy Edwards.

In the production the panto tradition of having males playing the 'Ugly Sisters' was adopted. The two sisters in this production were Ted Durante and Kenneth Williams.

In 1959 Harold Fielding imported another American television musical 'Aladdin' for the London stage. It starred Bob Monkhouse and Doretta Morrow. Some of the American productions were changed to provide a more spectacular decor and a happy ending, which his patrons liked.

Harold Fielding became more prominent when the motorways were built in this country and the development of the American tourist industry started booming. He started forging links with New York, first by importing Broadway shows and bringing over stars such as Danny Kaye and Nat 'King' Cole and of course sending over some of his shows to New York.

Some of the shows he sent over were, 'Half a Sixpence', 'Mame' and 'The Great Waltz.'

In 1960, his foray into the London's West End produced Alex Coppel's, 'The Gazebo,' which just broke even. He also suffered a series of setbacks, including an ill judged attempt to revive music hall at the Prince Charles Theatre, in Leicester Square.

In 1961, he brought over another American musical 'The Music Man', which starred Van Johnson. It was put on at the Adelphi Theatre, London.

'The Music Man' was the story of a small American town, with, (as Harold put it) "...old fashioned charm and rousing songs." The most popular song from that show was 'Seventy-Six Trombones'. 'The Music Man' ran for 395 performances.

From 1961 to 1964 Harold Fielding presented to the public a series of twice-nightly summer shows at the Winter Gardens, Bournemouth. His stars included the Beverley Sisters, Alma Cogan, Ted Ray, Arthur Askey, Ken Dodd, Tommy Steele and Petula Clark.

In 1962, his production of 'Sail Away' by Noel Coward suffered a threatened Musicians Union strike. Harold resigned from the 'Society of West End Managers' and reached a private agreement with an orchestra that hired local musicians.

Fielding who had invested £40,000 in the production of 'Sail Away' made them sign a petition ensuring that they would not strike for two years. 'Sail Away' ran for seven months. Its main star was Elaine Strich.

In 1963, he got David Henecker and Beverley Cross to write 'Half a Sixpence' for Tommy. It ran at 'The Cambridge Theatre' for 679 performances, only closing so that he could take it over to Broadway. 'Half a Sixpence' played at 'The Broadhurst Theatre,' New York for 512 performances. It was nominated for five 'Tony' awards, including the best musical.

'Half a Sixpence' was made into a film in 1967.

In 1963, he brought to the West End, Philip King's 'How are you Jonnie.' This was another of his productions, which just broke even.

In 1965, he brought to the West End, 'Charlie Girl' which ran for 2,202 performances. It became one of the most popular musicals of the decade. One of the reasons why this show became so popular was the opening up of the coach trade from the provinces. The cast of 'Charlie Girl' were Anna Neagle, Derek Nimmo, Hy Hazell and Joe Brown. When it opened, the critics were far from enthusiastic about its potential. When Joe Brown left the show his part was given to Gerry Marsden.

In 1967, Harold Fielding co-produced with Bernard Delfont, Neil Simon's 'Sweet Charity' at the Prince of Wales, which starred Juliet Prowse.

In 1969, he brought over another American musical and co-produced it with Bernard Delfont. The musical was called 'Mame'. The star of 'Mame' was Ginger Rogers.

Ginger Rogers wrote,

"... When the boat docked, I walked down the gangplank to a full orchestra playing tunes from the show. At the railway station in London, a horse drawn carriage was waiting for me, so that I could wave to all the people on the way to the hotel..."

For Fielding 'Phil The Fluter' was a big flop, he lost around 150 thousand pounds on this production, but it did not stop him from thinking that in the future he could bring it out again in a revised form, but he never did.

In 1970, he made an investment in a sex review, 'Let My People Come' but said, "I would never invest in a Sondheim show because the heroine was always an adulteress, and my people would not stand for a show like that." He also put on at Drury lane that year 'The Great Waltz'.

'The Great Waltz' was directed by Wendy Troy; it was co-produced by Bernard Delfont and ran for more than 600 performances.

In 1971, he revived 'Showboat' at The Adelpi Theatre, for which he received a 'Tony' award. The stars of 'Showboat' were Cleo Laine and Lorna Dallas.

In 1972, he put on 'Gone With The Wind' at Drury Lane. It starred June Ritchie, but it was not liked by the members of the public and closed costing Fielding a small fortune.

When he put on a revival of 'Charlie Girl' in South Africa he was to state, "... I'm a good marketer, but I'm much more proud to be known as a showman".

In 1980, he put on 'Biograph Girl', which was also a miss with the public.

In 1981, he put on 'Barnum', which starred Michael Crawford. This show was a definite hit both with the critics and the public.

In 1985, his wife died. She was cremated at Mortlake crematorium, and he went into nosedive. The only lavish production he tried to put on without her was met with disastrous reviews.

In 1986, he put on another revival of 'Charlie Girl', which starred Cyd Charise, and Dora Bryan, who was a personal hit. But the show wasn't.

In 1988, he put on 'Ziegfeld'.

Ziefeld was the biography of a legendary producer; Harold Fielding said this about the show, "... I put the problem with this show, on the unsympathetic central character - people don't want to go to a musical to hear nasty things. After a few weeks, the star of the show, Len Carrou left. I tried to save it by extensive revision and bringing in Topol and having Tommy Steele take over the direction but after investing 2.5 million pounds it closed after seven months, losing over 3 million pounds".

In 1990, after the failure of the civil war musical 'Someone Like You' was written by and starring Petula Clark. It closed after only one month; he went into voluntary liquidation. He predicted ... that he would bounce back. But the curtain had come down on his career, and he never did.

His stars moved to other producers.

In 1996, he received the 'Gold Badge of Merit ' from the British Academy of Songwriters, Composers and Authors, at the Savoy Hotel for his services to the British entertainment industry.

In 1998, he suffered a series of strokes and went to live in a private nursing home.

On the 27th of September 2003, he passed away."

His Friends said of him, "...Although he and his wife had no children, the shows were his children, his family were his employees. He was in his day, one of the most powerful figures in the industry with a long and varied career. He was known to keep a show on ice until he thought the time was right to put it on. Sometimes he would make changes to make it a better show. Then he would put it on either in London or abroad".

His death and the funeral arrangements were reported in all the national newspapers and many of his friends turned up.

The funeral took place on the 4th October 2003 at the Chiswick Parish Church, the place where he married his wife Maisie some forty odd years earlier. Tommy Steele, one of his closest friends made a special journey from Birmingham where he was rehearsing for the opening of 'Scrooge The Musical' for Bill Kenwright, and gave a tribute to this impresario and friend. Up to the time of his death, although very frail, Harold Fielding enjoyed being taken out to see many first night performances in the West End.

Kurt Littner

Kurt Littner was an Austrian who was a tourist waiter aboard the Mauritania and shared the same cabin as Tommy, he was better known to everybody by Tommy's nickname for him, 'Brushes'.

Tommy stated that 'Brushes' used to brush and lay out his clothes for him before he went out on stage in the concerts the crew put on for the tourists.

"He would be my manager, my band, my audience, applauding every time I used to practise a new number, or a play a joke on him. He was always telling me that I was wasting my time working on boats and that I ought to go on the stage". He told me, "Let me tell you, one day you will be a big star" and he would laugh. "Whenever I was down in the dumps he would know, for he would start telling stories of the days when he was in the Foreign Legion. In the months that followed, we would make up sketches and I would put them in my act."

"When I got fired he was most upset, and I used to talk about him a lot to my manager John Kennedy, so much in fact that when we arrived at the dressing room in Sunderland after Harold Fielding made me top of the bill, they let me go in first, and I got the biggest surprise of my life! There in the centre of the Dressing Room was my old mate from the ship - Kurt "Brushes" Littner".

He rushed to him and at once burst into tears. He was so pleased to see him. He thought he had come to see the show, but when John told him, "You talked about him so much in the first weeks of starting out I just had to have him as your dresser". He could have killed John for not informing him. Kurt stayed with Tommy for quite a long time but did not really take to all the travelling around. In 2007 Tommy said he died quite a few years ago, I did keep in touch with him until the end came.

Memories from Denmark

From Eddie Skoller
A Danish artist, who hosted a Swedish Entertainment programme in 1994 with Tommy Steele as one of his guests:
"I saw Tommy Steele for the first time in the 1970s and I especially remember a number, where he was riding a horse with a film running in the background to make it look real. I also remember his first visit to Denmark in 1957, I was 12 years old, but not allowed to go and see him. My first meeting with Tommy was at the Waldorff in London, where we were to discuss the proposed Swedish/Danish television programme with him. We had 'High Tea' and Tommy was immaculately dressed in a chequered tweed-jacket and impressed me by being much more cultured and knowledgeable than I had expected. Another memory from this introductory meeting was his management, who seemed to be very 'protective' of him, making us understand that we should not expect Tommy Steele to practise more than the allocated times in the studio and setting certain demands for his dressing room. However, following our meeting at The Waldorff we became good friends and agreed to meet at his hotel room soon after his arrival in Gothenburg. We discussed which songs to sing, and suddenly everything was fine and his dressing room could have been a

shed for all he cared. Besides being a super professional artist - of the old school, with respect for his job, Tommy was also a very nice person. He had a huge knowledge of history and we both shared an interest in the origins of words i.e. the reason for the words we use in our daily life. I learned a lot and was even able to add some interesting explanations to Tommy's collection. There was a funny incident at the Hotel Park Avenue, where we stayed in Gothenburg. The switchboard lady almost fainted, when she heard Tommy's voice on the phone and she pleaded with room service to be allowed to bring him his breakfast in the morning. Permission was given and she had both his autograph and a hug before she returned to her desk."

# Extra! Extra! Read all about him

## Read more about Tommy Steele

Tommy Steele My Own Story: 1956
Autobiography by Tommy Steele, a sixty-four page booklet
writing about his childhood days in London and his
adventures at sea. The skyrocket to success with over one
hundred pictures most of which were taken at Tommy's home.

Tommy Steele, the facts about a teenage idol and an 'inside'
picture of show business:  by John Kennedy, his manager (at
that time) and friend. Published by Souvenir Press 1958.
Even after all these years is still a good read, it goes into great
detail about the behind the scenes of show business – a thing
that Tommy's 2006 autobiography skims over.
Check out eBay auction sites to get a copy.

A Boy From Bermondsey:
A biography of Tommy Steele by Derek Mathews, 1996, takes
you from the beginning of Tommy's life enjoyably and
informatively to 1996 when Tommy's talent is as formidable as
ever. In it he provides you with a wealth of information, which
will enchant not only Tommy's legion of admirers, but also
anyone who enjoys a good read.

<u>Tommy Steele – Reflections,</u>

A Personal Journey.

By Pat Richardson (Secretary of The Official Tommy Steele Society in the UK).

A memoir of her beginnings with Tommy in the late 1950 through to today, wonderful, exciting reading! <u>Dean1942@talktalk.net</u>

<u>Tommy Steele, His Life His Songs</u>

By Derek Mathews 2006

Derek's second book on Tommy Steele

A well researched, highly – detailed, fascinating book, containing more intimate details of Tommy's life up to 2006 than Tommy's own autobiography.

<u>Memories of a Forgotten World: By Tommy Steele</u>

First instalment of Tommy's autobiography published by Michael Joseph.

The book contains memories of his childhood and the start of his life upon the stage concluding at the end of his rock and roll career. Available from the eBay auction site.

# The complete works

# THE TOMMY STEELE DISCOGRAPHY

MORTEN REFF

# The Tommy Steele Discography
# Morten Reff

*Thomas Hicks,* the ever-smiling, open-faced Cockney, was born on December 17, 1936, in Bermondsey, South London. Tommy was the very first rocker coming out of The United Kingdom, as a matter of fact; he was ahead of any other in Europe. His first record "Rock With The Caveman" hit the U.K. charts in October 1956. The song was co-written by Tommy Steele, however, he like so many of the other upcoming rock'n'roll artists in England also had success with American covers, though his best rockers were probably the ones he wrote himself or in collaboration with Michael Pratt and Lionel Bart. Besides being a songwriter and an actor, Tommy is also a novelist, sculptor and painter.

This survey includes his U.K. releases (also some very rare ones) from the early start and up to date. Also the U.S. releases are here, and all the singles and EPs which came out in Denmark, Norway and Sweden, because he was the first rocker to tour these countries, in the autumn of 1957. Also included are records released in France, Germany and several other countries around the world.

Since the early 1990s there have been quite a few CD releases and the ones I know about are here. (Additions are welcome!) In later years there's been plenty of titles like "Music Year 1957", "Top Hits of 1958", "Rock'n'Roll Years", "Hits of the 1950s", "British Hit Parade" etc., etc., many of them containing a Tommy Steele track or more, especially if released in Europe. The most important ones are featured. The CDs are compiled in a separate section.

You will also find sections containing movies, videos and DVDs, and finally Tommy's influence on other artists.

237

I won't go into any serious discussions, but Elton John, Cliff Richard and Paul McCartney have all been honored with a Sir title, so why not Tommy Steele?

However, Tommy did get an honor as early as 1979, when he was given the OBE – Order of British Empire. Without regard to, he should have been Sir Tommy by now.

A special thank you to *Terje Dalene* of Norway, whose help has been very valuable and much appreciated and this 'publication' would have been much the poorer without him. Others who have been of great support are Derek Mathews, Pat Richardson and Fred Rothwell.

*This set up © November 2013*

Morten Reff

**U.K. Singles**

All the 45s carried the prefix 45.  The numbers after the titles are the UK hit positions.

**Rock With The Caveman / Rock Around The Town**  #13
**Decca F-10795 • 1956**
**Elevator Rock / Doomsday Rock**
**Decca F-10808 • 1956**
**Singing The Blues / Rebel Rock**  #1
**Decca F-10819 • 1956**
**Knee Deep In The Blues / Teenage Party**  #15
**Decca F-10849 •   1957**
**Buttefingers / Cannibal Pot**  #8
**Decca F-10877 • 1957**
**Shiralee / Grandad's Rock**  #11
**Decca F-10896 •   1957**
**"All-Star Hit Parade No. 2"**   - Lord's Taverners Record
(*Various artists*)  #15
*Tommy Steele track :* **Butterfly**
**Decca F-10915 • 1957**

*As a 78rpm this came with a Decca art sleeve.  The entire profits from this record were donated to The National Playing Fields Association.  Other artists were Max Bygraves, The Beverly Sisters, The Johnston Brothers, Billy Cotton and Jimmy Young.  Not actually your favourite rock'n'roll stars!*

239

**Water, Water / A Handful Of Songs**  #5
**Decca F-10923 •    1957**
**Hey You! / Plant A Kiss**  #28
**Decca F-10941 •    1957**
**Happy Guitar / Princess**  #20
**Decca F-10976 •    1958**
**Nairobi / Neon Sign**  #3
**Decca F-10991 • 1958**
**The Only Man On The Island / I Puts The Lightie On**  #16
**Decca F-11041 •    1958**

*All the above singles with The Steelmen.*

**It's All Happening / What Do You Do**
**Decca F-11026 • 1958**
**Come On, Let's Go / Put A Ring On her Finger**  #10
**Decca F-11072 • 1958**
**Marriage Type Love / A Lovely Night**  *w/ The Roland Shaw Orchestra*
**Decca F-11089 • 1958**
**Hiawatha / The Trial**
**Decca F-11117 •    1959**
**Tallahassee Lassie / Give! Give! Give!**  #16
**Decca F-11152 • 1959**
**You Were Mine / Young Ideas**
**Decca F-11162 •    1959**
**The Little White Bull / Singing Time**  #6
**Decca F-11177 • 1959**  *(art sleeve)*
   *All the above 45s originally came with triangular-centre, but you can also find them with round-centre which are later pressings.  Decca F-1117 was reissued in 1963 with a square Decca logo on top.*
Note: *A special promo (CP 2100) of "Little White Bull" was released with a spoken intro by Tommy and Pete Murray. Same song on both sides.*
**What a Mouth (What A North And South) / Kookaburra**
#5
**Decca F-11245 •    1960**
   *All the above singles were also released as 78rpm's.*

**Drunken Guitar** *(instr)* / <u>**Light Up The Sky**</u>
**Decca F-11258 • 1960**

Note: *In various discographies this is proclaimed to be unreleased, but a copy turned up on eBay (England) in the summer of 2001. And Terje Dalene (Norway) has a nice original Decca blue label copy (see image below). Accidentally, he also has a demo copy of "Light Up The Sky"(DRF-26762) coupled with "Drunken Guitar"(DRF-27126). So it exists, really!!* (See also the discography from Australia)

UK *rare* Decca single 11258
UK Decca single 10795                          *(Coll. Terje Dalene)*

**Happy-Go-Lucky Blues / (The Girl With The) Long Black Hair**
**Decca F-11275 •     1960**
**Must Be Santa / Boys And Girls**   #40
**Decca F-11299 •     1960**
**My Big Best Shoes / The Dit-Dit Song**
**Decca F-11361 • 1961**
**The Writing On The Wall / Drunken Guitar** *(instr)*   #30
**Decca F-11372 • 1961**
**Hit Record / What A Little Darlin'**
**Decca F-11479 • 1962**
**Butter Wouldn't Melt In Your Mouth / Where Have All The Flowers Gone**
**Decca F-11532 • 1962**
**He's Got Love / Green Eye**
**Decca F-11551 • 1962**
**Flash, Bang, Wallop! / She's Too Far Above Me**
**Decca F-11615 •     1963**

*Note:* Demostration sample records (promos) of Tommy's Decca output, until 1961, were all issued as one-sided demos, some had printed labels and some were handwritten, which means that they were pressed with each song on one side and a blank side.   In that way the radio stations could play the new Tommy Steele record consecutive.   This   at   least continued up to F-11361 which is the last one I have seen as a one-sided. Variations might have happened. Labels were blue. Also take notice that all the demos followed the matrix numbers and not the usual Decca catalogue numbers, "Singing The Blues" DRF.22655 / "Rebel Rock" DRF.22533 (The matrix numbers are the ones that's printed upside down on the original Decca labels.) One interesting thing happened with F-11245 "What A Mouth..." as the B-side was not blank, but had Pat Boone and "Walkin' The Floor Over You" on the orange London promo label.

Another unusual thing occured with the first three one sided demos as they had Tommy's name printed as *Tommy Steel*.

**The Truth About Me**   *Exclusively by Tommy Steele*
**Weekend Mail • 1957**
   *This is a small one-sided 6" 78rpm. record where Tommy tells it all (at the time).   It was presented with Weekend Magazine in April 1957.   See also the CD release, "The Real Steele" from 2009.*

**"No.1 Spanish Romance"**   *Screen test Starring* **Tommy Steele and You**
**Marylin Screen Test  33 1/3rpm  Flexi-disc • 1959**
   *This is a one-sided disc were YOU can read your own part from the script (which actually is the fold out sleeve) and play a love scene with Tommy Steele.  Picture of Tommy on front and on  the flexi-disc itself; a very early picture-disc, so to speak.*

**The Dream Maker / Maximum Plus  w/Marion Ryan**
Columbia DB-7070 *(white label promo)* • 1963
  *From the movie "It's All Happening" w/ John Barry & His Orchestra.  This single is very rare as the B-side was switched when released officially.*
**The Dream maker / Egg And Chips**
Columbia DB-7070 • 1963
  *From the movie "It's All Happening".  w/ John Barry & His Orchestra.*
**Money To Burn / If The Rain's Got To Fall**
Star Sound Studios (London, England) *acetate* • 1967
  ***This particular single is pretty rare as a 45, since the A-side was switched with "Half A Sixpence" before ordinary release.***
**Half A Sixpence / If The Rain's Got To Fall**
RCA Victor  RCA 1654 • 1967
  *From the soundtrack "Half A Sixpence".  The regular issue of this has black label, and the promo has green label.*
RCA Victor  RCA 1654 • 1967
  *From the soundtrack "Half A Sixpence".  The regular issue of this has black label, and the promo has green label.*

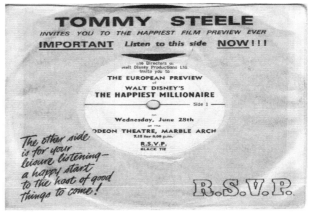

UK Promotional 45   *(Coll. Terje Dalene)*

  *Above is the promo for the European (London) preview of the movie "The Happiest Millionaire".*
Tommy Steele is speaking and inviting the listener to the film preview.  B-side is the recording of
"Fortuosity".   This promo was sent out to special people (V.I.P.) in the business.  Not to be broadcast.
**Fortuosity / I'm A Brass Band Today** *w/picture sleeve*

**Buena Vista DF-457 • 1967**

*The A-side is from the Walt Disney movie "The Happiest Millionaire". Issued also as a white label promo. The B-side, written by Tommy Steele, is available only on this rare single and the same one issued in the USA. The picture sleeve is different from the US one, although both sleeves says* printed in USA.

**Rock With The Caveman / Elevator Rock**
**Decca F 13813 • 1972** *(Blue label- 2 variations)*
**Rock With The Caveman/ Elevator Rock**
**Decca F-13813 • 1973** *(Red label)*
**Singing The Blues / Knee Deep In The Blues**
**Decca F-13814 • 1973** *(Red label)*
**Give! Give! Give! / Doomsday Rock**
**Decca F-13855 • 1973** *(Red label)*
Kings New Clothes / Wonderful Copenhagen
Pye 7N 45393 • 1974 ***w/picture sleeve***

***Both songs are edited versions. This was also issued as a promo.***

**Singing In The Rain / You Are My Lucky Star**
**Safari SAFE-61 (stereo) • 1984** *w/ colour picture sleeve*

*From the Original London Palladium Cast recording.*

**Singing The Blues / Come On, Let's Go**
**Old Gold OG-9536 • 1985**

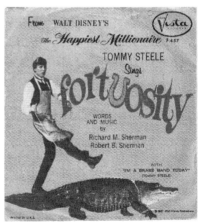

UK single sleeve PYE 7N 45303 (1974)
UK single sleeve Vista F-457 (1967)

The first pressings of the EPs had triangular centres (except the last two DFE-6607 & 6660 which only came with round centres), later pressings had round centres.

**"YOUNG LOVE"**
Decca DFE 6388 • 1957
**Young Love / Doomsday Rock / Wedding Bells / Rock With The Caveman.**
*The latter two songs are taken from the Decca LP LF-1287 "Tommy Steele Stage Show"*
**"SINGING THE BLUES"**
**Decca DFE 6389** • 1957
Singing The Blues / Rebel Rock / Knee Deep In The Blues / Elevator Rock.
**"THE TOMMY STEELE STORY No. 1"**
**Decca DFE 6398** • **1957**
Take Me Back Baby / Water, Water / Will It Be You? / Build Up.
**"TOPS IN POPS, No.1"** *Various*
**Decca DFE 6411** • **1957**
*Tommy Steele track:* Butterfingers
**"THE TOMMY STEELE STORY No. 2"**
**Decca DFE 6424** • **1957**
A Handful Of Songs / Cannibal Pot / Time To Kill / You Gotta Go.
**"THE DUKE WORE JEANS"** *Soundtrack*
**Decca DFE 6472** • **1958**
Photograph *-duet w/June Laverick* / Hair-Down, Hoe-Down / Princess / Happy Guitar.
**"TOMMY STEELE"** *(Also known as "Come On, Let's Go")*
**Decca DFE 6551** • **1958**
Come On, Let's Go / Put A Ring On Her Finger / The Only Man On The Island / Number Twenty-Two Across The Way.

**"TOPS IN POPS, No.7"**
**Decca DFE 6583** • **1959**
*Tommy Steele track:* Hiawatha.
**"TOMMY"** *(Also known as "Sweet Georgia Brown")*
**Decca DFE 6592** • **1959**
I'm A Little Blackbird / Georgia On My Mind / Sweet Georgia Brown / Mandy, Make Up Your Mind.

**"TOMMY THE TOREADOR"** *Soundtrack*
**Decca DFE 6607 • 1959**
Tommy The Toreador / Take A Ride / Where's The Birdie w/*Sidney James & Bernard Cribbens* / Little White Bull / Singing Time / Amanda.

**"WHAT A MOUTH !"** *w/Harry Robinson and his Orchestra*
**Decca DFE 6660 • 1960**
What A Mouth (What A North And South) / Kookaburra / Hollerin' And Screamin' / Little Darlin'.

*See also Decca LP LK-4351 .*

| UK EP Decca 6388 | UK EP Decca 6660 |
|---|---|

In the UK special EP Charts first appeared in March 1960 and continued up to December 1967. Music Mentor Books, York, England published in September 2001 a very comprehensive book titled "35 Years of British Hit EPs". The book includes chart data of EPs making the Top EP charts and single charts from 1955-1989. To my surprise only one Tommy Steele EP ever made the charts, **"Tommy The Toreador"** Decca DFE-6607, which entered the charts on 12 March, 1960, went to #4 and stayed for 10 weeks. On 28 May it made its first re-entry, reaching #15 – 2 weeks, again 2 July, #17 – 1 week, again 16 July, #13 – 1 week, and finally 13 August, #15 – 1 week.

## "IT'S TIME FOR TOMMY STEELE" *(Picture cover)*
Diamond DR3005 (33-1/3 rpm) • *unknown year*
Tallahassee Lassie / Come On, Let's Go / Give! Give! Give! /
Rock With The Caveman / Elevator Rock / Rebel Rock
    *The cover has liner notes in English, looks great and not like the bootlegs we are used to. Don't know the origin of this record or year of release.*

UK bootleg EP Diamond 3005    Bootleg 45 with US single
RCA Victor 47-9458
    I was fooled buying a single on RCA Victor 45-9458 (US single) with a picture sleeve that I thought was from West Germany. A 1963 single with a picture sleeve from 1957 looked pretty suspicious but you never know. It turned out to be homemade. On eBay it looked very professional but I saw it right away when I got it that it was a fake. It's the same front cover as the Swedish EP Decca 6389 but with the titles switched. *(See picture.)* I bought it from Germany but it could have been made anywhere.

### U.K. LPs

## "TOMMY STEELE STAGE SHOW" (10") Decca LF 1287 • 1957
Giddy-Up A Ding Dong / Treasure Of Love / Honky-Tonk Blues / Razzle-Dazzle / Kaw-Liga / Teenage Party / Wedding Bells / What Is This Thing Called Love / On The Move / Rock With The Caveman
***Reissued in 1981 in its original form. See also the CD section for a double feature from 2008.***
## "THE TOMMY STEELE STORY" (10")

**Decca  LF 1288 • 1957**
Take Me Back Baby / <u>Butterfingers</u> / I Like / <u>A Handful Of Songs</u> / You Gotta Go / Water, Water / Cannibal Pot / Will It Be You / Two Eyes / Build Up / Time To Kill / Elevator Rock / Doomsday Rock / <u>Teenage Party</u>

*The underlined titles are different versions than the ones released on singles and EPs.  Also released in USA on London LL-1770 (12") as "Rock Aorund The World".  Reissued in 1981 in its original form.*
***See also the CD section for a double feature from 2008.***
<u>**"STARS OF THE SIX-FIVE SPECIAL"**</u>  (10")  *Various*
Decca LF 1299 • 1957
***Tommy Steele tracks :* Swaller Tail Coat / Singing The Blues**

*Also featuring tracks by Lonnie Donegan, Terry Dene, The Bob Cort Skiffle, Wee Willie Harris, George Melly, Chris Barber's Jazz Band and The Worried Men.  See also "40 Years Of Television" BBC Records and Tapes REB 252, Compilation Album (1976)*
**"THE DUKE WORE JEANS"  (10")  *Soundtrack***
Decca LF 1308 • 1958
It's All Happening / What Do You Do / Family Tree / Happy Guitar / Hair-Down, Hoe-Down / Princess / Photograph / Thanks A Lot.
<u>**"CINDERELLA"**</u>   *Various artists from the Musical*
Decca LK 4303 **(mono)** SKL 4050 **(stereo)** • 1959
Overture / In My Own Little Corner / <u>A Very Special Day</u> / Do I Love You Because You're Beautiful? / The prince Is Giving A Ball / <u>Marriage Type Love</u> / Stepsisters' Lament / Your Majesties, A List of The Bare Necessities / <u>When You're Driving Through The Moonlight - A Lovely Night</u> / A Lovely Night / Impossible / No Other Love / Ten Minutes Ago / <u>You And Me</u> / <u>Finale</u>

*The underlined titles are featuring Tommy Steele. Music and lyrics by Richard Rodgers & Oscar Hammerstein, except "You And Me" by Tommy Steele.  Album reissued in 1983 on That's Entertainment Records TER-1045.  Also reissued in 2002 on Bayview Records CD RBNW-018.*
<u>**"HAIL VARIETY"**</u>   *Various*
Oriole MG. 20033 • 1959
***Tommy Steele track:* Rock With The Caveman  *(original Decca recording)***
*No picture of Tommy on the cover.*

## "GET HAPPY WITH TOMMY"
Decca LK 4351 • 1960

*Medley:* Hollerin' And Screamin'- Lonesome Traveller / A Handful Of Songs / Nairobi / Little Darlin' / Old Obadiah / What A Mouth (What A North And South) / Shiralee / Kookaburra / Tommy The Toreador / Shout / So Long

*This was recorded in the Decca studios with a number of fortunate fans present. Orchestra conducted by Harry Robinson. Also released in USA on London LL-3180 (mono) / PS-201(stereo). As far as we know this was not available in stereo in UK.*

## "HALF A SIXPENCE" *Original London Cast recording*
Decca LK/SKL 4521 • 1963

Overture / All In The Cause Of Economy / Half A Sixpence / Money To Burn / Oak And The Ash / She's Too Far Above Me / I'm Not Talking To You / If The Rain's Got To Fall / Flash, Bang, Wallop! / I Know What I Am / I'll Build A Palace-I Only Want A Little House / Finale

*Tommy is featured on all tracks except "The Oak And The Ash" and "I Know What I Am". This is not the same as the Broadway Cast issued in USA on RCA LSO-1110 in 1965. See also UK reissue in 1983, That's Entertainment Records TER-1041.*

## "IT'S ALL HAPPENING" *Original Soundtrack*
Columbia 33SX1537 **(mono)** SCX 3486 **(stereo)** • 1963

Overture / Wind And The Rain / <u>Dream Maker</u> / Meeting You / Casbah / <u>Maximum Plus</u> / Somebody Else, Not Me / That's Livin', That's Lovin' / Flamenco / <u>Egg And Chips</u> / Day Without You / The George Mitchell Show –*Medley* / *Finale* - <u>The Dream Maker</u>

*The underlined titles are performed by Tommy. Tracks by Shane Fenton, Russ Conway, John Barry, Danny Williams a.o. This movie was also shown in the USA but then the title was changed to "The Dream Maker". Although, I have never seen a US LP release of this.*

## "SO THIS IS BROADWAY"
Columbia 33SX1674 **(mono)** SCX 3536 **(stereo)** • 1964

Something's Coming / Hey There! / If I Were A Bell / Hey Look Me Over / The Girl That I Marry / Too Close For Comfort / Everything's Coming Up Roses / I Talk To The Trees / I Wish I Were In Love Again / Happy Talk / They Say It's Wonderful / There Once Was A Man

*Reissued in 1967 on World Records TP-610, different cover and updated liner notes. Have also seen this as a reel-to-reel tape TT-610. Reissued again in 1972 on EMI One-Up OU-2066, different cover and updated liner notes. The album first came out in USA titled "Everything's Coming Up Broadway" Liberty LRP-3426 / LST-7426. Different liner notes.*

**"HALF A SIXPENCE"** *Original Motion Picture Soundtrack*
**RCA Victor RB-6735** (mono) **SB-6735** (stereo) • **1967**

Overture / All In The Cause Of Economy / Half A Sixpence / Money To Burn / I Don't Believe A Word Of It– I'm Not Talking To You / A Proper Gentleman / She's Too Far Above Me / If The Rain's Got To Fall / Lady Botting's Boating Regatta Cup Racing Song (The Race Is On) / Entr'acte – Flash, Bang, Wallop! / I Know What I Am / This Is My World / Half A Sixpence (reprise) – Flash, Bang, Wallop! (reprise)

*Tommy is featured on all songs, except "Overture" and "I Know What I Am". Featuring a fold-out cover with photos from the movie. Original album issued in USA with a different cover. See also the US disco for an Open End Interview album with Tommy.*

**"THE HAPPIEST MILLIONAIRE"** *Original Cast Soundtrack*
Buena Vista BV 5001 **(mono)** BVS 5001 **(stereo)** • 1967
Overture / <u>Fortuosity</u> / What's Wrong With That / Watch Your Footwork / Valentine Candy / Strenghten The Dwelling / <u>I'll Always Be Irish</u> / Bye-Yum Pum Pum / Are We Dancing / I Believe In This Country / Detroit / When A man Has A Daughter / <u>There Are Those</u> / <u>Let's Have A Drink On It</u> / <u>Finale</u>

*The underlined titles are performed by Tommy. A Walt Disney film Production. Original album released in USA on Buena Vista BV/BVS-5001 with a <u>fold-out cover</u>.*

**"FINIAN'S RAINBOW"** *Original Motion Picture Soundtrack*
Warner Brothers WF 2550 • 1968
Prelude (Main Title) / This Time Of The Year / How Are Things In Glocca Morra? / Look To The Rainbow / If This Isn't Love / <u>Something Sort Of Grandish</u> / That Great Come-And-Get-It-Day / Old Devil Moon / When The Idle Poor Become The Idle Rich / <u>When I'm Not Near The Girl I Love</u> / Necessity / Rain Dance Ballet / The Begat / <u>How Are Things In Glocca Morra?</u> (Finale)

*The underlined titles are featuring Tommy Steele. Starring Fred Astaire and Petula Clark. (See also the CD section).*

**"WHERE'S JACK?"** *Original Score Soundtrack*

**Paramount SPFL-254 • 1969** *Tommy Steele only acts in the movie, no singing. The music is performed by Mary Hopkin and Danny Doyle. Picture of Tommy, Stanley Baker and Fiona Lewis on cover.*

**"THE HAPPY WORLD OF TOMMY STEELE"**
Decca PA 24 **(mono)** SPA 24 **(stereo)** • 1969
Nairobi / A Handful Of Songs / Little White Bull / Flash, Band, Wallop! / Rock With The Caveman / The Only Man On The Island / What A Mouth (What A North And South) / Singing The Blues / Marriage Type Love / Hit Record / Shiralee / Sweet Georgia Brown

**"THE WORLD OF TOMMY STEELE Vol. 2"**
**Decca SPA 137 • 1971**
Hiawatha / It's All Happening / Kaw-Liga / Young Love / The Writing On The Wall / Happy Guitar / Come On, Let's Go / Green Eye / Wishing Star / Butterfingers / Young Ideas / She's Too Far Above Me

**"MY LIFE, MY SONG"**
**Pye TS 101 • 1974**
*The album is divided into 12 chapters:*
My Life, My Song / Conceived / War / Youngest Love / Work / Adventure / Revolution / Ambition / Wilderness / Marriage / Fatherhood / Hope

*Fold-out cover containing several sheets of lyrics and paintings by Tommy. All songs written and composed by Tommy Steele. Album produced by George Martin.*

**"TOMMY STEELE'S 40 FAVOURITES"**
Arcade ADE P14 • 1974
*Side A:* Medley #1: Consider Yourself - Get Me To The Church On Time – I'm Henry The Eighth I Am – Knees Up Mother Brown – Roll Out The Barrel. Medley #2: Singing In The Rain – Ramblin' Rose – Tiptoe Through The Tulips – When The Red Red Robin – On A Slow Boat To China. Medley #3: Carolina In The Morning – My Mammy – April Showers – Is It True What They Say About Dixie – Baby Face. Medley #4: Que Sera, Sera – Cruising Down The River – Wonderful Copenhagen – Tulips From Amsterdam – Delilah.
*Side B:* Medley #1: You Made Me Love You – On Mother Kelly's Doorstep – I'll Be With You In Apple Blossom Time – In A shanty In Old Shanty Town – Underneath The Arches. Medley #2: I Wonder Who's Kissing Her Now – Hey Good Looking – Sunny Side Of The Street – Zip A Dee Doo Dah – When You're Smiling. Medley #3: For Me And

My Gal – You Are My Lucky Star – You Must Have Been A Bautiful Baby – Oh You Beautiful Doll.  Medley #4: Boiled Beef And Carrots – Any Old Iron – Wotcher – My Old Man's A Dustman – Don't Dilly Dally On The Way – I've Got A Lovely Bunch Of Coconuts

**"HANS ANDERSEN"**    *Original London Palladium Cast recording*

**Pye NSPL-18451    • 1974**

Overture / <u>This Town</u> / Thumbelina / Truly Loved / <u>For Hans Tonight</u> / Jenny Kissed Me / Inchworm / Ecclesiastious (I Can Spell) / Wonderful Copenhagen / Anywhere I Wander / I'm Hans Christian Andersen / The Ugly Duckling / No Two People / The King's New Clothes / Anywhere I Wander *(reprise). (15 tracks)*

   *Recorded in London on December 8, 1974.  Produced by Harold Fielding.  This is the original London Cast recording.  See also the years 1977 (PYE PRT-8080) and 1978 (Pye NSPL-18551).  The two underlined titles above are not on these two releases.*

**"HANS ANDERSEN**"   *London Palladium production*

PYE PRT-8080 • 1977

Overture / Thumbelina / *Dare To Take A Chance* / Truly Loved / *Dare To Take A Chance  -reprise* / Jenny Kissed Me / Inchworm /    Ecclesiastious (I Can Spell) / Anywhere I Wander / Wonderful Copenhagen / I'm Hans Christian Andersen / *Happy Days* / *Have I Stayed Away Too Long* / The Ugly Duckling / No Two People / The King's New Clothes / Anywhere I Wander –*reprise*   *(17 tracks)*

   *Recorded in London on December 8, 1974 and December 11, 1977.  This differs slightly from the 1974 release of the Palladium production.  The underlined titles are new to this release.*

**"FOCUS ON TOMMY STEELE"**  (2-LP set)

Decca FOS 21/22 • 1977

*LP 1:* A Handful Of Songs / Rock With The Caveman / Elevator Rock / Nairobi / Happy Guitar / Shiralee / Young Love / Singing The Blues / Water, Water / Razzle Dazzle / The Only Man On The Island / Sweet Georgia brown / Marriage Type Love / Kaw-Liga

*LP 2:* Little White Bull / Butterfingers / Rebel Rock / Gerogia On My Mind / Cannibal Pot / Kookaburra / Knee Deep In The Blues / Flash, Bang, Wallop! / Where Have All The Flowers Gone / Giddy-Up A Ding Dong / Hiawatha / Come

On, Let's Go / She's Too Far Above Me / What A Mouth (What A North And South)

*There is also a pink promo label of this album-set, a factory sample with FOS 21 and FOS 22 stamped on each label side. No Decca, artist name or titles printed on the labels.*


**"HANS ANDERSEN"**  *London Palladium production*
Pye NSPL-18551     • 1978

*Same tracks as the 1977 PYE PRT-8080 album above. Different cover.*

**"TOMMY STEELE'S FAMILY ALBUM"**
Ronco RTD 2041 • 1979
A Handful Of Songs / Matchstalk Men And Matchstalk Cats And Dogs / Flash, Bang, Wallop! / Sometimes When We Touch / High Hopes / The Runaway Train / Bridge Over Troubled Water / Singing In the Rain / Bright Eyes / Wonderful Copenhagen / Windmills In Old Amsterdam / Half A Sixpence / What A Mouth (What A North And South) / Sweet Caroline / King Of The Road / Little White Bull / Singing The Blues / Puff (The Magic Dragon) / When I'm 64 / Superbird

*20 Golden Family Favourite songs on one album. It has a fold-out cover with many family pictures. Several of these songs are often performed by Tommy on stage.*

**"LIVE AT THE FESTIVAL"** OAKS Oaks-1001 • 1979
Tommy Baby / I'm A Song / A Handful Of Songs / Flash, Bang, Wallop! / Bridge Over Troubled Water / Little White Bull / Rock On / Johnny B. Goode / Sweet Caroline / Rock With The Caveman / Nairobi / Water, Water / Happy Guitar / Butterfingers / Singing The Blues / Hey Jude / Maybe It's Because I'm A Londoner

*This is the only live album by Tommy in more recent years. Unfortunately the liner notes on this album don't tell us when the album was recorded, or exactly where. However, everything points at that this was recorded in 1977 at The Festival Theatre, Paignton, where Tommy did his show from July 15 until September 24, 1977.*

**"TOMMY STEELE STAGE SHOW"**   (10")
Decca LFT 1287     • 1981     *Reissue of original album from 1957.*

**"THE TOMMY STEELE STORY"** **(10")**
Decca LFT 1288 • 1981       *Reissue of original album from 1957.*

 **"20 GREATEST HITS**" SPOT Records SPR 8531 • 1983
Singing The Blues / Rock With The Caveman / Butterfingers / Come On, Let's Go / Water, Water / The Only Man On The Island / Marriage Type Love / **Light Up The Sky** / Elevator Rock / Little White Bull / A Handful Of Songs / It's All Happening / Happy Guitar / Shiralee / Knee Deep In The Blues / Nairobi / Tallahassee Lassie / She's Too Far Above Me / What A Mouth (What A North And South / Flash, Bang, Wallop!

*As far as I know, this LP is the only place you can actually find the song "**Light Up The Sky**" featured on an album, except for the two rare single releases from the UK and Australia.*


**"HALF A SIXPENCE**"   *Original London Cast recording*
That's Entertainment Records TER-1041 **(stereo)** • 1983
*Reissue of original Decca SKL-4521 from 1963, same cover.*


**"CINDERELLA**"   *Various artists from the Musical*
That's Entertainment Records TER-1045 • 1983
*Reissue of original Decca SKL-4050 album from 1959. Same cover.*

**"SINGIN' IN THE RAIN"**   *Original London Cast recording*
Safari RAIN 1 • 1984
**Overture** / Fit As A Fiddle / Temptation / **I Can't Give You Anything But Love** / **Be A Clown** / Too Marvellous For Words / You Are My Lucky Star / Moses Supposes / Good Morning / Singin' In The Rain / **Would You?** / Fascinating Rhythm / Finale

*First performance at the London Palladium, June 30, 1983. The above album recorded in London at EMI Studios on 20-21 February, 1984. The four titles in bold letterings are **not** featuring Tommy Steele. Nice fold-out cover with many colour pictures.*

**"HANS ANDERSEN**"   *Original London production*
Flashback FBLP-8080 • 1985
***Same as the Pye PRT-8080*** *album from 1977 and Pye NSPL-18551 from 1978. Different cover.*

## "THE ROCK'N'ROLL YEARS"

See For Miles SEE-203 • 1987
Rock With The Caveman / Come On, Let's Go / Butterfly / Give! Give! Give! / Elevator Rock / Rebel Rock / You Gotta Go / Build Up / Put A Ring On Her Finger / You Were Mine / Swaller Tail Coat / Singing The Blues –*live 1957* / Singing The Blues –*studio 1956* / Doomsday Rock / Knee Deep In the Blues / Two Eyes / Take Me Back Baby / The Writing On The Wall / Hey You! / Teenage Party / Plant A Kiss / Rock Around The Town / Drunken Guitar *(instr)* / Tallahassee Lassie

*It is strange that so many compilers often ignore one of Tommy's best rockers, "Hair-Down, Hoe-Down". And where is "Happy Guitar"? Anyway, great cover and good extensive liner notes.*

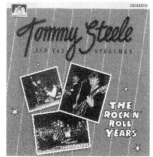

**UK LP "Rock'n'Roll Years" 1987**

## "HALF A SIXPENCE"    *Original Broadway Cast recording*
Deram LP 820 589-1 • 1988
*Same tracks as the US album release on RCA Victor 1110 from 1965.*

## "REBEL ROCK"    (2-LP set)
Pickwick Ditto DTO-10287 • *unknown year*
*LP 1:* Rock With The Caveman / Shout! / Nairobi / It's All Happening / Put A Ring On Her Finger / Butterfingers / Come On, Let's Go / Razzle Dazzle / Hey You! / Young Love / Grandad's Rock / Knee Deep In The Blues
*LP 2:* Singing The Blues / Boys And Girls / Little Darlin' / Doomsday Rock / Hollerin' And Screamin' / Rock Around The Town / Water, Water / Teenage Party / Happy Guitar / Rebel Rock / Elevator Rock / Shiralee

## "THE VERY BEST OF TOMMY STEELE"

Carlton (Pickwick) PWKM-4071 P ● 1991

Nairobi / Tallahassee Lassie / Kookaburra / Flash, Bang Wallop! / She's Too Far Above Me / Happy Guitar / Young Love / Butterfingers / Green Eye / Where Have All The Flowers Gone / A Handful Of Songs / Marriage Type Love / Georgia On My Mind / Come On, Let's Go / Sweet Georgia Brown / It's All Happening / Only Man On The Island / Princess / Writing On The Wall / What A Mouth (What A North And South)

*In 1991 they usually released LP and CD simultaneously, however, the catalog number above is for the CD as I have never seen any LP set of this.*

**Please turn to the CD section to follow Tommy's releases into the '90s and the next century.**

### BBC RADIO Programmes

In 1964 and 1965 Tommy had a series of shows recorded for the BBC.  LPs with one show on each side were made by the BBC Transcription Service for use on various radio stations throughout the country. The first show went out on the 5th January 1964. Tommy was supported by 'The Raindrops,' The Johnnie Spence Orchestra' and Jackie Lee. The series were recorded in front of a live audience. In all 'The Tommy Steele Show' ran for nineteen programmes, each show of twenty- seven minutes making nine hours of programmes over three months of 1964 and two months of 1965.

The contents of the following shows are right from Tommy's master recording from the producer of the radio stations in England including dates of the shows sent out on the air.  If necessary, the number sequence of the shows can have been changed before transmitting.  The songs in Italics are the ones performed by Tommy, however, this only applies to the first five shows as I haven't heard the rest.

Thanks to *Derek Mathews* for individual help in this section.

### *BBC Transcription Service*

113006   **"THE TOMMY STEELE SHOW - 1"**   27 minutes 5 Jan 1964  (Expiry date 30.9.67)

Featuring **Tommy Steele**, The Raindrops incl. Jackie Lee, Johnnie Spence & His Orchestra.

Short signature Fanfare based on 'Singing The Blues' / **Come On In** / **I'm All Right** / A New Kind Of Love / Cherokee / **The Ugly Duckling /** Down Our Street / **What A Mouth (What A North And South) /** My Colouring Book / **Comedy /** *Medley:* Hit The Road Jack - **Take These Chains From My Heart – What'd I Say** / Closing Signature 'Thanks A Lot'.

113007 **"THE TOMMY STEELE SHOW - 2"** 27 minutes 12 Jan 1964 (Expiry date 30.9.67)

Featuring **Tommy Steele**, The Raindrops incl. Jackie Lee, Johnnie Spence & His Orchestra.

Good Morning / Comedy / Early In The Morning / Teach Me Tonight / C-Jam Blues / Puff (The Magic Dragon) / short Comedy / I Only Want To Be With You / Beep Beep / When Sunny Gets Blue / Comedy / Little Liza Jane / Closing Signature 'Thanks A Lot'.


113008 **"THE TOMMY STEELE SHOW - 3"** 27 minutes 26 Jan 1964 (Expiry date 30.9.67)

Featuring **Tommy Steele**, The Raindrops incl. Jackie Lee, Johnnie Spence & His Orchestra. Len Beadle

Short signature Fanfare based on 'Singing The Blues' / Goody Goody / Money / When I see an Elephant Fly / Fantail / King's New Clothes / Swinging on a Star / If You Like Beetroot / Small World / Fire Down Below / Closing Signature 'Thanks A Lot'.

113009 **"THE TOMMY STEELE SHOW - 4"** 27 minutes 2 Feb 1964 (Expiry date 30.9.67)

Featuring **Tommy Steele**, The Raindrops incl. Jackie Lee, Johnnie Spence & His Orchestra. Len Beadle

Short signature Fanfare based on 'Singing The Blues' / **My Big Best Shoes / Green, Green /** Baubles, Bangles, And Beads / Woodchoppers Ball / **Give A Little Whistle /** Twenty-Four Hours from Tulsa / **Hit Record /** If You Love Me / **For My Good Fortune** / Closing Signature 'Thanks A Lot'.

113010 **"THE TOMMY STEELE SHOW - 5"** 27 minutes 9 Feb 1964 (Expiry date 30.9.67)

Featuring **Tommy Steele**, The Raindrops incl. Jackie Lee, Johnnie Spence & His Orchestra. Len Beadle

Short signature Fanfare based on 'Singing The Blues'/ **Sitting On Top Of The World / Come On, Let's Go** / Lazy Bones / Perdido / **The Little White Duck** / I Think Of You / **Messing About On The River** / My Special Dream / One O'Clock Jump / **That's Right** / Thanks A Lot.

113011 **"THE TOMMY STEELE SHOW - 6"** 27 minutes 15 Feb 1964 (Expiry date 30.9.67)
Featuring **Tommy Steele**, The Raindrops incl. Jackie Lee, Johnnie Spence & His Orchestra. Len Beadle
Short signature Fanfare based on "Singing The Blues" / Zip A Dee Do Da / Acapulco 1922 / Sunset Strip / Hallelujah Gathering / Candy Man / High Hopes / Candy Man / Tychee Fair/Sunday / Instrumental / Lonesome Traveller / Thanks A Lot.
113012 **"THE TOMMY STEELE SHOW - 7"** 27 minutes 23 Feb 1964 (Expiry date 30.9.67)
Featuring **Tommy Steele**, The Raindrops incl. Jackie Lee, Johnnie Spence & His Orchestra. Len Beadle
Short signature Fanfare based on 'Singing The Blues'/ When You're Smiling / Hallelujah I Love Her So /They Can't Take That Away From Me / Intermission Rift / There's A Tiny House / I'm The One / I'm The One / Busted / Anyone Who Had A Heart /Yes Indeed /Thanks A Lot.
113013 **"THE TOMMY STEELE SHOW - 8"** 27 minutes 1 March 1964 (Expiry date 30.9.67)
Featuring **Tommy Steele**, The Raindrops incl. Jackie Lee, Johnnie Spence & His Orchestra. Len Beadle.
Short signature Fanfare based on 'Singing The Blues'/ Alright You Win / This Little
Girl of Mine / The Square on the Hypotenuse / Hoe Down / Popo the Puppet /You Don't Know / I put The Lightie On / There's A Place For Us / Lonesome Road / Thanks A Lot.
113014 **"THE TOMMY STEELE SHOW - 9"** 27 minutes 8 March 1964 (Expiry date 30.9.67)
Featuring **Tommy Steele**, The Raindrops incl. Jackie Lee, Johnnie Spence & His Orchestra.
Short signature Fanfare based on 'Singing The Blues' / The Start of Something Big / Rave On /You Make Me Feel So Young / Moaning / Inchworm / Over You/ I Could Write A Book / Down By The Riverside / Thanks A Lot.
113015 **"THE TOMMY STEELE SHOW - 10"** 27 minutes 15 March 1964 (Expiry date 30.9.67)
Featuring **Tommy Steele**, The Raindrops incl. Jackie Lee, Johnnie Spence & His Orchestra.
Short signature Fanfare based on 'Singing The Blues'/ An Awful Lot Of Coffee In Brazil / Shout Shout / Old New York/ Sugar Beat/ I Taut I Saw A Puddy Cat/ South Town USA / Point of No Return / No Regrets / Personality / Thanks A Lot.

113016 **"THE TOMMY STEELE SHOW -11"** 27 minutes 22 March 1964 (Expiry date 30.9.67)
Featuring **Tommy Steele**, The Raindrops incl. Jackie Lee, Johnnie Spence & His Orchestra.
Short signature Fanfare based on 'Singing The Blues'/ Let's Get Away From It All / Alright / To Be Worthy Of You / Kareba / Dream Maker / Little Children / Things / As Long As He Needs Me / Dem Bones/ Thanks a Lot.

113017 **"THE TOMMY STEELE SHOW - 12"** 27 minutes 29 March 1964 (Expiry date 30.9.67)
Featuring **Tommy Steele**, The Raindrops incl. Jackie Lee, Johnnie Spence & His Orchestra.
Short signature Fanfare based on 'Singing The Blues'/ Good Morning / Early In The Morning / Candy Man / Fantail / Kings New Clothes / Come on Dream / What A Mouth (What A North And South) / Anyone Who Had A Heart / What'd I Say / Thanks A Lot.

113018 **"THE TOMMY STEELE SHOW - 1"** 27 minutes 3 Jan 1965 (Expiry date 30.9.67)
Featuring **Tommy Steele**, The Raindrops incl. Jackie Lee, Johnnie Spence & His Orchestra.
Short signature Fanfare based on 'Singing The Blues'/ Sitting On Top Of The World / Early In The Morning / Gal In Calico / June Is Busting Out All Over / Puff The Magic Dragon / I've Fallen In Love With A Snowman / Beep Beep / Somewhere / Lonesome Road / Thanks A Lot .

113019 **"THE TOMMY STEELE SHOW - 2"** 27 minutes 10 Jan 1965 (Expiry date 30.9.67)
Featuring **Tommy Steele**, The Raindrops incl. Jackie Lee, Johnnie Spence & His Orchestra.
Short signature Fanfare based on 'Singing The Blues' / Zip a Dee Doo Dah / Sing Halleluiah / Tangerine / Ugly Duckling / Real Live Girl / What A Mouth (What A North And South) / Like A Child / Lonesome Traveller / Thanks A Lot.

113020 **"THE TOMMY STEELE SHOW - 3"** 27 minutes 17 Jan 1965 (Expiry date 30.9.67)
Featuring **Tommy Steele**, The Raindrops incl. Jackie Lee, Johnnie Spence & His Orchestra.
Short signature Fanfare based on 'Singing The Blues'/ Hey Look Me Over / Happy Talk / Take A Message To Martha / Creve / Inch Worm / Messing About On The River / Tax Inspector Sketch / My Colouring Book / Five Down Below / Thanks A Lot.

113021 **"THE TOMMY STEELE SHOW - 4"** 27 minutes 27 Jan 1965 (Expiry date 30.9.67)

Featuring **Tommy Steele**, The Raindrops incl. Jackie Lee, Johnnie Spence & His Orchestra.

Short signature Fanfare based on 'Singing The Blues'/ Hallelujah I Love Her So / Arthur Honeybell sketch / One O'clock Jump / Give A Little Whistle / Yeah Yeah / I Wish I were In Love Again / But Now / Everything's Coming Up Roses /Thank A Lot.

113022 **"THE TOMMY STEELE SHOW - 5"** 27 minutes 31 Jan 1965 (Expiry date 30.9.67)

Featuring **Tommy Steele**, The Raindrops incl. Jackie Lee, Johnnie Spence & His Orchestra.

Short signature Fanfare based on 'Singing The Blues'/ This Could Be The Start Of Something New / I Think Your Wonderful / Thud Ville / Little White Duck / I'd Rather Be Rich / High Hopes / There Once Was A Man / Thanks A Lot.

113023 **"THE TOMMY STEELE SHOW - 6"** 27 minutes 7 Feb 1965 (Expiry date 30.9.67)

Featuring **Tommy Steele**, The Raindrops incl. Jackie Lee, Johnnie Spence & His Orchestra.

Short signature Fanfare based on 'Singing The Blues' / An Awful Lot Of Coffee In Brazil / Lullaby Of Broadway / Fantail / Surrey With The Fringe On Top / When I Grow Up To Be A Man / A Taste Of Honey / To Close For Comfort /Thank A Lot.

113024 **"THE TOMMY STEELE SHOW -7"** 27 minutes 14 Feb 1965 (Expiry date 30.9.67)

Featuring **Tommy Steele**, The Raindrops incl. Jackie Lee, Johnnie Spence & His Orchestra.

Short signature Fanfare based on 'Singing The Blues' / Alright You Win / Baubles Bangles And Beads / Sugar Beet / Kings New Clothes / Didn't It Rain / Changing The Guard At Buckingham Palace / I Cry Alone/ Little Lisa Jane / Thanks A Lot.

UK Radio LP – Show

UK Decca Promo F-11245                    *(Coll. Terje Dalene)*

## VARIOUS ARTISTS (LPs)

This survey include all countries containing albums featuring Tommy Steele recordings. This is probably quite unsufficient and is not ment to be complete.

**"MUSIC FOR HAND JIVING"** (USA)
**London LL-3034 • 1958**
*Tommy Steele track:* Swaller Tail Coat
*A pretty rare album. Compilation of English artists varying from the Worried Men, Terry Dene, the Blue Jeans, the Baron to the Graham Stewart Seven, the Bob Cort Skiffle and the Four Jacks.*
**"WALT DISNEY HAPPIEST SONGS"** (USA)
**Disneyland LP DL-3509 • 1967**
*Tommy Steele track:* Fortuosity
*(A Gulf Oil promotion)* From The Happiest Millionaire.
**"WALT DISNEY'S WUNDERLAND"** (West Germany)
**Hör Zu Records SHEL-56 • late '60s**
*Tommy Steele track:* Fortuosity

*("Music Für Grosse und Kleine Leute")* From The Happiest Millionaire.

**"THEY CALLED IT ROCK'N'ROLL"** (UK)
**Decca LP DTA-3087 • 1970s**
*Tommy Steele tracks:* Rock With The Caveman / Singing The Blues / Rebel Rock / Elevator Rock

*A compilation covering a variety of British rockn'n'roll artists.*

**"THEY CALLED IT ROCK'N'ROLL"** (West Germany)
**Decca 6.28526 DP • 1970s**
*Tommy Steele tracks:* Rock With The Caveman / Singing The Blues / Rebel Rock / Elevator Rock

*A compilation covering a variety of British rockn'n'roll artists.*

**"GOLDEN DECADE 1960-61"**
**Decca SPA-477 • 1971**
*Tommy Steele track:* What A Mouth (What A North And South)

Also featuring artists like Ken Dodd, Joe Brown, Max Bygraves, Julie Andrews, Billy Fury etc... 12 tracks.

**"The GOLDEN ERA OF HITS Vol. 2"** (2-LP set) (West Germany)
**Decca LP DS-3158/1-2 • 1973**
*Tommy Steele track:* Put A Ring On Her Finger


**"The GOLDEN ERA OF HITS – 2nd Edition"** (2-LP set) (West Germany) Decca LP DS-3257/1-2 • 1974
*Tommy Steele track:* Tallahassie Lassie

**"ROOTS OF BRITISH ROCK"** (2-LP set) (USA)
**Sire SASH-3711-2 • 1975**
*Tommy Steele track:* Singing The Blues

This is actually a very good compilation containing the best from the '50s and early '60s, but roots of British rock? Among the other artists are: Lonnie Donegan, Emile Ford, Laurie London, Petula Clark, Helen Shapiro, Kenny Ball, Acker Bilk, Johnny Kidd, Jet Harris, Cliff Richard, The Shadows, Mike Berry, Eden Kane and many more. Kenny Ball, Acker Bilk, Laurie London, they were hit artists in England, but far from rock'n'roll. Where's Don Lang & His Frantic Five, Wee Willie Harris, Tony Crombie & His Rockets etc. That's rock'n'roll ! "Singing The Blues" was Tommy's biggest hit in UK..

*This double-LP bubbled under in the US album charts, reaching #205 and stayed for only 1 week.*

**"SIX-FIVE SPECIAL- 40 Years Of Television"** (UK)
**BBC Records LP REB-252 • 1976**
*Tommy Steele Track:* Singing The Blues  *(Original Decca studio recording)*
      *15 tracks album released as part of the BBC's 40th Anniversary celebration.  This has nothing to do with the Decca LF-1299 10" album from 1957.*
**"BRITISH GRAFFITI"** (2-LP set)  (Sweden)
**Decca  LP DPA-3079/80 • 1979**
"32 Original Oldies From Decca Records"
*Tommy Steele track:*  Rock With The Caveman
**"STAR GOLD"** (4-LP Box set)  (UK)
**Ronco EGS-4/5012 • early '80s**
**Tommy Steele – Max Bygraves – Kenny Ball – Lena Martell**
***Tommy Steele tracks:* Taken from the 1979 "TOMMY STEELE'S FAMILY ALBUM" Ronco RTD 2041.**
**"ROCK 'N' ROLLING BRITAIN"** (UK)
Decca TAB-85 • 1985
*Tommy Steele tracks:* Rock With The Caveman / Rebel Rock / Elevator Rock  *(14 tracks)*

**"INTERNATIONAL TOP HITS 1958"** (Germany)
**Polyphon LP 840 707-1 • 1990**
*Tommy Steele track :*  Nairobi  *(16 tracks)*
**"UK ROCK 'N' ROLL – The Rock'n'Roll Era"** (2-LP set) (Holland)
***Time Life* TL-514/33 • 1992**
*Tommy Steele tracks*: Knee Deep In The Blues / Nairobi / Happy Guitar / Teenage Party / Elevator Rock / Rebel Rock
     *Also featured are Billy Fury, Marty Wilde and Lonnie Donegan with one side each.  No picture of Tommy,*
just Billy Fury.  Fold-out cover with liner-notes.  Also available on CD, Time Life TL-516/33.

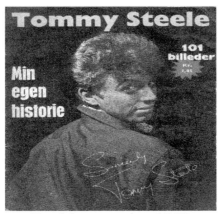
Danish magazine 1958

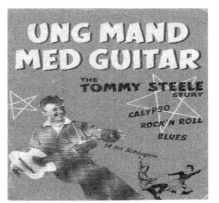
Danish film programme 1957

I believe that most countries in one way or another released Tommy Steele records in the late '50s and early '60s. We're talking about singles and EPs in particular. In the '60s during his movie and stage appearances his albums seemed popular enough to be released throughout the world. Unfortunately no survey of all the releases has ever turned up. So the following is what we know have been available of Tommy Steele records in various countries

## ARGENTINA

**78s:**
Singing The Blues / Knee Deep In The Blues
London 343138 • 1957

Rebel Rock / Elevator Rock
London 343152 • 1957

**EP:**

**"AMOR JOVEN"** ("Young Love")
*London* **DLM/E 5538 • 1957**
Young Love *(Amor Joven)* / Doomsday Rock *(El Ultimo Rock)* / Wedding Bells *(Campanas De Boda)* / Rock With The Caveman *(Rock Con El Hombre De Las Cavernas)*
    *Dark brownish Decca label with light tan letterings.*

**LPs:**

**"La HISTORIA de TOMMY STEELE"** ("The Tommy Steele Story")
**London LLM-16315 • 1957**
    *Despite a little colour difference, same as original UK LP Decca LF-1288, blue label.*
**"EN SEIS MONEDAS POR TUS SUENOS"** ("Half A Sixpence") *Original Motion Picture Soundtrack*
**RCA Victor AVL-3803 • 1967**
    *Same as original album release RCA Victor 6735 (UK) and RCA Victor 1146 (USA). (Not sure if the album above is in mono or stereo.)*

I am sure that most of Tommy's original UK singles and EPs were also issued in Australia. Several were released in New Zealand (see this country). I would also assume that most of Tommy's original albums came out in Australia. The Decca 45rpm label was dark blue with gold print. The 78rpm label was black and silver in an old fashion style. After so many years checking the net I wonder why Tolmmy's first singles from "Rock With The Caveman" to "Nairobi" have never turned up. Did they get a release in Australia?

**78:**
**Hey You! / Plant A Kiss**
Decca Y6961 • 1957

**45s:** *(Blue Decca label with round centre.)*
**Water, Water / A Handful Of Songs**
Decca 45-Y6933 • 1957
**Hey You! / Plant A Kiss**
Decca 45-Y6961 • 1957
**The Only Man On The Island / I Puts The Lightie On**
Decca 45-Y6991 • 1958
*This and the ones above have gold letterings. Not sure when they they changed to silver letterings, as on Y7028.*
**Come On, Let's Go / Put A Ring On Her Finger**
Decca 45-Y7003 • 1958
**Talahassee Lassie / Give ! Give! Give!**
Decca 45-Y7010 • 1959
**Little White Bull / Singing Time**
Decca 45-Y7012 • 1959
**What A Mouth (What A North And South) / Kookaburra**
Decca Y7021 • 1960
**Drunken Guitar** *(instr)* / **Light Up The Sky**
Decca Y7028 • 1960
*Has silver letterings. This particular single was not supposed to have been released in the UK. A promo copy has been found and also a regular issue, so this Australian one must also be a rare treat. (See the UK singles.)*

**Happy-Go-Lucky Blues / (The Girl With The) Long Black Hair**
Decca Y7032 • 1960

**Flash, Bang, Wallop! / She's Too Far Above Me**
**Decca Y7288 •** 1963
**I'll Always Be Irish / Furtuosity**
**Disneyland D-23  •** 1967
*Both sides from the movie "The Happiest Millionaire".*
**Half A Sixpence / If The Rain's Got To Fall**
**RCA 47-9458 •** 1968
*From the Paramount Picture.*
**The Dream Maker / Egg And Chips**
**Columbia (black label) DO-4448 •** 1963
**What A Mouth (What A North And South) / Little White**
**Bull** *(reissue)* **Decca 882 082-7  •** 1960 *(grey-blue label)*

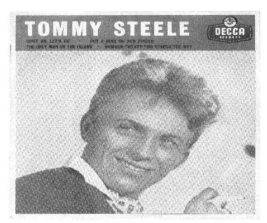

**Aussie EP Decca 6551**

**EPs:**
The covers were thinner, more like sleeves.  And were are the two "The Tommy Steele Story" EPs?

**"SINGING THE BLUES"**
Decca  DFEA 6389 • 1957 *(green label)*
*Same tracks as UK EP DFE-6389.*
**"TOMMY STEELE"**
**Decca DFEA 6551 •** 1958
*Same tracks as UK EP DFE-6551.*
**"TOMMY"**
**Decca DFEA 6592 •** 1959
*Same tracks as UK EP DFE-6592.*
**"TOMMY THE TOREADOR"**    *Soundtrack from film*
**Decca DFEA 6607 •** 1959
*Same tracks as UK EP DFE-6607.*

**LPs:**

**"TOMMY STEELE STAGE SHOW" (10")**
Decca LFA 1287 • 1957
*Identical to UK issue.*
**"THE TOMMY STEELE STORY"** (10")
**Decca LFA 1288 • 1957**
*Identical to UK issue.*
**"THE DUKE WORE JEANS"** (10") *Soundtrack*
**Decca LFA 1308 • 1958**
*Identical to UK issue.*
**"HALF A SIXPENCE"** *Oiginal soundtrack*
Decca SKLA-7614 (Stereo) • 1963
**Same tracks and cover as UK album Decca LK/SKL-4521.**
**"SO THIS IS BROADWAY"**
Columbia SOEX-10207 • 1964
*Same as UK LP Columbia SCX-3536.*
**"HALF A SIXPENCE"** *Original Broadway Cast recording*
RCA Victor LOC-1110 (mono) LSO-1110 (stereo) • 1965
*Same tracks and cover as US. album LOC/LSO-1110*
**"FINIAN'S RAINBOW"** *Original Motion Picture Soundtrack*
Warner Brothers B 2550 (mono) BS 2550 (stereo) • 1968
*Same as US issue.*
**"THE WORLD OF TOMMY STEELE Vol.2"**
**Decca SPA-137 • 1971**
*Same as UK LP.*
**"THE HAPPY WORLD OF TOMMY STEELE"**
World Record Club S-5356 • 1970s
Nairobi / A Handful Of Songs / Little White Bull / Flash, Bang, Wallop! / Rock With The Caveman / The Only Man On The Island / What A Mouth (What A North And South) / Singing The Blues / Marriage Type Love / Hit Record / Shiralee / Sweet Georgia Brown
*Album front cover is similar to the two UK Decca albums "The World Of Tommy Steele" Vol.1 (1969) and Vol.2 (1971), however, different colours.*

**BELGIUM**


**45s:** *(Blue Decca label without centre.)*

**Singing The Blues / Rebel Rock**
Decca 9.22.667 • 1957
**Shiralee / Grandad's Rock**

Decca 9.22.716 • 1957
**Hey You! / Plant A Kiss**
Decca 9.22.754 • 1957
**Happy Guitar / Princess**
Decca 9.22.836    • 1958
**Come On Let's Go / Put A Ring On Her Finger**
Decca 9.22.917 • 1958
**The Trial / Hiawatha**
Decca 9.22.975 • 1958


**LP:**


**"BILLY FURY / TOMMY STEELE"**        **(2-LP set)**
Decca DA 207/208 • 1970s
*Tommy Steele tracks:* Rock Around The Town / Rock With
The Caveman / Elevator Rock / Rebel Rock / Teenage Party /
Grandad's Rock / Hey You! / Take Me Back Baby / Build Up
/ You Gotta Go / Come On, Lets Go / Tallahassee Lassie /
Doomsday Rock / Singing The Blues / Knee Deep In The
Blues / Water, Water

The most interesting thing about this album is that it
includes a good bunch of Tommy's best rockers. The other
album has 16 tracks by Billy Fury. Fold-out cover but photos
of Tommy and Billy are only featured on the front cover. The
inside of the fold-out cover has a survey of all the other
albums in the series.


### CANADA


Usually, most of the records that came out in the USA
were also issued in Canada. Unfortunately no complete
survey is available for Canada. However, it seems the London
45s followed the American catalogue numbers, except the
first #309 which so far has never turned up in the USA.

**78s:**

**Rock With Caveman / Rock Around The Town**
London FC.309 • 1956
**Elevator Rock / Doomsday Rock**
London L.1706 • 1956
**Singing The Blues / Rebel Rock**
London L.1714 • 1957

**45s:** *(Black London label)*

**Rock With Caveman / Rock Around The Town**
London 45-PC-309 • 1956
**Elevator Rock / Doomsday Rock**
London 45-L.1706 • 1956
**Singing The Blues / Rebel Rock**
London 45-L.1714 • 1957
**Butterfingers / Teenage Party**
London 45-L.1735 • 1957

**LPs:**

**"HALF A SIXPENCE"**   *Original Broadway Cast recording*
RCA Victor LSO-1110 • 1965

**"SO THIS IS BROADWAY"**
**Capitol T-6124** (mono)  **ST-6124** (stereo) • **1965**
    *Same songs as UK album Columbia 33SX1674 / SCX-3536 from 1964 and US LP Liberty LRP-3426 / LST-7426 but slightly different cover and different liner notes.*

**"THE HAPPIEST MILLIONAIRE"**   *Original Cast Soundtrack*
**Buena Vista STER-5001** • **1967**
    *Same as US album Buena Vista BVS-5001 with the fold-out cover and book.*

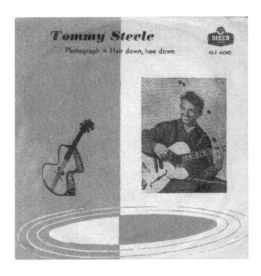

Denmark single sleeve Decca F-44345

The singles released in this country carried special and typical Danish *picture sleeves*, well worth checking out. The singles followed the UK issues with record numbers and tracks, except two. The EPs were identical to the UK issues with both sleeves, record numbers and tracks (except one). Both the singles and EPs were on the Danish blue Decca label. 78 rpm's came without the 45-prefix (of course) and also had the blue Decca label. However, not quite sure when they stopped issuing 78s, but F-11152 is a good guess.
There is no complete survey of what's been released by Tommy in Denmark, so what you have here are mostly the records collected through the years.

**45s:** *(Blue Decca label with round centre.)*

**Singing The Blues / Rebel Rock**
Decca 45-F 10819 ● 1956
**Butterfingers / Cannibal Pot**
Decca 45-F 10877 ● 1957
**Water, Water / A Handful Of Songs**
Decca 45-F 10923 ● 1957

**Hey You! / Butterfingers**

Decca 45-F 44343 ● 1957

Note: *This number didn't follow the others as the coupling was exclusive for Denmark.*

**Happy Guitar / Princess**
Decca 45-F 10976 ● 1958
**Photograph / Hair-Down, Hoe-Down**
Decca 45-F 44345 ● 1958

Note: *This number didn't follow the others as the coupling was exclusive for Denmark.*

**The Only Man On The Island / I Puts The Lightie On**
Decca 45-F 11041 ● 1958
**Tallahassee Lassie / Give! Give! Give!**
Decca 45-F 11152 ● 1959
*(Probably the last 78rpm issue.)*
**Happy-Go-Lucky Blues / (The Girl With The) Long Black Hair**
Decca 45-F 11275 ● 1960
**The Writing On The Wall / Drunken Guitar** *(instr)*
Decca 45-F 11372 ● 1961

*The latter two singles here came with Danish picture sleeves and English records.*


**EPs:** *(Blue Decca label with round centre.)*


**"YOUNG LOVE"**
Decca DFE 6388      ● 1957
**"SINGING THE BLUES"**
Decca DFE 6389      ● 1957
**"THE TOMMY STEELE STORY No.1"**
Decca DFE 6398      ● 1957

*The Danish releases all had round centres, however, I have a copy of this EP with a big centre hole, probably aimed at jukeboxes (?)*

**"THE TOMMY STEELE STORY No.2"**
Decca DFE 6424      ● 1957


**"THE DUKE WORE JEANS"**
Decca DFE  6472 ● 1958

*This has a different picture of Tommy on the back cover.*


**"4 SMASH HITS"**
Decca SDE-7085 ● 1958  *Art cover.*

*Tommy Steele track:* **Plant A Kiss**
Other tracks by Edmundo Ross: "Melodie D'Amour", Terry Dene: "Teernage Dream", The Southlanders: "Alone".

Denmark single sleeve Decca F-11372

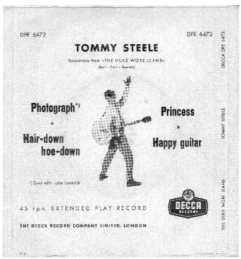

Denmark EP Decca DFE-6472 (back cover)

## "16 GREATEST HITS"

Music Stars  MC 870190 • early '80s

A Handful Of Songs / Elevator Rock / Rock With The Caveman / Water, Water / Razzle Dazzle / The Only Man On The Island / Knee Deep In The Blues / Come On, Let's Go / Singing The Blues / Happy Guitar / Young Love / Rebel Rock / Butterfingers / Cannibal Pot / Giddy-Up A Ding Dong / What A Mouth (What A North And South)

*The only interesting thing about this release is the picture of Tommy on the front cover.  I haven't seen any LP of this album.*

## FINLAND

**EPs:**

## "THE TOMMY STEELE STORY No. 1"

Decca DFE-6398 • 1957

Take Me Back Baby / Water, Water / Will It Be You? / Build Up

*Same tracks and same number as UK issue.  BUT ! the front cover is completely different ! It has a very nice blueish photgraph of Tommy and the band from the movie itself.  I have never seen anything like it, and so many countries have released this EP and all have followed the UK issue.  The back-side of cover is almost identical to the UK issue, except it doesn't say 'Made in England.   As of this the cover was probably printed in Finland.*

## "THE TOMMY STEELE STORY No. 2"

Decca DFE-6424     • 1957

*I haven't seen this EP so I can't verify if the front cover carried the same picture as No.1.*

## "MELODIE d'AMOUR"

Decca DX-1975 • 1957

*Tommy Steele tracks:* Water, Water / A Handful Of Songs
*Edmundo Ross:*  Melodie d'Amour.  *Bob Sharples*:  In The Middle Of An Island

*No picture of any artists. This EP was also issued in West-Germany with a different cover and title "Schlager-Telegramm Aus London – Nr.1" Decca DX-1975.*

# FRANCE

Some of the releases in France during the late '50s carried obviously the same catalog numbers as the UK issues, as you will notice in the EP and LP surveys.

## 45s:

**Tallahassee Lassie / Give! Give! Give!**
Decca F. 11.152 • 1959 *(yellow label)*
*France didn't press singles for the common market until around 1968, so this was aimed at jukeboxes.*
**Fortuosity / (Bye-Yum Pum Pum) Joyce Bulifant & Lesley Ann Warren**
Vista VS-613 F • 1968 *(picture sleeve)*
*From "The Happiest Millionaire". This feature the same colour sleeve as the original US LP.*
**Singing The Blues / Rock With The Caveman**
Decca 79096 • (early '70s) *(art sleeve)*

**EPs:** *(Blue Decca label without centre)*

### *"TOMMY STEELE No 1"*
Decca 457.000 • 1957
Rock With The Caveman / +Rock Around The Town / Rebel Rock / Singing The Blues
*Front cover is red with a drawing of Tommy's face.*
### *"TOMMY STEELE 2"* *(Tommy Steele No.2)*
Decca 457.001 • 1957
Doomsday Rock / Young Love / Elevator Rock / Knee Deep In The Blues
*Front cover is blue but otherwise identical to No.1.*

### *"The TOMMY STEELE STORY (No.1)"*
**Decca DFE 6398 • 1957**
Take Me Back Baby / Water, Water / Will It Be You? / Build Up.
### *"TOPS IN POPS"* *Various*
**Decca DFE 6411 • 1957**
*Tommy Steele track:* Butterfingers
*Almost same cover as the UK one, but a different photo of Tommy.*

France EP Decca 457.000

**"The TOMMY STEELE STORY (No.2)"**
Decca DFE 6424      • 1957
A Handful Of Songs / Cannibal Pot / Time To Kill / You Gotta
Go.
**"The TOMMY STEELE STORY"**     *(Tommy Steele No.5)*
Decca 457.005 •      1958
Hey You! / Nairobi / Plant A kiss / Neon Sign
      *Same front cover as No. 3 (DFE 6398)*
**"THE JUKE WORE JEANS"**
Decca DFE 6472 • 1958
Photograph  /  Hair-Down,  Hoe-Down  /  Princess  /  Happy
Guitar
      *Same cover as UK EP.*
**"TOMMY THE TOREADOR"**
Decca DFE 6607      • 1959
Tommy  The  Toreador  /  Take  A  Ride  /  Where's  The  Birdie
w/*Sidney James & Bernard Cribbens* / Little White Bull /
Singing Time / Amanda
      *Different cover from the UK album, front and back.*

**LPs:**
**"TOMMY STEELE STAGE SHOW"**   (10")
Decca LF-1287 • 1957
**"THE TOMMY STEELE STORY"**   (10")
**Decca LF 1288 • 1957**
      *Both the two albums above have the same front cover
picture, similar to the UK 10" issue of "Tommy Steele Stage
Show". However, the photo is in black & white (sort of) and the
bottom half is blue on LF-1287 and green on LF-1288.*

**"THE HAPPIEST MILLIONAIRE"** *Original Cast Soundtrack*
Buena VISTA VS-5001 F • 1968
   *French issue of the UK album Buena Vista BVS-5001 (1967). Except for the title all text are in French.*


## WEST GERMANY

78:
**Singing The Blues / Rebel Rock**
Decca F 46427 • 1957

45s:

**Singing The Blues / Rebel Rock**
Decca D 18 427 • 1957
**Rock With The Caveman / Rock Around The Town**
Decca D 18 447 • 1957
**Elevator Rock / Doomsday Rock**
Decca D 18 448 • 1957
**Knee Deep In The Blues / Teenage Party**
Decca DL 18 463 • 1957
**Water, Water / A Handful Of Songs**
Decca DL 18 631 • 1957
**Butterfingers / Cannibal Pot**
Decca DP 18 632 • 1957
**Nairobi / Neon Sign**
Decca DP 18 754 • 1958
**The Only Man On The Island / I Puts The  Lightie On**
Decca DP 18 810 • 1958
**Come On, Let's Go / Put A Ring On her Finger**
Decca DL  25 010 • 1958

*The above 45s all have Decca blue label with a tri-centre.*

**Tallahassee Lassie / Give! Give! Give!**
Decca DL 25 016 • 1959
**The Writing On The Wall / Drunken Guitar *(instr)***
Decca DL 25 049 • 1961

**My Big Best Shoes / The Dit-Dit Song**
Decca DL 11 361 • 1961
**Hit Record / What A Little Darlin'**
Decca DL 25 079 • 1962

*The above singles have maroon label without tri-centre.*

**Fortuosity / I'll Always Be Irish**

Buena Vista F-460 • 1968

*Both songs from the Walt Disney Musical "The Happiest Millionaire".*

**"Oldies but Goldies"**

**Tallahassee Lassie / Put A Ring On Her Finger**

Decca DL 25 539 • 1981 *(art cover)*

**"Big Hits 1955-65"**

Tallahassee Lassie / *Screamin' Lord Sutch*: Jack The Ripper

Decca 6.14918 • 1987 *(art cover)*

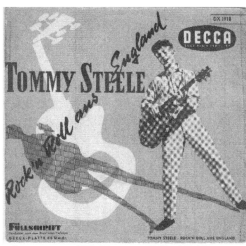

Germany EP Decca DX-1918

**EPs:**  *(Blue Decca label with tri-centre.)*

**"ROCK'n'ROLL  AUS  ENGLAND"**  *(Tommy  Steele,  der englische Elvis)*

Decca DX-1918     • 1956

Elevator Rock / Doomsday Rock / Rock With The Caveman / Rock Around The Town

*Nice cover.*

**"TEENAGE PARTY"**

Decca DX-1927     • 1957

Teenage  Party  /  Knee  Deep  In  The  Blues     + tracks  by **Winifred Atwell**

*This EP was also released in Yugoslavia, Decca (Yugoton) EP-DC-9045.*

## "ROCK'n'ROLL SESSION Nr.1"

Decca DX-1953 • 1957

Razzle Dazzle / Kaw Liga / Teenage Party / Wedding Bells
> *All live.*

## "ROCK'n'ROLL SESSION Nr.2"

Decca DX-1957 • 1957

What Is This Thing Called Love / Rock With The Caveman / Giddy-Up A Ding Dong / Honky Tonk Blues
> *All live.*

*The above two "Rock'n'Roll Session" EPs have the same cover, and all songs are taken from the "Tommy Steele Stage Show" album.*

## "SCHLAGER-TELEGRAMM AUS LONDON – Nr.1"

Decca DX-1975 • 1957

*Tommy Steele tracks:* Water, Water / A Handful Of Songs / *Plus one track each by Bob Sharples and Edmundo Ros.*

**This EP was also issued in Finland with a different cover and title "Melodie d'Amour" Decca DX-1975.**

## LPs:

## "HALF A SIXPENCE" *Original Motion Picture Soundtrack*

RCA Victor LSO-1146 (stereo) • 1967

*Except for a single cover (no fold-out) the album is identical to the UK issue, however, using the US catalog number.*

## "FINIAN'S RAINBOW" *Original Motion Picture Soundtrack*

Warner Brothers BS-2550 • 1968

*Same as US album.*

*We can assume that most (if not all) of Tommy's musical albums were released in Germany, and carrying the same catalog numbers as the US albums. No more info.*

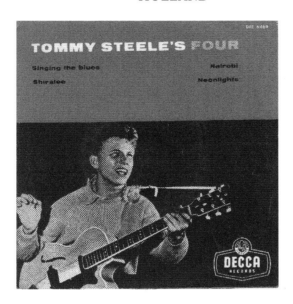

Holland EP Decca DFE-6469

**78s:**

**Singing The Blues / Rebel Rock**
Decca M 35019 • 1957
**Knee Deep In The Blues / Young Love**
Decca M 35020 • 1957
**Butterfingers / Cannibal Pot**
Decca M 35032 • 1957
**Shiralee / Water, Water**
Decca M 35043 • 1957

**45s:** *(Blue Decca label with silver letterings. Round centre.)*

**Singing The Blues / Rebel Rock**
Decca FM 235 019 • 1957
**Shiralee / Water, Water**
Decca FM 235 043 • 1957
**A Handful Of Songs / Hey You!**
Decca FM 235 066 • 1957
**The Only Man On The Island / I Puts The Lightie On**
Decca FM 235 091 • 1958

**Tallahassee Lassie / Give! Give! Give!**
Decca FM 235 153 • 1959

**Dream Maker / Egg And Chips**
Columbia DB 7070 • 1963 *(Picture sleeve)*
*From the movie "It's All Happening" (aka "Dream Maker" USA). Nice picture from the movie.*

**EPs:**

**"TOMMY STEELE's FOUR"**
Decca DFE-6469 • 1958
Singing The Blues / Shiralee / Nairobi / Neon Sign
*This was made exclusively in Holland. "Neon Sign" misprinted on cover as Neonlight see picture pevious pages.*

## INDIA

**78:**
**The Only Man On The Island / I Puts The Lightie On**
Decca F-11041 • 1958
*Comes in an original India Decca sleeve.*
**45:**
**Come On, Let's Go / Put A Ring On Her Finger**
Decca 45-F.11072 • 1958
**EP:**
**"TOMMY THE TOREADOR"**
**Decca DFE-6607 • 1959**
*Same as the UK release, slightly different letterings.*

## IRELAND

**45:**

**Happy-Go-Lucky Blues / (The Girl With The) Long Black Hair**
**Decca 45-F. 11275 • 1960**
*Label almost identical to the British one, however,* Made in Eire *is printed between the Decca logo and the round push-out centre.*

## ITALY

**45s:** *(Blue Decca label with silver letterings. Without centre.)*

**Butterfingers / Cannibal Pot**
Decca 45-F 10877 • 1957
**Water, Water/ A Handful Of Songs**
Decca 45-F 10923 • 1957
**Nairobi / Neon Sign**
Decca 45-F 10991 • 1958
**The Only Man On The Island / I Puts The Lightie On**
Decca 45-F 11041 • 1958


**EPs:** *(Blue Decca label with silver letterings. Without centre.)*


**"YOUNG LOVE"**
Decca DFE-6388      • 1957
   *Same as UK EP issue. Same front cover.*
**"SINGING THE BLUES"**
Decca DFE-6389 • 1957
   *Same as UK EP issue. Same front cover.*
**"THE TOMMY STEELE STORY"  Selezione n. 1**
Decca DFE-6398 • 1958
   *Same as UK EP issue. Same front cover.*


**LPs:**


**"THE TOMMY STEELE STORY"**
Decca LF-1288 • 1958
   *Same as UK issue. Same front cover.*
**"FINIAN'S RAINBOW"** ('Sulle Ali Dell'arcobaleno') *Original Soundtrack*
Warner Brothers  WLS-2550 • 1969
   *Same as all the other issues, except liner notes in Italien*


**ISRAEL**


**LP:**


**"THE TOMMY STEELE STORY"**  (10")
Decca LF-1288 • 1957
   *Same tracks and front cover as original UK LP.*

**45s:**

**Butterfingers / Cannibal Pot**
London LED.53 • 1958
*(King Record Co.Ltd.) Maroon label.*
**Grandad's Rock / Shiralee**
London LED.72 • 1958
*(King Record Co.Ltd.) Maroon label.*
**Half A Sixpence / If The Rain's Got To Fall**
Victor SS-1806 • 1967   *w/picture sleeve*
*From the soundtrack "Half A Sixpence".*

**LP:**

**"HALF A SIXPENCE"**
Victor SRA-5118 • 1967
*Same tracks and front cover as original US LP. Has a fold-out cover with lyrics to all songs.*

## MEXICO

**45:**

**Tallahassie Lassie** (Mi Chica Alocada) **/ Young Ideas** (Ideas Jovenes)
London 45/154 • 1959   *(Maroon label)*

## NEW ZEALAND

It seems like most of Tommy's UK singles also came out in New Zealand. Unfortunately there's no survey and the ones below are just a small part, probably. The label was dark blue with silver letterings. The Decca DEC-185 single featured a square push-out centre (45 degrees), the other four have round centre. They came in special New Zealand London/Decca sleeves. The EPs also had round centre.

**45s:**

**Water, Water / A Handful Of Songs**
Decca 45-DEC.161 • 1957
**Happy Guitar / Princess**
Decca 45-DEC.185 • 1958
**The Only Man On The Island / I Put The Lightie On**
Decca 45-DEC.191 • 1958
**Come On, Let's Go / I Put A Ring On Her Finger**
Decca 45-DEC.194 • 1958
**Tallahassie Lassie / Give! Give! Give!**
Decca 45-DEC.206 • 1959
**What A Mouth (What A North And South) / Kookaburra**
　　　　　Decca 45-DEC.218 • 1960

**EPS**

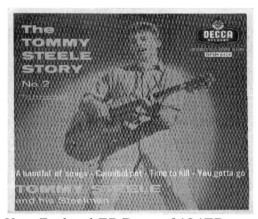

New Zealand EP Decca 6424EPs:
All the EPs were almost identical to the UK issues, except
they all had a white edge on the front covers. The covers all
seems like they were inferior copies of the UK ones. That
applies especially to DFEM-6607 where also the back side is
quite poor.

**"SINGING THE BLUES"**
Decca DFEM-6389 • 1957
**"THE TOMMY STEELE STORY No. 1"**
Decca DFEM-6398 • 1957
**"THE TOMMY STEELE STORY No. 2"**
Decca DFEM-6424 • 1957
**"THE DUKE WORE JEANS"**
Decca DFEM-6472 • 1958
**"TOMMY"**

Decca DFEM 6592 • 1959
*The front -over is in black & white except for the title which is in yellow*
**"TOMMY THE TOREADOR"** *Soundtrack*
Decca DFEM-6607 • 1959


**LPs:**
I would think that most of if not all of Tommy's original Decca albums came out in New Zealand, but no complete survey is available.

**"TOMMY STEELE STAGE SHOW"** (10")
Decca LFM-1287 • 1957
*Same as the UK issue*
**"TOMMY STEELE STORY"** (10")
Decca LFM-1288 • 1957
*Same as the UK issue.*
**"HALF A SIXPENCE"** *Original Cast recording*
Decca LKM-4521 • 1963
*Same cover and tracks as UK release LK-4521*


## NORWAY

The singles released in this country carried Norwegian blue/white Decca company sleeves, but followed the UK record numbers and tracks. The EP sleeves and tracks were identical to the UK issues, record numbers and tracks. However, both the singles and EPs were on the darker blue Norwegian Decca label. All 45rpm's had round push-out centres (except one). The 78rpm's carried the prefix NF.


**78s:**

**Elevator Rock / Doomsday Rock**
Decca NF-10808 • 1956
**Knee Deep In The Blues / Teenage Party**

Decca NF-10849 • 1957
**Butterfingers / Cannibal Pot**
Decca NF-10877 • 1957
**Shiralee / Grandad's Rock**
Decca NF-10896 • 1957
**Water, Water / A Handful Of Songs**
Decca NF-10923 • 1957

Norway 78 Decca NF-10877

**45s:**

**Butteringers / Cannibal Pot**
Decca 45-F 10877 • 1957
**Water, Water / A Handful Of Songs**
Decca 45-F 10923 • 1957
**Hey You! / Plant A Kiss**
Decca 45-F 10941 • 1957
**Princess / Happy Guitar**
Decca 45-F 10976 • 1958
*Here "Princess" became the A-side. It could be a misprint on the label though.*
**Nairobi / Neon Sign**
Decca 45-F 10991 • 1958
**It's All Happening / What Do You Do**
Decca 45-F 11026 • 1958
**The Only Man On The Island / I Puts The Lightie On**
Decca 45-F 11041 • 1958
**Come On, Let's Go / Put a Ring On Her Finger**
Decca 45-F 11072 • 1958
*This came out with both a small round centre and a push-out centre.*
**A Lovely Night / Marriage Type Love**

Decca 45-F 11089 • 1958
**Tallahassee Lassie / Give! Give! Give!**
Decca 45-F 11152 • 1959

*In the Spring of 1959, the pressing plant in Oslo, A/S Proton, ceased pressing vinyl so the records were imported from England.*

**EPs:**

**"YOUNG LOVE"**
Decca DFE-6388      • 1957
**"SINGING THE BLUES"**
Decca DFE-6389 • 1957
**"THE TOMMY STEELE STORY No.1"**
Decca DFE-6398 • 1957
**"THE TOMMY STEELE STORY No.2"**
Decca DFE-6424      • 1957
**"THE DUKE WORE JEANS"**
Decca DFE-6472      • 1958
**"TOMMY STEELE"**
Decca DFE-6551      • 1958


## POLAND

**Rebel Rock**
Postcard single • 1960
*This is a Polish postcard with a childish colour drawing on the front where the grooves are. The only thing that links this to Tommy Steele is that it's written on the back side: "Elevator Rock" T. Steel. But it plays "Rebel Rock", though.*


## PORTUGAL

**45:**

**Must Be Santa** ("Deve Ser O Pai Natal") **/ Boys And Girls** ("Rapazes E Raparigas")
Decca P45-F 11299 • 1960
*Picture sleeve. Pressed in four different vinyl variations, blue, green, red and yellow.*

**LP:**

**"HALF A SIXPENCE"** ("Este É O Meu Mundo")  *Original Soundtrack*
        RCA Victor TPL-389 • 1960
        Same cover and tracks as original US album.  (This has only turned up once on the Internet and the record number could be 308 or 388)

## RUSSIA

**LPs:**

**AROUND THE WORLD**  (10")  *Various*
VSG (Vsesoyuznaya Studia Gramzapisi) ROCT-  ? • *unknown year*
*Tommy Steele tracks:*  Knee Deep In The Blues / Wedding Bells
**AROUND THE WORLD Part 6**  (10")  *Various*
VSG (Vsesoyuznaya Studia Gramzapisi) ROCT-5289-56 • *unknown year*
*Tommy Steele track:*  Young Love
**AROUND THE WORLD**  (10")  *Various*
VSG (Vsesoyuznaya Studia Gramzapisi) ROCT-5289-61 • *unknown year*
*Tommy Steele track:*  A Handful Of Songs

*Have no idea of any release dates here.  No picture of any artist on the above three albums, and came in just ordinary brown CCCP sleeves.  The VSG record label later became Melodiya (Melody).*

## SOUTH AFRICA

I am sure most of Tommy's UK records were released in this country.  However, as you will notice, especially on the 78s, the songs didn't always have the same coupling, and the song "I Like" wasn't even included on any UK single releases!  The label was blue and the 45s had tri-centre.

**78s:**

**Singing The Blues / Elevator Rock**
Decca FM-6445 • 1957
**Teenage Party / I Like**
Decca FM-6540 • 1957
**A Handful Of Songs / Water, Water**
Decca FM-6528 • 1957
**The Writing On The Wall / Drunken Guitar** *(instr)*
Decca FM-6826 • 1961

**45s:**

**Hit Record / What A Little Darlin'**
Decca FM.7-6894 • 1962
**Butter Wouldn't Melt In Your Mouth / Where Have All The Flowers Gone**
Decca FM-7-6965 • 1962   *(Picture sleeve)*

South Africa 45 Decca FM-7-6965

**EPs:**

**"YOUNG LOVE"**
Decca DFE-6388      • 1957
   *Same as UK issue, w/ Tri centre, almost same front cover except it's pink tinted.*
**"THE TOMMY STEELE STORY No.1"**

289

Decca DFE-6398 • 1957
 *This is identical to the UK issue.*
**"TOPS IN POPS, No.1"** *Various*
Decca DFE-6411 • 1957
*Tommy Steele track:* Butterfingers
**"THE TOMMY STEELE STORY No.2"**
Decca DFE-6424 • 1957
 *Same as UK issue, w/Tri centre, same photo of Tommy, however, the cover is light blue and title and Tommy's name are in red.*

**LPs:**

**"TOMMY STEELE"** (10")
Decca LF-1287 • 1957
 *Same cover as UK LP LF-1287. Dark blue label.*

**"THE TOMMY STEELE STORY"** (10")
Decca LF-1288 • 1957
 *Same cover as UK LP LF-1288.*
**"GET HAPPY WITH TOMMY"**
Decca LK- 4351 • 1960
 *Same cover as UK LP LK-4351.*

**SPAIN**

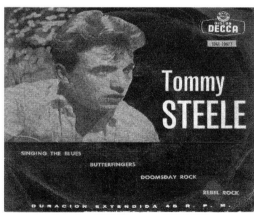
Spain EP Decca 70677

**EPs :**

290

**"TOMMY STEELE"**   Decca EDGE 70677 • 1957
Singing The Blues / Buttefingers / Doomsday Rock / Rebel
Rock
    *This was probably  the first EP by Tommy released in*
*Spain.  Green Decca label with gold printing and small round*
*centre.  The front cover feature the same but a smaller picture*
*of Tommy (in black & pink) as on the first UK EP DFE-6388*
*"Young Love".  The cover has liner notes in Spanish.*
**"TOMMY STEELE"**   Decca EDGE 70724 • 1957
Teenage Party / Knee Deep In The Blues / Young Love /
Wedding Bells
    *Green Decca label with gold printing and small round*
*centre.  Later it  was reissued with a black Decca label with*
*silver printing and TRI centre. The cover is the same as the one*
*above but in black & white and has liner notes in Spanish.*

**"THE TOMMY STEELE STORY"** ("La   Historia   de   Tommy
Steele")
Decca EDGE 70820 • 1958
A Handful Of Songs *(Un Punado de Canciones)* / Cannibal Pot
*(Puchero de Canibal)* / Time To Kill *(Tiempo Para Matar)* / You
Gotta Go *(Tienes Que Marchar)*
    *Green label.  Same front cover as the UK issue but the*
*colour is red-brownish and the printings in yellow.  Liner notes*
*in Spanish.*
**"THE TOMMY STEELE STORY"** ("La   Historia   de   Tommy
Steele")
Decca EDGE 70821 • 1958
Take Me Back Baby *(Tomame Otra Vez, Nena)* / Water, Water
*(Agua, Agua)* / Will It Be You *(Seras Tu)* / Build Up *(Construye)*
    *Black label with Tri centre.  Same front cover as the UK*
*issue.  Liner notes in Spanish.*
**"TOMMY"  ( ? )**
Decca EDGE 71240 • 1959
I'm A Little Blackbird *(Soy un Pequeno Mirlo)* / Georgia On My
Mind *(Georgia en mi Pensamiento)* / Sweet Georgia Brown
*(Dulce Georgia Brown)* / Mandy, Make Up Your Mind *(Mandy
Decidete)*
    *The title of this EP is a little uncertain.  The following*
*Decca EP 71480 has the title of "Tommy", so this 71240 might*
*be different.*
**"TOMMY"**
Decca EDGE 71480 • 1960

What A Mouth (What A North And South) / Kookaburra / Holerin' And Screamin' / Little Darlin'
*Black label.*
**"HALF A SIXPENCE"**   ("La Mitad De Seis Peniques")
RCA Victor EP3-21039 • 1968
Overture / Half A Sixpence / Flash, Bang, Wallop / If The Rain's Got To Fall
*As far as I know this is the only EP released from the original Broadway Cast recording. (US RCA LP LOC-1110 in 1965.)*
**"WHERE'S JACK"**
**Paramount HDT 537-01 • 1969**
*As we know Tommy only acts in this movie, no singing. However, this feature the same cover as on the original UK album (Paramount SPFL-254) so Tommy is on the cover. I have never seen any other EP released from the movie, so this must be pretty unique.*

**LPs:**

**THE TOMMY STEELE STORY**   (10")   **("La Historia De Tommy Steele")**
Decca LF-1288 • 1957
*Same tracks and front cover as original UK LP. However, full Spanish text on the back cover. Green Decca label.*
**"HALF A SIXPENCE"**   **("La Mitad De Seis Peniques")**
*Original Soundtrack*
**(Historia de La Musica en el Cine) Belter 2-90.009 • 1972**
*This is the same as the US RCA album LSO-1146 "Half A Sixpence", original Motion Picture  Soundtrack, but a sligthly different cover.*
**"HISTORIA DE LA MUSICA ROCK  #39"**
Decca 9-LP 013 • 1982
*Tommy Steele tracks :* A Handful Of Songs / Rock With The Caveman / Singing The Blues / Come On, Let's Go / Nairobi / Water, Water
*Side A featuring 6 tracks by **LULU**. Only  picture of Lulu appears on the front cover.*

Sweden never issued any singles (78 or 45), however, they released a whole bunch of EPs and many with picture covers not available anywhere else. Some photos of Tommy on these special EPs were taken in Sweden when he toured there in the late '50s. The EPs were on the Swedish lighter blue Decca label and had round push-out centre.

### "Klingande Post"
Decca  Provskiva (***promo***) • April 1958
**Nairobi                     (from     the     Decca     EP     SDE-7096)**

*This is something the Swedish Decca Company sent out to dealers to promote new releases. Devided into part 1 and part 2 (instead of side 1 and 2). Just a small snippet is heard of each song. Little Richard, Larry Williams and Chuck Berry are some of the other artists featured. "Klingande Post" means Musical Mail.*

### "Klingande Post"
**Decca Provskiva** *(promo)* • **December 1959**
*This one contained various current releases and just mentions Tommy Steele, no specific song.*

*The interesting thing, though, is that these kind of records rarely turns up on the market, and probably most (if not all) of the EPs in Sweden were promoted like this.*

### EPs:

### "YOUNG LOVE"
Decca DFE 6388      • 1957
*Identical to the UK issue, same cover and tracks.*
### "SINGING THE BLUES"
Decca DFE 6389      • 1957
*Same tracks as the UK issue, but different Swedish cover – "The Sensational new rock'n'roll voice !"*
### "THE TOMMY STEELE STORY No. 1"

Decca DFE 6398 • 1957
*Cover and tracks same as UK issue.*
**"TOPS IN POPS"** *Various*
Decca DFE 6411 • 1957
*Same as UK issue.*
**"THE TOMMY STEELE STORY No. 2"**
Decca DFE 6424 • 1957
*Same as UK issue, except that the cover is also printed in Sweden.*
**"HERE'S TOMMY"**
Decca SDE 7078 • 1957
Shiralee / Grandad's Rock / Razzle Dazzle / Honky Tonk Blues
**"TOMMY STEELE And THE STEELMEN"**
Decca SDE 7086 • 1958
Butterfingers / I Like / Two Eyes / Time To Kill
**"TOMMY STEELE And THE STEELMEN"**
Decca SDE 7087 • 1958
On The Move / Kaw-Liga / Teenage Party / Treasure Of Love
**"SINGS NAIROBI"**
Decca SDE 7096 • 1958
Nairobi / Neon Sign / Plant A Kiss / Hey You !

**"TOMMY STEELE"**
Decca SDE 7118 • 1958
The Only Man On The Island / I Put The Lightie On / Rock Around The Town / Swaller Tail Coat
**"LONDON ROCK"**
Decca SDE 7142 • 1958
Put A Ring On Her Finger / Come On, Let's Go    + *two tracks by* **Terry Dene**
**"TOMMY STEELE"**   *w/The Roland Shaw Orchestra*
Decca SDE 7164 • 1959
Number Twenty-two Across The Way / Hiawatha / The Trial / A Lovely Night
*This has the same front cover as the UK EP DFE-6551.*
**"TOMMY STEELE"**
Decca SDE 7175 • 1959
Give! Give! Give! / Tallahassee Lassie / Young Ideas / You Were Mine
*This has almost the same front cover as UK EP DFE-6592.*

Sweden EP Decca SDE-7142

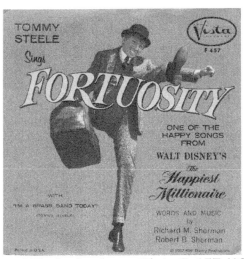

US single sleeve Vista F-457 (1967)

**45s:**

**Elevator Rock / Doomsday Rock**
London 45-1706     • 1956

**Singing The Blues / Rebel Rock**
London 45-1714 • 1957

**Butterfingers / Teenage Party**
London 45-1735 • 1957

**A Handful Of Songs / Water, Water**
London 45-1760 • 1958
**Nairobi / Neon Sign**
London 45-1795 • March 1958
**The Only Man On The Island / Swaller Tail Coat**
London 45-1824 • 1958
**Hey You!** (DRF-23730) **/ No. 22 Across The Way** (DRF-24982)
London 45-1838 • Dec.1958
*Pretty obscure coupling as the A-side was a 1957 recording and the B-side (actually "Number 22 Across The Way") from 1958. Also the B-side is a pretty obscure track, taken from an UK EP DFE-6551.*

**Give! Give! Give! / The Trial**
London 45-1878-V • Sept. 1959

**Happy-Go-Lucky Blues** (DRF-27390) **/ She's My Baby** (DRF-27125)
London 45-1950-V • 1960
Note: *The B-side here is not available anywhere else. As you can see it has a lower matrix-number than the A-side and is therefore from an earlier session. It was written by one 'Smith' and music directed by Ian Fraser.*
**Doomsday Rock / Elevator Rock**
WAM 45-1 • *unknown year*
**Half A Sixpence** *(edited)* **/ If The Rain's Got To Fall** *(edited)*
RCA Victor 47-8602 • 1967
*From the Broadway production "Half A Sixpence".*
**Half A Sixpence / If The Rain's Got To Fall**
RCA Victor promo MB-22499 / MB-22500 • 1967
*Promotional record with sleeve in connection with Tommy being selected "Star of the Future" by the National association of Theatre Owners. "Not for sale or Air play" printed on the white label. The two songs taken from the Paramount Picture release of "Half A Sixpence" runs for (5:16) and( 6:40) respectively, which explains why they were not suited for air play at the time. (see picture below)*

296

**"PARAMOUNT PICTURES Presents: HALF A SIXPENCE"**
**(Thaddeus Suski Productions Inc.)**
**Five Radio Spot Announcements,** 1&2 -60 seconds; 3&4 -
30 seconds, 5 -10 seconds.
**Promo • 1967**
*10" one-sided promo album.*
**Half a Sixpence** *(edited)* **/ If The Rain's Got To Fall** *(edited)*
RCA Victor 47-9458 • 1967
*The promo release carried a yellow label. From the
Paramount Picture "Half A Sixpence".*

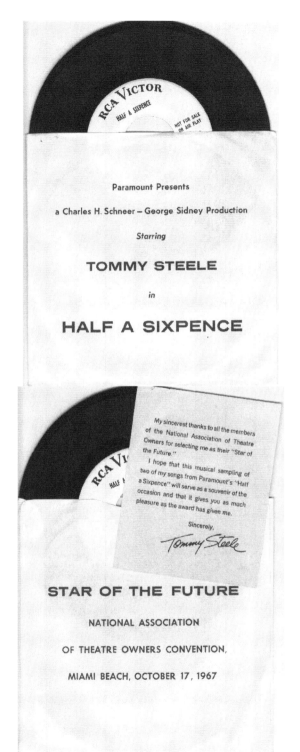

Paramount Presents

a Charles H. Schneer — George Sidney Production

*Starring*

**TOMMY STEELE**

*in*

**HALF A SIXPENCE**

My sincerest thanks to all the members of the National Association of Theatre Owners for selecting me as their "Star of the Future."

I hope that this musical sampling of two of my songs from Paramount's "Half a Sixpence" will serve as a souvenir of the occasion and that it gives you as much pleasure as the award has given me.

Sincerely,

*Tommy Steele*

**STAR OF THE FUTURE**

NATIONAL ASSOCIATION

OF THEATRE OWNERS CONVENTION,

MIAMI BEACH, OCTOBER 17, 1967

US Promotional 45  *(see info above)*   *(Coll. Terje Dalene)*

**Fortuosity / I'm A Brass Band Today**
London Buena Vista F-457 • (1967) *( picture sleeve)*

*The promo release with picture sleeve carried a white label. B-side exclusive for this single (also UK). The US picture sleeve is different than the UK one.*

*Note:* There's a US single from 1976 by one *Tommy Steele* on Slippery Rock Records #001 titled "Face In The Shadows" / "If I Were A Clown", both written by T. O. Steele. The A-side is kinda white disco and the B-side is an uptempo pop song. Just to set the record straight, this is not the English Tommy Steele.

## LPs:

### "ROCK AROUND THE WORLD" (12")
London LL-1770 • 1957
*Actually "The Tommy Steele Story", with a different cover. Maroon label. See also the movie section for more information about this movie in the USA.*

### "GET HAPPY WITH TOMMY"
London LL-3180 (mono) PS-201 (stereo) • 1960
*Same tracks as UK Decca LP LK-4351 "Get Happy With Tommy". As you can see this one was also released in stereo! which didn't happen in England. Therefore the particular stereo album is quite rare. As a matter of fact the album itself is so rare I have till this day never seen a stereo copy.*

### "EVERYTHING'S COMING UP BROADWAY"
Liberty LRP-3426 (mono) LST-7426 (stereo)        • 1964
Something's Coming / Hey There! / If I Were A Bell / Hey Look Me Over / The Girl That I Marry / Too Close For Comfort / Everything's Coming Up Roses / I Talk To The Trees / I Wish I Were In Love Again / Happy Talk / They Say It's Wonderful / There Once Was A Man
*Tommy's tribute to the many Broadway musicals that he admired. With Geoff Love and His Orchestra. This album also issued in UK on Columbia 33SX1674 / SCX 3536 (1964) and Canada on Capitol ST-6124 (1965) as "So This Is Broadway". Different liner notes.*

### "HALF A SIXPENCE" *Original Broadway Cast Production*

RCA Victor LOC-1110 (mono) LSO-1110 (stereo) • 1965
Overture / All In The Cause Of Economy / Half A Sixpence / Money To Burn (Tommy Steele –banjo solo / A Proper Gentleman / She's Too far Above Me / If The Rain's Got To Fall / Long Ago / Flash, Bang Wallop! / I Know What I Am / The Party's On The House / Finale

*Tommy is featured on all songs except "I Know What I Am". I haven't seen a UK issue of this album until much later when it came out on a Deram CD 820 589 "Half A Sixpence" in 1988, with the same front cover.*

**"THE HAPPIEST MILLIONAIRE"**   *Original Cast Soundtrack*
Buena Vista BV 5001 (mono) BVS 5001 (stereo) • 1967

*Same as UK issue, but with a nice fold-out cover which includes a booklet with pictures from the film and lyrics to the songs. This is the original album release.*

**"WALT DISNEY'S THE HAPPIEST MILLIONAIRE – COMMERCIAL RADIO ANNOUNCEMENTS"**
Buena Vista CR-2833/2834 • 1967

*Album containing nine 55 seconds, four 25 seconds, two 15 seconds and one 10 seconds **Radio Spots** for the movie "The Happiest Millionaire". All of them have something to do with Tommy Steele's involvement in the movie, even his rock'n'roll days are mentioned a few times in there.*

**"HALF A SIXPENCE"**   *Original Motion Picture Soundtrack*
RCA Victor LOC-1146 (mono) LSO-1146 (stereo) • 1967
Overture / All In The Cause Of Economy / Half A Sixpence / Money To Burn / I  Don't Believe A Word Of It – I'm Not Talking To You / A Proper Gentleman / She's Too Far Above Me / If The Rain's Got To Fall / Lady Botting's Boating Regatta Cup Racing Song (The Race Is On) / Entr'acte – Flash, Bang, Wallop! / I Know What I Am / This Is My World / Half A Sixpence (reprise) – Flash, Bang, Wallop! (reprise)

*Tommy is featured on all songs, except "Overture" and "I Know What I Am". I have seen a reel-to-reel tape, 3 ¾ ips, of this US release, but no more info availbale.    Album       also issued in UK on RCA Victor 6735 in 1967, and in Germany as LSO-1146.*

**"HALF A SIXPENCE"   OPEN-END INTERVIEW – RADIO SPECIAL**
Paramount Pictures • 1967
Tommy is talking about the movie and music from the film is heard.

*Recorded on location in England during the production of "Half A Sixpence".*

**"FINIAN'S RAINBOW"**   *Original Motion Picture* Soundtrack
Warner Brothers B 2550 (mono) BS 2550 (stereo) • 1968
Prelude (Main Title) / This Time Of The Year / How Are Things In Glocca Morra? / Look To The Rainbow / If This Isn't Love / <u>Something Sort Of Grandish</u> / That Great Come-And-Get-It-Day /Old Devil Moon / When The Idle Poor Become The Idle Rich / <u>When I'm Not Near The Girl I Love</u> / Necessity / Rain Dance Ballet / The Begat / <u>How Are Things In Glocca Morra?</u> (Finale)

*The underlined titles are sung by Tommy Steele. Also starring Fred Astaire and Petula Clark. See also the CD section.*

**"OPEN END INTERVIEW WITH THE STARS OF FINIAN'S RAINBOW"**   (2-LP set)
Warner Brothers - Seven Arts, Inc. PRO-292 • 1968
Interviews with *Tommy Steele*, Fred Astaire and Petula Clark.

*Each star is interviewed separately. Album sent to various radio-stations where the local disc jockey could ask the stars the questions by reading from an enclosed lyric sheet.*

**"...PRESENTS FINIAN'S RAINBOW"** – General release.
Warner Brothers  - Seven Arts, Inc. WBSA-5886 • 1968

*One-sided album containing four 30 and three 60 seconds Radio Spots for the film "Finian's Rainbow". Two of them have something to do with Tommy Steele's involvement in the movie.*

**"SIXPENNY MILLIONAIRE"**
Liberty LST-7566 • late 1968

*Contains the same tracks as the Liberty album LST-7426 "Everything's Coming Up Broadway" from 1964. Different cover.*

**"WHERE'S JACK?"**   *Original Score Soundtrack*
Paramount PAS-5005 • 1969

*Tommy Steele only acts in the movie, no singing. The music is performed by Mary Hopkin and Danny Doyle. Picture of Tommy, Stanley Baker and Fiona Lewis on front cover.*

*Note:* Terje Dalene from Norway got hold of a 10" one-sided promo (#22866) pressed by Dick Charles Recording Service, N.Y.C. featuring Tommy Steele playing a piano tune titled "The Wall". Don't know if any regular release was ever issued.    Probably a mid '60s recording.    But what's the background and story behind this? *(See picture below.)*

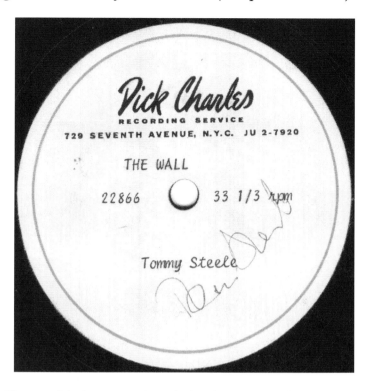

US 10" one-sided promo *(see info above)*   *(Coll. Terje Dalene)*

YUGOSLAVIA

45s:

**Butterfingers / Cannibal Pot**
Decca  (Jugoton) S-DC-8057 ● 1957 *(picture sleeve)*
    *Grey Decca label.  Came with a picture sleeve.*
**Hit Record / What A Little Darlin'**
Decca  (Jugoton) S-DC-8088 ● 1962
    *In Jugoton company sleeve.*

Yugoslavia EP Decca DC-9045

EP:

**"TOMMY STEELE"**
Decca (Jugoton) EP-DC-9045 • 1957
Teenage Party / Knee Deep In The Blues     + *tracks by* Winifred Atwell
   *Same as the one issued in Germany, "Teenage Party" Decca DX-1927, however, this came in a* sleeve *with two pictures of Tommy on both sides.*

TOMMY STEELE on CD :

All are UK releases except where mentioned otherwise.

**"HALF A SIXPENCE"**   *Original Broadway Cast recording*
Deram CD 820 589-2 • 1988
   *Same tracks as the US album release on RCA Victor 1110 from 1965.*
**"TOMMY STEELE'S GREATEST HITS"**
Deram CD 820 688-2 • 1988
Rock With The Caveman / Come On, Let's Go / Singing The Blues / Butterfingers / A Handful Of Songs / Shiralee / Little White Bull / Nairobi / The Only Man On The Island / Knee Deep In The Blues / Water, Water / Tallahassee Lassie / Happy Guitar / Hey You ! / Give! Give! Give! / Hit Record /

303

The Writing On The Wall / Flash, Bang, Wallop! / Must Be Santa / What A Mouth (What A North And South)  *(20 tracks)*

*I have never seen an LP issue of this album, but it's probably out there somewhere.*

**"THE ROCK'N'ROLL YEARS"**
See For Miles SEE CD-203 ● 1990
*Same tracks as LP See For Miles SEE 203.*

**"HANS CHRISTIAN ANDERSEN"**  *Original London Palladium Cast recording*
Marble Arch CMA CD-119 ● 1991
*Same as LP PYE NSPL-18451 from 1974.*

UK 2-CD set Decca 466 409-2 (1999)

**"THE VERY BEST OF TOMMY STEELE"**
Carlton (Pickwick) PWKM-4071 P ● 1991
Nairobi / Tallahassee Lassie / Kookaburra / Flash, Bang Wallop! / She's Too Far Above Me / Happy Guitar / Young Love / Butterfingers / Green Eye / Where Have All The Flowers Gone / A Handful Of Songs / Marriage Type Love / Georgia On My Mind / Come On, Let's Go / Sweet Georgia Brown / It's All Happening / Only Man On The Island / Princess / Writing On The Wall / What A Mouth (What A North And South)  *(20 tracks)*

**"HANS ANDERSEN"**  (USA)  *London Palladium production (1977)*
DRG Theater 13116 ● 1992
*Same cover as the UK LP PYE NSPL-18551 from 1978. Tracks are identical except they have added 'This Town' and 'For Hans Tonight' from the 1974 production, making it a 19 track compilation.*

*Not quite sure about the year of release for this CD. Nothing printed on the cover or label.*

## "THE EP COLLECTION"
See For Miles SEE CD-347 • 1992

Rock With The Caveman / Doomsday Rock / Singing The Blues / Take Me Back Baby / A Handful Of Songs / Rebel Rock / Will It Be You / Happy Guitar / Knee Deep In The Blues / Put A Ring On Her Finger / Young Love / Come On, Let's Go / Elevator Rock / The Only Man On The Island / Time To Kill / The Little White Bull / Number Twenty-Two Across The Way / You Gotta Go / Singing Time / Cannibal Pot / Build Up / Water, Water *(23 tracks)*

## "SOME LIKE IT HOT"
First Night Score CD-33 • 1992  *(Picture CD single)*

Some Like It Hot / It's Always Love

*Recorded at Angel Studios, Islington, London, December 1991. Producer: Tommy Steele.*

## "SOME LIKE IT HOT"  *Original London Cast recording*
First Night CAST CD-28 • 1992

*Overture*: "Some Like It Hot" / Maple Leaf Rag / Penniless Bums / Meet A Man In Chicago / Beauty That Drives A Man Mad / With The Sun On My Face / Dirty Old Men / Doing It For Sugar / Dirty Old Men (reprise) / What Do You Give A Man Who Has Everything / I'm Naive / Beautiful Through And Through / Magic Nights / It's Always Love / *Finale*: "Some Like It Hot"

*Recorded at Angel Studios, Islington, London, on 25th and 26th February 1992. Producer: Tommy Steele*

## "HANS CHRISTIAN ANDERSEN"  *Original London Palladium Cast recording (1974)*
Success CMA CD-119 (16080CD) • 1993

*This is the same as Marble Arch CD-119 from 1991, but with a different cover.*

## "HANS CHRISTIAN ANDERSEN"  (Australia)  *Original London Palladium Cast recording (1974)*
Pickwick PKD-3146 • 1993

*This is the same as UK Marble Arch CD-119, same cover.*

## "HANDFUL OF SONGS"
Spectrum CD 5500182 • 1993

A Handful Of Songs / Singing The Blues / Young Love / Water, Water / Cannibal Pot / It's All Happening / Where Have All The Flowers Gone / Nairobi / I Puts The Lightie On /

Georgia On My Mind / Where's The Birdie / Rock With The Caveman / Butterfingers / Shiralee / What A Little Darlin' / She's Too Far Above Me / Hey You! / Flash, Bang, Wallop! *(18 tracks)*

**"THE HIT COLLECTION"** (Sweden)
Scana CD 95033      ● 1995
Singing The Blues / Butterfingers / A Handful Of Songs / Rock With The Caveman / Come On, Let's Go / Shiralee / The Only Man On The Island / Give! Give! Give! / Little White Bull / Tallahassee Lassie / Happy Guitar / Nairobi / Must Be Santa / What A Mouth (What A North And South) / Knee Deep In The Blues / Water, Water / Hey You! *(17 tracks)*

**"SINGIN' IN THE RAIN AND OTHER GREAT STANDARDS"**
Hallmark CD 300742 ● 1995
   *Same as LP Arcade ADE-P14 "40 Favourites" from 1974, minus one medley: # 4 on side A. See also Double Play CD GRF-242 from 1996.*

**"TOMMY STEELE"**
Tring Double Play GRF-242 ● 1996
   *See Hallmark CD 300742 from 1995.*


**"THE WORLD OF TOMMY STEELE"** (Germany)
Spectrum CD 552 016-2 ● 1996
Singing The Blues / The Little White Bull / A Handful Of Songs / Shiralee / Half A Sixpence / Rock With The Caveman / Water, Water / Come On, Let's Go / Sweet Georgia Brown / Where's The Birdie / Nairobi / What A Mouth (What A North And South) / If The Rain's Got To Fall / Where Have All The Flowers Gone / The Only Man On The Island / Knee Deep In The Blues / Butterfingers / Number Twenty-Two Across The Way / She's Too far Above Me / Happy Guitar *(20 tracks.)*

**"SINGIN' IN THE RAIN"** *Original Cast recording*
First Night OCR CD-6013   ● 1997
   *First released on LP in 1984, Safari RAIN-1. Also released as CD in New Zealand with the same label and number.*

**"SOME LIKE IT HOT"** *Original London Cast recording*
First Night OCR CD-6028   ● 1998
   *Same as First Night CD-28 from 1992*

**"THE DECCA YEARS 1956-1963"** (2-CD set)
Decca 466 409-2      ● 1999
*CD1:* Rock With The Caveman / Rock Around The Town / Doomsday Rock / Elevator Rock / Singing The Blues / Rebel Rock / Knee Deep In The Blues / Teenage Party / Butterfingers / Cannibal Pot / Shiralee / Grandad's Rock /

Butterfly / Water, Water / A Handful Of Songs / Hey You! / Plant A Kiss / Nairobi / Neon Sign / Happy Guitar / Princess / It's All Happening / What Do You Do / The Only Man On The Island / I Puts The Lightie On / Come On, Let's Go / Put A Ring On Her Finger / A Lovely Night / Marriage Type Love / Hiawatha / The Trial / Tallahassee Lassie / Give! Give! Give! / You Were Mine / Young Ideas.

*CD2:* Little White Bull / Singing Time / What A Mouth (What A North And South) / Kookaburra / Happy-Go-Lucky Blues / (The Girl With The) Long Black Hair / Must be Santa / Boys And Girls / The Dit-Dit Song / My Big Best Shoes / The Writing On The Wall / Drunken Guitar / Hit Record / What A Little Darlin' / He's Got Love / Green Eye / Butter Wouldn't Melt In Your Mouth / Where Have All The Flowers Gone / Flash, Bang, Wallop! / She's Too Far Above Me / Half A Sixpence / Giddy-Up-A-Ding Dong / Kaw-Liga / Young Love / Take Me Back Baby / Build Up / Time To Kill / Hair-Down, Hoe-Down / Sweet Georgia Brown /Tommy The Toreador / Hollerin' And Screamin' / Lonesome Traveller / So Long (It's Been Good To Know You) *(68 tracks)*

*Several songs are making their first appearance on CD. Great compilation and includes a nice booklet.*

*Finally they have included one of Tommy's best rockers, "Hair-Down, Hoe-Down". This particular track was missing from both the See for Miles' "The Rock'n'Roll Years" (1990) and "EP Collection" (1992) albums.*

**"THE BEST OF TOMMY STEELE"**
Universal Spectrum 544 172-2 • 1999
Rock With The Caveman / Singing The Blues / Knee Deep In The Blues / Butterfingers / Water, Water / A Handful Of Songs / Shiralee / Hey You! / Nairobi / Happy Guitar / The Only Man On The Island /Come On, Let's Go / Tallahassee Lassie / Give! Give! Give! / The Little White Bull / What A Mouth (What A North And South) / Writing On The Wall / Half A Sixpence / Sweet Georgia Brown / Must Be Santa *(20 tracks)*

**"A WORLD OF ROCK'N'ROLL** - THE ORIGINAL VERSION"
(France)
RDM Edition CD-269 • 1990s

 *This is actually the "The Tommy Steele Story" Decca LF 1288 (1957).*

**"HALF A SIXPENCE"** (USA) *Original Broadway Cast Recording*
RCA Victor (BMG) 09026-63691-2 • 2000

 *Recorded on 2 May, 1965, in Webster Hall, New York City. Contains a nice booklet with revised liner-notes and updated information.*

**"THE HAPPIEST MILLIONAIRE" (UK)** *Original Soundtrack*
Buena Vista 5099921610028 • 2002

 *Containing the original 15 songs with two bonus tracks which doesn't feature Tommy Steele.*
*Bonus tracks:* It Won't Be Long 'Til Christmas / Off Rittenhouse Square *(demo)*

 *The latter is the original opening number that was shelved when Tommy Steele was signed onto the project. The other ditty is a song that was cut from the final film. However, the version included here is a cover performed by Anne Shelton and the John Aldis Singers and released in the UK.*

 **"THE HAPPIEST MILLIONAIRE**" (Canada) *Original Soundtrack*
Buena Vista DIS 607817 • 2002
*Containing the original 15 songs with two bonus tracks which doesn't feature Tommy Steele.*
*Bonus tracks:* It Won't Be Long 'Til Christmas / Off Rittenhouse Square *(demo)*

**"CINDERELLA**" *Original Cast Recording*
Bayview Records RNBW-018 • 2002

 *Originally issued in 1959 on Decca LK-4303 / SKL-4050.*

**Many Sides Of Rock And Roll - "THE BEST OF TOMMY STEELE"** (unknown country) *Bootleg(?)*
(*Unknown label and number*) • 2000s
Rock With The Caveman / Rock Around The Town / Hey You! / Doomsday Rock / Elevator Rock / Singing The Blues / Rebel Rock / Knee Deep In The Blues / Teenage Party / Butterfly / Cannibal Pot / Grandad's Rock / A Handful Of Songs / Plant A Kiss / Neon Sign / Happy Guitar / Come On,

Let's Go / I Puts The Lightie On / Hiawatha / Put A Ring On Her Finger / The Trial / Tallahassee Lassie / Give! Give! Give! / You Were Mine / Young Ideas / Happy-Go-Lucky Blues / Drunken Guitar *(instr)* / Giddy-Up A Ding Dong / Kaw Liga / Young Love / Take Me Back Baby / Build Up / Time To Kill / Hair-Down, Hoe-Down / Sweet Georgia Brown / Hollerin' And Screamin' / Lonesome Traveller *(37 tracks)*

*Don't know the origin of this release as it doesn't feature any record label or number as far as I can see. It seems to be from one of the used-to-be east-block countries, however, it was released after the 1999 double CD "The Decca Years 1956-1963" as it has the same front cover picture. Ten other CDs in the same "Many Sides Of Rock And Roll" series are printed on the inside of the cover.*

**"ROCK WITH THE CAVEMAN"** (2-CD set)
SPECTRUM (Decca) CD-982 479-8 ● 2005
*CD1*: Rock With The Caveman / Elevator Rock* / Singing The Blues / Knee Deep In The Blues / Butterfingers / Water, Water / A Handful Of Songs / Shiralee / Hey You! / Nairobi / Happy Guitar / The Only Man On The Island / Come On, Let's Go / Tallahassee Lassie / Give! Give! Give! / Little White Bull / What A Mouth (What A North And South) / Must Be Santa / The Writing On The Wall / *medley:* Hollerin' And Screamin'*- Lonesome Traveller*.
*CD2*: Little Darlin' / Old Obadiah / Kookaburra / Tommy The Toreador / Shout / So Long / Doomsday Rock / Wedding Bells / Honky Tonk Blues / Kaw-Liga / Razzle-Dazzle / Giddy-Up A Ding Dong / Young Love / Photograph / Hair-Down, Hoe-Down / Princess / Take A Ride / Where's The Birdie / Flash, Bang Wallop! / She's Too Far Above Me / You Gotta Go / Time To Kill. *(43 tracks)*

*CD 1 is interesting, as all tracks except * are Tommy's UK hits in correct year sequence from 1956-1961. "Elevator Rock" was his second Decca release and should have been a hit. "A Handful Of Songs" is the alternative, slower version from the Tommy Steele Story.*

**"SCROOGE"** *London Palladium Cast recording*
BK Records BK002CD ● 2005 *(The official release.)*
Bill Kenwright presents Tommy Steele In Scrooge.
Sing A Christmas Carol / M.O.N.E.Y. / Christmas Children / Mister Christmas / I Hate People / Make The Most Of This World / It's Not My Fault / / December The Twenty-Fifth / Happiness / You...You / Love While You Can / I Like Life /

Finale Act 1 / The Milk Of Human Kindness / The Beautiful Day / The Minister's Cat / A Better Life / Thank You Very Much / I'll Begin Again / Finale Act 2

*There's also an unofficial release out there, with a blue cover.*

**"FINIAN'S RAINBOW"** (USA) *Original Motion Picture Soundtrack*

Collector's Choice Music CCM-729 ● 2006

Prelude (Main Title) / This Time Of The Year / How Are Things In Glocca Morra? / Look To The Rainbow / If This Isn't Love / <u>Something Sort Of Grandish</u> / That Great Come-And-Get-It-Day / Old Devil Moon / When The Idle Poor Become The Idle Rich / <u>When I'm Not Near The Girl I Love</u> / Necessity / Rain Dance Ballet / The Begat / <u>How Are Things In Glocca Morra?</u> (Finale)

*The underlined titles are featuring Tommy Steele. Also starring Fred Astaire and Petula Clark. Originally this album came out in 1968 on Warner Brothers BS-2550 (USA) and Warner Brothers WF-2550 (UK). In 2004 Rhino Handmade (USA) released a limited CD edition (RHM2-7852) of this record which soon became sold out.*

**"HEY YOU !"**

Rex Records REXX-118 ● 2008

Take Me Back Baby / Butterfingers / I Like / A Handful Of Songs / You Gotta Go / Water, Water / Cannibal Pot / Will It Be You / Two Eyes / Build Up / Time To Kill / Elevator Rock / Doomsday Rock / Teenage Party / Giddy-Up A Ding Dong / Treasure Of Love / Honky-Tonk Blues / Razzle-Dazzle / Kaw-Liga / Teenage Party / Wedding Bells / What Is This Thing Called Love / On The Move / Rock With The Caveman / Hey You! / Singing The Blues / Knee Deep In The Blues / Shiralee / Grandad's Rock

*Interesting release. 'The Tommy Steele Story' and 'The Tommy Steele Stage Show' together on one CD, plus five bonus tracks. Check out the two original albums in the UK disco.*

**"THE TOMMY STEELE STORY"** (Holland)

Hallmark 706872 ● 2008

Take Me Back Baby / Butterfingers / I Like / A Handful Of Songs / You Gotta Go / Water, Water / Cannibal Pot / Will It Be You / Two Eyes / Build Up / Time To Kill / Elevator Rock / Doomsday Rock / Teenage Party / Giddy-Up A Ding Dong / Treasure Of Love / Honky-Tonk Blues / Razzle-Dazzle / Kaw-Liga / Wedding Bells / What Is This Thing Called Love / On The Move / Rock With The Caveman

*Much the same as the one above except the bonus tracks, however, different cover, and they left out one track from the 'Stage Show' album, namely 'Teenage Party'. They probably thought it was the same version (which it's not) and didn't want it included twice.*

## "RAZZLE DAZZLE"
Pegasus Entertainment PEG CD-662 • 2008
Butterfingers / Cannibal Pot / Razzle Dazzle / Teenage Party / Treasure Of Love / Wedding Bells / Young Love / You Gotta Go / Will It Be You? / Two Eyes/ Time To Kill / Take Me Back Baby / Plant A Kiss / Singing Time / Number 22 Across The Way / I Like / Hey You! / Butterfly / Build Up / A Handful Of Songs

*20 of the more obscure Tommy songs, not so much rock'n'roll as the title would indicate. Interesting compilation, though. It also makes the first appearance on CD of "Number 22 Across The Way".*

## "THE WORLD OF TOMMY STEELE"
Decca 531 145-0 • 2009
A Handful Of Songs / Singing The Blues / Knee Deep In The Blues / Water, Water / Nairobi / The Only Man On The Island / Shiralee / Happy Guitar / Butterfingers / Rock With The Caveman / Tallahassee Lassie / Give! Give! Give! / Come On, Let's Go / Hey You! / The Writing On The Wall / It's All Happening / Hit Records / Half A Sixpence / Flash, Bang, Wallop / Little White Bull / What A Mouth (What A North And South)

*21 classic Tommy Steele recordings that embraces all of the musical styles he's known for. Also includes a nice 12 page booklet.*

## "THE REAL STEELE"
Blue Orchid BLUE134CD • 2009
Rock With The Caveman / What Is This Thing Called Love / Doomsday Rock / Young Love / Singing The Blues / Giddy-Up A Ding Dong / Knee Deep In The Blues / Teenage Party / Butterfingers / Razzle Dazzle / Shiralee / Take Me Back Baby / Water, Water / Kaw-Liga / A Handful Of Songs / You Gotta Go / Hey You! / Honky Tonk Blues / Happy Guitar / Time To Kill / Nairobi / On The Move / Only Man On The Island / The Truth About Me / Butterfly / Family Tree / It's All Happening / Will It Be You / Come On, Let's Go / Treasure Of Love / Put A Ring On Her Finger / Thanks A Lot / A Lovely Night / Photograph / Number 22 Across The Way / Hair-Down, Hoe-Down / I Like

*Not bad, 37 tracks on one CD! And even some obscure ones too. The most unusual have to be "The Truth About Me" making it's first appearance on CD. Originally this was a small 6" 78rpm record from 1957 where Tommy spoke about himself to the fans (see UK disco). Stylish blue cover including a booklet with necessary info on all tracks.*

## "SINGING THE BLUES"

d Performance 38297● 2009

*CD 1:* Singing The Blues / Rock With The Caveman / Nairobi / Butterfingers / Water, Water / Rebel Rock / Happy Guitar / Doomsday Rock / Neon Sign / You Gotta Go / A Lovely Night / Butterfly / Photograph / Time To Kill / Build Up / It's All Happening / Princess / Cannibal Pot / I Like / Rock Around The Town / Giddy-Up A Ding Dong

*CD 2 :* A Handful Of Songs / Come On, Let's Go / Hey You! / The Only Man On The Island / Shiralee / Young Love / Elevator Rock / Teenage Party / Knee Deep In The Blues / Grandad's Rock / Marriage Type Love / Number 22 Across The Way / Two Eyes / What Do You Do / I Puts The Lightie On / Hair Down, Hoe Down / Wedding Bells / Plant A Kiss / Take Me Back Baby / Will It Be You? / Kaw Liga

## "THE VERY BEST OF TOMMY STEELE"  (2-CD set)

Universal 5321840 ● 2009

*CD 1 - The Rock'n'Roll Years*

Rock With The Caveman / Singing The Blues / Rock Around The Town / Doomsday Rock / Eleveator Rock / Young Love / Wedding Bells / Rebel Rock / Knee Deep In The Blues / Teenage Party / Giddy-Up A Ding Dong / What Is This Thing Called Love? / Butterfingers / Cannibal Pot / Shiralee / Grandad's Rock / Butterfly / Water, Water / Build Up / Will It Be You? / Two Eyes / You Gotta Go / Hey You! / Plant A Kiss / Happy Guitar / Neon Sign / Come On, Let's Go / Tallahassee Lassie / Give! Give! Give! / The Writing On The Wall

*CD 2 - Musicals, Movies and More*

A Handful Of Songs / Hit Record / What Do You Do / Princess / It's All Happening / Nairobi / The Only Man On The Island / A Lovely Night / Little White Bull / Singing Time / What A Mouth (What A North And South) / Where Have All The Flowers Gone / Flash, Bang, Wallop / Half A Sixpence / She's Too Far Above Me / Fortuosity / Finale - Some Like It Hot / Fascinating Rhythm / Singing In The Rain / Thank You Very Much

*Now this is a fine compilation of tracks, although "Hair Down, Hoe Down" is missing on CD1. It also has a nice and informative booklet, plus a very unusual picture on the front cover.*

**"THE DEFINITIVE COLLECTION"** (UK) (3-CD set)
Reader's Digest RDCD7021-3 ● 2009
*CD 1* "Singing The Blues"
Rock With The Caveman / Rock Around The Town / Doomsday Rock / Elevator Rock / Singing The Blues / Rebel Rock / Knee Deep In The Blues / Teenage Party / Butterfingers / Cannibal Pot / Water, Water / A Handful Of Songs / Shiralee / Grandad's Rock / Hey You! / Plant A Kiss / Nairobi / Neon Sign / Happy Guitar / Princess / What Do You Do / Hair-Down, Hoe-Down / The Only Man On The Island / Come On, Let's Go
*CD 2* "Half A Sixpence"
Young Love / Butterfly / Kaw-Liga / Put A Ring On Her Finger / I Puts The Lightie On / Hiawatha / The Trial / Tallahassee Lassie / Give! Give! Give! / Young Ideas / Tommy The Toreador / Little White Bull / Singing Time / What A Mouth (What A North And South) / Giddy-Up A Ding Dong / Kookaburra / Happy-Go-Lucky Blues / (The Girl With The) Long Black Hair / Take Me Back Baby / Build Up / A Lovely Night / Time To Kill / Half A Sixpence
*CD 3* "Flash, Bang, Wallop"
Flash, Bang, Wallop / She's Too Far Above Me / Where ave All The Flowers Gone / Green Eye / Butter Wouldn't Melt In Your Mouth / What A Little Darlin' / Hit Record / The Writing On The Wall / Drunken Guitar / The Dit-Dit Song / Sweet Georgia Brown / My Big Best Shoes / It's All Happening / Marriage Type Love / Boys And Girls / Hollerin' And Screamin' - Lonesome Traveller / So Long (It's Been Good To Know You) / You Were Mine / He's Got Love / Must Be Santa / Wonderful Copenhagen

*'Definitive' is always a difficult word to use, however, all the hits are here plus some good ones that weren't, and songs from various soundtracks. So yes, you get the most of the most. The front cover is great too, and an informative booklet written by Spencer Leigh.*

**"THE COLLECTION"**
The Red Box THERB-158 • 2010
A Handful Of Songs / Rock With The Caveman / Singing The Blues / <u>Butterfingers</u> / Water, Water / Knee Deep In The Blues / Nairobi / Come On, Let's Go / Tallahassee Lassie / Little White Bull / Shiralee / Happy Guitar / Hey You! / The Only Man On The Island / Give! Give! Give! / Tommy The Toreador / I Puts The Lightie On / Elevator Rock

*The only interesting thing about this rather anonymus release is that it includes a different version of "Butterfingers" available no where else!!! You never know where or when to find them.*

**"COME ON, LET'S GO! - The Very Best Of TOMMY STEELE"** (3-CD set)
Uni SPECSIG-2047 • 2010
*CD 1:* Rock With The Caveman / Singing The Blues / Knee Deep In The Blues / Butterfly / Hey You! / Plant A Kiss / Nairobi / The Only Man On The Island / Come On, Let's Go / Put A Ring On Her Finger / The Trial / Hiawatha / Tallahassee Lassie / Give! Give! Give! / You Were Mine / Young Ideas / What A Mouth (What A North And South) / Happy-Go-Lucky Blues / (The Girl With The) Long Black Hair / The Writing On The Wall / What A Little Darlin' / Hit Record
*CD 2:* A Handful Of Songs / Butterfingers / Take Me Back Baby / Time To Kill / Cannibal Pot / Build Up / Doomsday Rock / Elevator Rock / Teenage Party / Shiralee / Grandad's Rock / Happy Guitar / Princess / It's All Happening / What Do You Do / Hair-Down Hoe-Down / Tommy The Toreador / Singing Time / Little White Bull / She's Too far Above Me / Half A Sixpence / Flash, Bang, Wallop
*CD 3:* Young Love / Butter Wouldn't Melt In Your Mouth / A Lovely Night / Marriage Type Love / Neon Sign / Green Eye / Sweet Georgia Brown / Where Have All The Flowers Gone / Drunken Guitar / Kookaburra / The Dit-Dit Song / Boys And Girls / I Puts The Lightie On / My Big Best Shoes / Must Be Santa / He's Got Love / Rebel Rock / Rock Around The Town / Giddy- Up A Ding Dong / Kaw-Liga / Lonesome Traveller / Hollerin' And Screamin' / So Long (It's Been Good To Know You)

**"A WORLD OF ROCK'N'ROLL - THE ORIGINAL VERSION"**
(France)
RDM Edition CD-269 • 2010

314

*Same 14 tracks as the original Tommy Steele Story album.*

**TOMMY STEELE & COLIN HICKS – *The Rock'n'Roll Years 1956-1960***
**"HOLLERIN' 'N' SCREAMIN'"** (UK) (2-CD set)
Pink & Black PBCD-019 • 2012
*Tommy Steele tracks:* Tallahassee Lassie /Drunken Guitar / Rock Around The Town / Plant A Kiss / Teenage Party / Hey You! / Take Me Back Baby / Two Eyes / Knee Deep In The Blues / Doomsday Rock / Singing The Blues / Swaller Tail Coat / You Were Mine / Put A Ring On Her Finger / Build Up / You Gotta Go / Rebel Rock / Elevator Rock / Give! Give! Give! / Butterfly / Come On, Let's Go / Rock With The Caveman / Happy Guitar / Young Love / Time To Kill / Singing Time / Cannibal Pot / Water, Water / Grandad's Rock / Razzle Dazzle / Honky Tonk Blues / She's My Baby / Hollerin' And Screamin'

*34 songs by Tommy and 33 by Colin Hicks, one CD each. Interesting concept, combining the two brothers onto one specific release. The most interesting thing is that we finally get the song "She's My Baby" on CD, previously only available on the rare US single London 45-1950-V coupled with "Happy-Go-Lucky Blues" from 1960 (See US disco).*

UK 2-CD Pink & Black PBCD-019 (2012)

All are UK releases except where mentioned otherwise. Since 2005 a lot of CD compilations have seen the light of day. They are released as wild fire, usually only containing one track by Tommy. Interesting? It depends on the compilation itself. Anyway, here's a survey of the most important ones.

**"UK ROCK 'N' ROLL – The Rock'n'Roll Era"** (Holland)
*Time Life* TL-516/33 • 1992
*Tommy Steele tracks*: Knee Deep In The Blues / Nairobi / Happy Guitar / Teenage Party / Elevator Rock / Rebel Rock
*Also featured are Billy Fury, Marty Wilde and Lonnie Donegan with one side each. No picture of Tommy, just Billy Fury. Fold-out cover with liner-notes.* Also available as a 2-LPset, Time Life TL-514/33.

**"BRITISH BEAT BEFORE THE BEATLES"**
(7 CDs - 140 track selections) • 1993
EMI CDGO 2046    Volume 1  (1955-56)
*Tommy Steele tracks:* Rock With The Caveman / Singing The Blues
EMI CDGO 2047  Volume 2  (1957)
*Tommy Steele track:* Butterfly
EMI CDGO 2048  Volume 3  (1958)
*Tommy Steele track:* Come On, Let's Go
EMI CDGO 2029  Volume 4  (1959)
*Tommy Steele track:* Tallahassee Lassie

**"TOMMY-ELVIS-CLIFF / THE 3 LOVE TENORS"** (Sweden)
Scana CD 95032    • 1995
*Tommy Steele tracks :* Singing The Blues / Butterfingers / A Handful Of Songs / The Only Man On The Island / Shiralee / Come On, Let's Go
*Also 6 tracks each by* Elvis Presley *and* Cliff Richard.

***THE IVOR NOVELLO AWARDS* – THE WINNERS**
**"40 YEARS OF OUTSTANDING BRITISH SONGS 1955-1995" (2-CD set)**
EMI 7243 8 33680 2 • 1995
*Tommy Steele track:* A Handful Of Songs
*BASCA – the British Academy of Songwriters, Composers and Authors has been presenting the Ivor Novello Awards since 1955 to Britain's writing community. Unlike other musical accolades, the Ivors are not based upon statistics or sales. The winners are selected by songwriters and composers.*

**"HAIL VARIETY"**
Lismor LCOM-5249 • 1995
*Tommy Steele track:* Rock With The Caveman  *(original Decca recording, 40 seconds)*
*Highlights and memories of 48 stars of the Great British Music Hall, narrated by George Elrick. The earliest recording is from 1901, the latest being from 1957. All recordings are edited down to some 45 seconds.*
*This particular album was originally released for the Variety Club of Great Britain in 1983 on Oriole Records. However, also refering to the 1959 UK LP on Oriole MG. 20033 featuring the same Tommy track but in its full length (see UK disco).*

**"HAVE YOURSELF AN EASY LISTENING CHRISTMAS"**
(Germany)
Spectrum (Karusell) CD 552 110-2 • 1996
*Tommy Steele track:* Must Be Santa
*It's the first time I have seen this Tommy Steele track included on a compilation album. Also interesting because it's one of two Christmas songs recorded by Tommy, and it makes it easier to be played at the Yuletide. Further artists being Bing Crosby, Connie Francis, David Essex, RogerWhittaker, The Anita Kerr Singers, The Statler Brothers, The Blue Diamonds, Harry Simeone Chorale among others.*

**"SHOWTIME** – Songs From The Golden Age Of Musicals"
Marks & Spencer CMD-615 • mid '90s
*Tommy Steele track:* Half A Sixpence

**"THE HITS & THE MISSES"**   (2-CD set)
Play CD-007 • 1998
*Tommy Steele track:*  Dream Maker *(stereo)*
*Includes a 16 page booklet. The rest of this compilation contain mostly lesser known UK artists; the exception being Adam Faith, Marty Wilde, John Barry and Shirley Bassey.*

**"DECCA ORIGINALS : "THE ROCK'N'ROLL SCENE"**
Deram 844 892-2 • 1999
Tommy Steele track:  Elevator Rock     *Contains various skiffle and rock'n'roll songs (a total of 25) from the likes of Bob Cort Skiffle, Ken Colyer's Skiffle Group, Michael Cox, Billy Fury, Wee Willie Harris, Freddie Starr & Midnighters, Screamin' Lord Sutch, Lonnie Donegan and others. Good stuff!*

**"SKEIVE SKIVER"**   (Norway)
Arcade CD-9100021 • 1999
*Tommy Steele track :* Happy Guitar

*A compilation of various '50s, '60s and '70s artists and groups (26 tracks), put together by Norwegian DJ Rune Halland from his Radio programme "Skeive Skiver", which was on the air for many years. Includes a nice booklet.*

**"MUSIC OF THE YEAR – 1957"**
Spectrum CD-544 148 • 1999
*Tommy Steele track:* Shiralee

**"MUSIC OF THE YEAR – 1958"**
Spectrum CD-545 058 • 1999
*Tommy Steele track:* Come On, Let's Go

**"MUSIC OF THE YEAR – 1959"**
Spectrum CD-564 938 • 1999
*Tommy Steele track:* Tallahassee Lassie

**"MUSIC OF THE YEAR – 1960"**
Spectrum CD-544 155 • 1999
*Tommy Steele track:* What A Mouth (What A North And South)

**"MUSIC OF THE YEAR – 1961"**
Spectrum CD-544 140 • 1999
*Tommy Steele track:* Writing On The Wall

**No. 1s of THE FIFTIES**
Marks & Spencer MS-4930 • 2001
*Tommy Steele track:* Singing The Blues

**"THE TEDDY BOY GENERATION"**
CD / CMF-683 • 2003
*Tommy Steele track:* Doomsday Rock

**"ROCK YOU SINNERS! – The Dawn Of British Rock'n'Roll"**
Rev-Ola Bandstand CR BAND-10 • 2006
*Tommy Steele tracks:* Rock Around The Town / Doomsday Rock / Rock With The Caveman.

**GREAT BRTISH ROCK'n'ROLL – As Good As It Gets!"**
**(2-CD set)**
Smith & Co. SCCD-1124 • 2007
*Tommy Steele tracks:* Rock With The Caveman / Elevator Rock / Doomsday Rock / Rebel Rock / Rock Around The Town / Singing The Blues
*Picture of Tommy on the front cover.*


**"ROCK'n'SKIFFLE – Brit Beat Beginnings"** (4-CD set)
Proper PROPERBOX 135 • 2007
*Tommy Steele tracks:* Rock With The Caveman / Rock Around The Town / Doomsday Rock / Elevator Rock / Rebel Rock / Singing The Blues

*The Tommy tracks are on Disc 4.  Picture of Tommy on the front cover.*

**"NOSTALGIA Vol. 2"**  (Sweden)
Universal 560807 • 2007
*Tommy Steele track:*  A Handful Of Songs

**"ICONS - ROCK'N'ROLL ORIGINALS"** (2-CD set)
Green Umbrella ICON2CD-2161 • 2007
*Tommy Steele track:*  Rock With The Caveman

**"THE 1956 BRITISH HIT PARADE"** Part 2 / July-December (4-CD set)
Acrobat ACQCD-7003 • 2007
*Tommy Steele tracks:* Rock With The Caveman / Singing The Blues

**"THE 1957 BRITISH HIT PARADE"** Part 1 / January-July (4-CD set)
Acrobat ACQCD-7004 • 2008
*Tommy Steele tracks:* Knee Deep In The Blues / Butterfingers

**"THE 1957 BRITISH HIT PARADE"** Part 2 / July-December (4-CD set)
Acrobat ACQCD-7005 • 2008
*Tommty Steele tracks:* Water, Water / A Handful Of Songs / Shiralee / Hey You!

The three CD sets above are quite good and feature all the hits from the actual periods, both English and American artists.  More CDs will follow.

**"GREAT BRITISH ROCK'n'ROLL** – As Good As It Gets! Vol. 2"** (2-CD set)
Smith & Co. SCCD-1146 • 2008
*Tommy Steele tracks:* Hey You! / Teenage Party / A Handful Of Songs / Butterfly
   *Picture of Tommy on the front cover.*

**1957 – WHEN SKIFFLE WAS KING**
Xtra 26589 • 2008
*Tommy Steele tracks:* Singing The Blues / Butterfingers / Water, Water

**ROCK AROUND THE CLOCK**  (2-CD set)
Marks & Spencer MS-2363 • 2008
*Tommy Steele tracks:* Singing The Blues / Come On Let's Go

**BRITISH ROCK'N'ROLL ANTHOLOGY**
Universal Spectrum 531 585-5 • 2009
*Tommy Steele tracks:* Rock With The Caveman / Tallahassee Lassie / Come On, Let's Go / Singing The Blues

**"BRITAIN LEARNS TO ROCK!"**
Fantastic Voyage FVCD005 • 2009
*Tommy Steele tracks:* Elevator Rock / Shiralee
*Great cover and booklet.*
**"BRITISH ROCK & ROLL"** (3-CD set)
Odeon BOBCD003 • 2009
*Tommy Steele tracks:* Elevator Rock / Rock With The Caveman / Singing The Blues / Tallahasse Lassie
*Picture of Tommy on the front cover together with Cliff Richard and Billy Fury.*
**"GREATEST HITS OF 1957"** (2-CD set)
Great Voices of the Century GVC-1957 • 2010
*Tommy Steele tracks:* Singing The Blues / A Handful Of Songs
*Picture of Tommy on the front cover together with Harry Belafonte, Fats Domino and Charlie Gracie.*
**"GREATEST HITS OF 1958"** (2-CD set)
Great Voices of the Century GVC-1958 • 2010
*Tommy Steele track:* Nairobi
**"ROCKIN' AT THE 2 I's COFFEE BAR"**
Delta DCD-26632 • 2010
*Tommy Steele tracks:* Singing The Blues / Rock With The Caveman
*25 tracks, also featuring Cliff Richard, Marty Wilde, Terry Dene, Adam Faith and many more.*
**"DRUM BEAT/SATURDAY CLUB and British Hits of the Late '50s"** (2-CD set)
Jasmine JASCD-580 • 2010
*Tommy Steele tracks:* Come On, Let's Go / Tallahassee Lassie
**"VINTAGE CHILDREN'S FAVOURITES 1926-1959"** (2-CD set)
Retrospective RTS-4162 • 2010
*Tommy Steele track:* Little White Bull
**"TEENAGERS & YOUTH IN MUSIC 1951-1960"**
Bear Family BCD-17242 • 2011
*Tommy Steele track:* Teenage Party
*A 34 track compilation of songs dealing with teenagers featuring Nat King Cole, Gene Vincent, Chuck Berry, Duane Eddy, Dion & The Belmonts, Eddie Cochran, Johnny Cash, Al Casey and 26 more. Compiled by John Savage. And as always with Bear Family Records, great booklet and liner-notes with many pictures.*

**"SIX-FIVE SPECIAL"** *Songs From The TV Series*
Delta DCD-26655 • 2011

*Tommy Steele tracks:* A Handful Of Songs / Come On, Let's Go

 *31 tracks, but only the first 14 are actual performances from the TV series. The rest, 16 bonus tracks, including the two Steele songs, are just original studio recordings by artists who performed on the show.*
*(Delta Cheating Music Corp.)*

**"GREAT BRITISH ROCK'n'ROLL INSTRUMENTALS** – As Good As It Gets! Vol. 2"** (2-CD set)
Smith & Co. SCCD-2443 ● 2011
*Tommy Steele track:* Drunken Guitar
 *Picture of Tommy on the front cover.*

**"BEST OF THE BEST"** (3-CD set) Tommy Steele – Lonnie Donegan – Chris Barber
Go Entertainment GO3CD-7143 ● 2012
*Tommmy Steele tracks:* Singing The Blues / Come On, Let's Go / What A Mouth (What A North And South) / Little White Bull / A Handful Of Songs / Nairobi / Give! Give! Give! / Tallahassee Lassie / Rock With The Cavemand / Doomsday Rock / Knee Deep In The Blues / Butterfingers / Shiralee / Water, Water / Hey You! / Happy Guitar / The Only Man On The Island / It's All Happening / A Lovely Night / Hiawatha / You Were Mine / Happy Go Lucky Blues / My Big Best Shoes / The Writing On The Wall / Must Be Santa
 *25 songs each from three legends of British music'. One CD each.*

# MOVIES

**"KILL ME TOMORROW"** (UK) • 1957  -80 min.  Black&White
*Drama*
    *Tommy plays himself and sings "Rebel Rock" in a nightclub scene.  His only appeerence in the movie.*
**"THE TOMMY STEELE STORY"** (UK) • 1957  -71 min. Black&White  *Rock Musical*
    *Tommy plays himself and performs the songs available on the 10" Decca album LF-1288.*
**"ROCK AROUND THE WORLD"** (USA) • 1957
    *This was the American version of "The Tommy Steele Story", but this included some extra scenes which were not shown in England featuring the legendary American west coast DJ, Hunter Hancock - "Huntin' with Hunter".*
**"SHIRALEE" (UK**) • 1957  Black&White  *Drama*
    *Tommy is not acting.  Two songs by Tommy are used in the movie:* Shiralee / Grandad's Rock.
**"THE DUKE WORE JEANS"** (UK / USA) • 1958  -90 min. Black&White  *Comedy*
*Tommy acts and performs:*  It's All Happening / What Do You Do / Family Tree / Happy Guitar / Hair-Down, Hoe-Down / Princess / Photograph / Thanks A Lot.
    *Tommy plays a dual role as Tony Whitecliff (the nobleman) and Tommy Hudson (the jeans bloke).*
**"TOMMY THE TOREADOR" (UK)** • **1959**  -90 min.  Colour *Comedy*
*Tommy acts and performs :* Tommy The Toreador / Take A Ride / Where's The Birdie / Little White Bull / Singing Time / Amanda.
    *Tommy plays Tommy Tomkins, a British sailor who ends up in Spain with bullfighters and smugglers.*
**"LIGHT UP THE SKY" (UK)** • **1960**  -90 min.  Black&White *Comedy*
    *Tommy plays the role of Eric McGaffey, together with Ian Carmichael and Benny Hill.  Pretty dull.*
**"SKYWATCH" (USA)** • **1960**
    *Same as "Light Up The Sky".*

**"IT'S ALL HAPPENING" (UK)** • **1963**  -74 min.  Colour *Musical*

*Tommy acts and sings:* Dream Maker / Maximum Plus / Egg And Chips / Finale. The Dream Maker.

*Tommy plays the character Billy Bowles as an A&R talent co-ordinator.*

**"THE DREAM MAKER"** **(USA)** • **1963** -74 min. Color *Musical*

*This is the same film as "It's All Happening" in UK.*

**"NEW YORK, NEW YORK"** **(USA)** • **1965** -45 min. Colour *Promotional*

*A movie made by American Airlines to promote the town of New York. Featuring Gene Kelly, Tommy Steele and Woody Allen. To show what was going on in the city and on Broadway, focusing on musicals.*

**"HALF A SIXPENCE"** **(UK)** • **1967** -148 min. Colour *Musical*

*Tommy acts and sings. He's playing the character Arthur Kipps. The movie is based on H.G. Wells story "Kipps".*

**"THE HAPPIEST MILLIONAIRE"** **(USA)** • **1967** -164 min. and 141 min. Colour *Musical*

*Tommy acts and sings:* Fortuosity / I'll Always Be Irish / There Are Those / Let's Have A Drink On It / Finale.

*He's playing the character John Lawless. w/Fred MacMurray. A Walt Disney production. The original first version had a lenght of 164 minutes but was edited down to 141 minutes. The later video version was 118 min. (See the DVD releases.)*

**"FINIANS RAINBOW"** **(USA)** • **1968** -141 min. Colour *Musical comedy / fantasy*

*Tommy acts and sings: He's playing the character Ogg the Leprechaun. w/Fred Astaire as Finian and Petula Clark as his daughter Sharon. Director: Francis Ford Coppola.*

**"WHERE'S JACK ?"** **(UK)** • **1969** -119 min. Colour *Adventure/Drama*

*Tommy plays the character Jack Sheppard.*

**"QUINCY'S QUEST"** **(USA)** • **1979** TV-Movie -80 min. Colour *Fantasy*

*Tommy plays the title role of Quincy. A Christmas toy story.*

**"TWELFTH NIGHT"** • **1969** -102 minutes (Original I.T.C. TV Entertainment VHS NTSC) (UK)
Starring **Tommy Steele**, Alec Guinnes, Ralph Richardson, Joan Plowright, Adrienne Corri etc.

*An Emmy Award winning William Shakespeare play, TV Special. Produced by John Dexter. Music composed by Marc Wilkinson.*

**"THE YEOMEN OF THE GUARD"** • **1978** -105 minutes (original I.T.C. TV Entertainment VHS NTSC) (UK)
Starring **Tommy Steele** (*as Jack Point*), Laureen Livingstone, Della Jones, Terry Jenkins, Paul Hudson etc.

*An Emmy Award winning operetta TV Special. Made at The H.M. Tower Of London for The Festival of The City Of London. Produced & directed by Stanley Doreman. The New World Philarmonic Orchestra conducted by David Lloyd-Jones.*

*The two special videos above were sold through the Internet in the early parts of 2003. Originally they were sent to various TV Stations programme managers for viewing.*

*The Tommy Steele Collection:*
**"TOMMY THE TOREADOR"** • **1989** -83 minutes, WB (Warner Home Video) PES-38250 (UK)
**"IT'S ALL HAPPENING"** • **1989** -97 minutes, WB (Warner Home Veideo) PES-38251 (UK)
**"HALF A SIXPENCE"** • **?** -140 minutes, Paramount VHS 634 870 3 (film version) (UK)
**"FINIAN'S RAINBOW"** • **1991** -145 minutes, WB (Warner Home Video) (USA)
**"FINIAN'S RAINBOW"** • **1997** -142 minutes WB Musicals SO11208 (UK)
**"THE TOMMY STEELE STORY"** • **1991** -82 minutes, WB (Warner Home Video) WTB 39281 (UK)
**Double Feature:**
**"TOMMY THE TOREADOR"** / **"IT'S ALL HAPPENING"** • **1994** -180 minutes, WB (Warner Home Video) (both) SO38341 (UK)

**"LIGHT UP THE SKY"** • **1997** -86 minutes, 4Front video 046 802 3 (UK)
**"THE HAPPIEST MILLIONAIRE"** • **1999** -164 minutes, 2 tape set SV-10768 VHS (Part 1 & 2) Anchor Bay *Disney* (USA) Widescreen (Road Show edition)

**"THE HAPPIEST MILLIONAIRE"** • **1999** -144 minutes, widescreen, Anchor Bay *Disney* SV-10769 (USA)

### Various:

Videos featuring Tommy Steele taken from various sources.

**"ROCK 'N' ROLL – THE GREATEST YEARS – 1950s Vol. 2"** • **1989** -45 minutes, Video Coll. VC-4083 (UK)
*Tommy Steele sings:* **Singing The Blues** with rare footage filmed in a concert in Sweden, 1957.
**"WHEN THE QUIFF WAS KING"** • **1990** -55 minutes, Virgin Music Video VVD-740 (UK)
*The Best Of British '60s Rock'n'Roll Film Music*
*Tommy Steele sings:* Elevator Rock / Happy Guitar / Tommy The Toreador
**"FILMAVISEN 1957-1958"** • **1993** WB (Warner Home Video) #90585 (Norway)
*From September 1957, and showing Tommy arriving at the Oslo airport and also some clips from his performance at the Colosseum Movie Theatre, but without any original sound. Great picture of Tommy on the front cover.*
**"THE BEST OF BRITISH CINEMA"** • **1995** -50 minutes, Tring Video REB054 (UK)
*Clips of Tommy Steele from "The Tommy Steele Story" (1957)*
**SWEDISH TV** has some great black & white clips from Tommy's arrival and performances in Sweden in 1957 or 1958. Unfortunately without original sound, but great to watch anyway.
In February 1967 **BBC TV** did show a 100 minute spectacular benefit show for the Aberfan disaster. Stanley Baker and Sean Connery read words. Among others Tommy Steele sang **The King's New Clothes**.

**"THE HAPPIEST MILLIONAIRE"** • **1999**  -144 minutes, Ancher Bay Entertainment  (USA)
**"THE HAPPIEST MILLIONAIRE"** • **2000**  -164 minutes, Anchor Bay Entertainment DV-10827 (USA)
*The complete 'Road Show' edition as it originally appeared for the 'trades' in 1967. Diferent cover.*
*Special features:  Widescreen, Road Show Presentation and Theatrical Overture.*
**"THE HAPPIEST MILLIONAIRE"** • **2004**  -172 minutes, Walt Disney Video (USA)
*This is an even longer restored 'Road Show' edition, different cover.*
**"HALF A SIXPENCE"** • **2004**  -145 minutes, Paramount Home Entertainment 06721 (USA)
*Widesrceen version.*
**"FINIAN'S RAINBOW"** • **2005**  -145 minutes, Warner Home Video 11208 (USA)
*Widescreen version. Special features: New Introduction by director Francis Ford Coppola, The World Premiere of Finian's Rainbow and Theatrical Trailer.*
**"LIGHT UP THE SKY"** • **2007**  - 90 minutes, Odeon Entertainment ODNF-100 (UK)
**"TWELFTH NIGHT"** • **2008**  - 102 minutes, Universal (UK)
*See more info under Videos for this.*
**"THE TOMMY STEELE COLLECTION"** • **January 2008** (4 DVDs) -344 minutes, Optimum OPTD-0994 (UK)
*Featuring:* **The Tommy Steele Story** (1957), **The Duke Wore Jeans** (1958), **Tommy The Toreador** (1959), **It's All Happening** (1963).
*Nice collection and these movies have not been out on DVD before, and it's good to finally get a monumental release of the Tommy Steele filmography.  After so many years he deserves it ! And the "Duke Wore Jeans" has been unavailable in any format previously.*
*Later on in 2010 these four movies were again available on separate DVDs, different front covers though.*

Notable TV shows:

**"TOMMY STEELE AND THINGS" • 1969 (BBC Omnibus series)**
*Written by Tommy, prose, verse and song, the programme became an highly personal autobiographical journey through memories and thoughts of his early childhood in London.*
**"TOMMY STEELE IN SEARCH OF CHARLIE CHAPLIN" • 1970 (BBC Omnibus special)**
**"THE TOMMY STEELE HOUR" • 1971 (London Weekend Television)**
**"A SPECIAL TOMMY STEELE" • 1972 (London Weekend Television)**
*Britain's entry at the Montreux Festival.*
**"TOMMY STEELE AND A SHOW" • 1977 (Thames Television)**
*A celebration of Tommy's 21 years in show business. Britain's entry at the Montreux Festival in, and was also nominated in the USA for an Emmy.*
**"A HANDFUL OF SONGS" • 1981 (BBC)**
*A tribute to Tommy's 25 years in show business.*

*This survey is just a small portion of releases by other artists containing songs associated with Tommy Steele. However, the following records by various artists in Norway, Sweden, Denmark, Germany, England and USA gives an evidence of the impact Tommy had in these countries, especially in Scandinavia. I have also included most of Tommy's brother Colin Hicks's record releases, for old time sake.*

**_JOHNNY BACH & THE MOONSHINE BOOZERS_** (UK)
"BACH ON THE BOTTLE AGAIN" Vinyl Japan JRCD-30 • 1997
**Rock Around The Town**
**_BIG AUDIO DYNAMITE_** (USA)
"FLINSTONES" MCA CD/ 11045 • 1994 *Original Soundtrack - various*
**Rock With The Caveman**
**_BOG-SHED_** (UK)
"STEP ON IT" Shellfish Records Shelfish 2 • 1986
**Tommy Steele Record**
　　　Some kind of punk-music, however, I can't understand a word of what they are singing about except they seem to include the line "buy a Tommy Steele record". Is it a tribute or what …?
**_BORIS_** (Sweden)
"DOOMSDAY ROCK" Sonet EP SXP-4003 • 1958
**Doomsday Rock** / Mean Woman Blues / **Take Me Back Baby** / Teenagers Romance
_IVO CARRARO_ **(West Germany)**
The Only Man On The Island **('Ich Bin der Könich auf Meiner Insel') / Come Prima**
**Decca D-18840 • 1958**
**_COUNT BASIE_ (USA)**
"Music From The Paramount Motion Picture HALF A SIXPENCE"
Dot DLP-25834 (stereo) DLP-3834 (mono) • 1967
Half A Sixpence / A Proper Gentelman / She's Too Far Above Me / Know What I Am / This Is My World / All In The Cause Of Economy / If The Rain's Got To Fall / I Don't Believe A Word / Flash, Bang, Wallop! / The Race Is On / I'm Not Talking To You / Money To Burn

*Recorded November 9 & 10, 1967, featuring the basic Basie personnel like Illinois Jaquet on tenor saxophone, Bobby Plater and Marshall Royal on alto saxophones, Charles Fowlkes on baritone sax, plus 5 trumpets, 4 trombones, Freddie Green on guitar, Norman Keenan on bass, Ed Shaughnessy on drums and of course Count Basie at the piano. Liner notes by Tommy Steele and a good picture of Tommy and the Count.*

**"Captures Walt Disney's THE HAPPIEST MILLIONAIRE" (USA)**
Coliseum DS-51003 (stereo) • 1967
Detroit / Strengthen The Dwelling / I'll Always Be Irish / Valentine Candy / Bye-Yum-Pum-Pum / Watch Your Footwork / What's Wrong With That / Let's Have A Drink On It / Are We Dancing / Fortuosity

**"Captures Walt Disney's THE HAPPIEST MILLIONAIRE" (UK)**
**London HAU-8347 (mono) / SHU-8347 (stereo) •1967**
*Same as above.*

**_SAMMY DAVIS JR._** (USA)
Lonely Is The Name / **Flash, Bang, Wallop!**
Reprise 0673 • 1968
*"Lonely Is The Name" reached #93 on the US charts. Both songs produced by Jimmy Bowen.*


**_COLIN HICKS_** (UK) *Brother of Tommy.*


**45s:**


**Wild Eyes And Tender Lips / Empty Arms Blues**
Pye 7N 15114 • 1957 *w/ Cabin Boys*


**La Dee Dah / Wasteland**
Pye 7N 15125 • 1958 *w/ The Beryl Stott Group*


**Little Boy Blue / Jambalaya**
Pye 7N 15163 • 1958


**Broadway (Italy)**
B-1021 Dream Lover / A Teenager In Love • 1959
B-1022 Tallahassee Lassie / Brand New Cadillac • 1959
B-1023 Oh Boy / Rock And Roll Shoes • 1959
B-1024 Giddy-Up A Ding Dong / Hanging Around • 1959
B-1025 Put Me Down / Lovin' Up A Storm • 1959

B-1026 All Because Of You / Hollering And Screaming • 1960
B-1027 Stop Me / That Little Girl Of Mine • 1960
B-1028 Sexy Rock / Johnny B. Goode • 1960
B-1029 Love's Made A Fool Of You / Blue Moon Of Kentucky • 1960
B-1030 In The Garden Of Eden / For Every Boy • 1960
B-1031 Swinging School / Robot Man • 1960
B-1032 La Valle Dell'eco / Ooltre Il Fiume, Oltre Il Mare • 1961
B-1033 Il Mondo De Suzie Wong / Hallelujah, I Love Her So • 1961

*Colin was extremely popular in Italy counting all the records released in that country during a three years time!*

**EPs:**

**"Tribute To Tommy"** (Denmark)
Metrnome MEP-1177 • 1958
Empty Arms / Wild Eyes And Tender Lips / La Dee Dah / Wasteland
**"Colin Hicks & His Cabin Boys In Italy"** (Italy)
**Broadway EPB-104 • 1958**
Johnny B. Goode / Mean Woman Blues / Tutti Frutti / Whole Lotta Shakin' Goin' On
**"Colin Hicks & His Cabin Boys In Italy"** (Italy)
**Broadway EPB-106 • 1958**
Yea Yea / Oh Boy / Book Of Love / Twenty Flight Rock
   *From the movie "Europa de Notte" (Europe By Night).*
**"Colin Hicks"** (Italy)
**Broadway EPB-108 • 1960**
Giddy-Up A Ding Dong / Put Me Down / Sexy Rock / Stop Me
"Colin Hicks" (Italy)
**Broadway EPB-109 • 1960**
In The Garden Of Eden / Love's Made A Fool Of You / For Every Boy / Blue Moon Of Kentucky
**"Colin Hicks y sus Cabin Boys"** (Italy)
Discophon 17.016 • ?
Iea Iea / Oh Boy / Book Of Love / Twenty Flight Rock
**"Colin Hicks"** (Spain)
Discophon 17.068 • ?
Sexy Rock / Giddy-Up A Ding Dong / Brand New Cadillac / Tuttu Frutti

**LP:**

Historia del Rock & Roll - No. 13   (Spain)
**"COLIN HICKS Y SUS CABIN BOYS"**
Records LP 560209 ● 1988
Empty Arms Blues / Wild Eyes / Ladida / Wasteland / Little Boy Blue / Jambalya / Book Of Love / Twenty Flight Rock / Iea Iea / Old Boys / Sexy Rock / Brand New Cadillac / Giddy-Up A Ding Dong / Tutti Frutti
     Note:  *In 1994 a 2-CD set containing 40 tracks was issued in Italy as a limited collectors edition with only 500 copies pressed.  The set was titled "Anthology 1957-1961" Rockin' Ghost Records RGR-500-RA.*
*In 2002 a 25 track CD compilation was released in the UK titled "Bermondsey Bop" Rigsby Records RIGCD-041.   Also check out the 2-CD set "Hollerin' 'N' Screamin" that came out in 2012 featuring one CD each with Tommy and Colin.*
----------

***DARREL HIGHAM***  (UK)
"CRAZY WITH LOVE"   CD/ Foot Tapping FT-042 ● 2006
**Butterfingers**
***THE JAGUARS***  (UK)
"GIT IT !"  King ED LP/CD 12-01 ● 1995
**Rock With The Caveman**
***JAMES & HIS JAMESMEN***  (Denmark)   *Real name: James Rasmussen*
Philips PF 355144 **En Håndful Musik** *(A Handful Of Songs)* / Hand Clap  (1958)
    *The Danish Tommy Steele.   He dressed like Tommy Steele, performed and played like him, later member of the Four Jacks.*
***THE JIVE ROMEROS***  (UK)
"BIM BAM !"
Raucous RAUCD-098 ● 2001
**Elevator Rock**
**"BUILD UP"**
Raucous RAUCD-175 ● 2005
**Build Up**
**"HERE COMES THE GREEN LIGHT"**  Foottapping FT-056 ● 2007 **Rebel Rock / Two Eyes / Teenage Party**

***MORRIS & MITCH***  (UK)
**The Tommy Rot Story** / What Is A Skiffler

Decca F-10929 • 1957
Introducing **"Butterfingers"** and **"Elevator Rock"**.
*Accompaniment directed by Harry Robinson*
**JOHNNY REBB & His Rebels** (Australia) *One of the best rockers from Australia. Had many Top 40 hits.*
**Rebel Rock** / Johnny B. Goode
Columbia DO-3967 • 1958
**ROCKE PELLE** (Norway) *Real name: Pelle Hartvig. Although he was a big Tommy Steele fan he didn't record any songs made famous by Tommy.*

**45s:**

**Tennessee Toddy / The Teenage Love Affair**
Fontana 268002 • 1958
**Goodnight My Love / Gonna Shake This Shack Tonight**
Fontana268003 TF • 1958
**Easy Goin' Heart / Good Rockin' Baby**
Fontana 268004 TF • 1958
**I Thank You, Mr. Moon / A Love That's A Lie**
Fontana 268006 TF • 1958 *as Pelle Hartvig*

**EPs:**

**"ROCKIN' RENDEZVOUS"**
Fontana EP 64252 TE • 1958
Goodnight My Love / Gonna Shake This Shack Tonight / Tennessee Toddy / Teenage Love Affair
**"HETE SEPTEMBERDAGER"**
Fontana 464250 TE • 1958
Dance With Me / Poor Miguel / Easy Goin' Heart / Splish Splash *as Pelle.*
    *From the movie "Hete Septemberdager" (Hot September Days).*
**SMILING TOMMY** (Norway) *Real name: Odd Gisløy*
Sail Along Silvery Moon / Dancing With My Rockin' Shoes
RCA NA-45-1012 • 1958

**PERCY STEELE** (Sweden) *Real name: Percy Jönson*
"PERCY STEELE"
Gazell GEP-18 • 1958
Diana / **Teenage Party** / You Got To Go / I Love You Baby
 **BECKY TAYLOR** (UK)
"DREAM COME TRUE"

EMI CD 57142 • 2001
**A Handful Of Songs**
***CATERINA VALENTE*** (West Germany)
**Shiralee** / La Strada del Amore
Decca D-18960 • 1959  *(Picture sleeve)*

*VARIOUS:*

**"HALF A SIXPENCE"**  *Songs from the Musical*
Embassy EP WEP-1091 (UK) • 1963
*Featuring* **Paul Rich**\* & **Leoni Page**\*\*, *Orchestra directed by Gordon Franks*
Flash, Bang, Wallop!\* / Long Ago\*\* / Half A Sixpence\* \*\* / She's Too Far Above Me\* / If The Rain's Got To Fall\*
*This has a picture on the front cover of Tommy & ensemble from the original musical.*
**"HALF A SIXPENCE / NO STRINGS"**  *Songs from the Musicals*
Senator WSR-818 (UK) • 1964
Featuring the Senator Singers, Chorus and Orchestra
*Half A Sixpence:* Flash, Bang, Wallop / Long Ago / Half A Sixpence / She's Too Far Above Me / If The Rain's Got To Fall

A special various artist LP on Secret Heart 1008 released in the UK in 1988 featuring unfamiliar names like Barbara Hunt, Johnny London, Jean-Paul Dionysus, Andrew Cunningham and more, carried the strange title **"In The Beginning Tommy Steele"**, which has nothing to do with Tommy at all. Why the title then? Haven't the slightest idea.

***BOB MERRILL*** (USA)  *He was one of the most prolific songwriters in popular music who besides "Nairobi" wrote many well-known songs like "How Much Is That Doggie In The Window", "Funny Girl", "Mambo Italiano", "People", to name just a few.*

**Nairobi / Jump When I Say Frog**
Nairobi / Jump When I Say Frog
Roulette R-4043 (USA) • 1958    Columbia DB-4086 (UK) • 1958

------------------

There must have been 100s no 1000s of articles/interviews have been printed about Tommy Steele during over 5 Decades. However, one special interview and very up to date, appeared in the May 2009 issue of the UK rock'n'roll mag **Now Dig This** (no.314). 5 full pages. *Here's What He Did When He Wanted to Rave – Tommy Steele talks to Spencer Leigh.* It is very seldom and rare that you see Tommy talk about his rock'n'roll days. This is quite interesting for every Tommy Steele fan, actually it is a MUST. Also the Swedish American Music Magazine had a great article in their #125 (December 2010) issue featuring 13 pages containing many pictures most of them regarding Sweden (also advertisements) but also several rare pictures from England. Although the text are in Swedish the pictures are worth the price alone. The same would apply for the 1993 issue.

UK fab mag Now Dig This (May 2009)

Swedish American Music magazine (1993)

334

Printed in Great Britain
by Amazon